INCLUSIVE EDUCATIONAL ADMINISTRATION

A case study approach

Mary Konya Weishaar

Southern Illinois University—Edwardsville

John C. Borsa

Southern Illinois University—Edwardsville

D1411539

Boston   Burr Ridge, IL   Dubuque, IA   Madison, WI   New York   San Francisco   St. Louis
Bangkok   Bogotá   Caracas   Lisbon   London   Madrid
Mexico City   Milan   New Delhi   Seoul   Singapore   Sydney   Taipei   Toronto

McGraw-Hill Higher Education ⊗

A Division of The McGraw-Hill Companies

INCLUSIVE EDUCATIONAL ADMINISTRATION: A CASE STUDY APPROACH

Published by McGraw-Hill, an imprint of The McGraw-Hill Companies, Inc., 1221 Avenue of the Americas, New York, NY 10020. Copyright © 2001 by The McGraw-Hill Companies, Inc. All rights reserved. No part of this publication may be reproduced or distributed in any form or by any means, or stored in a database or retrieval system, without the prior written consent of The McGraw-Hill Companies, Inc., including, but not limited to, in any network or other electronic storage or transmission, or broadcast for distance learning.

Some ancillaries, including electronic and print components, may not be available to customers outside the United States.

This book is printed on acid-free paper.

1 2 3 4 5 6 7 8 9 0 QPF/QPF 0 9 8 7 6 5 4 3 2 1 0

ISBN 0–07–290531–X

Vice president and editor-in-chief: *Thalia Dorwick*
Editorial director: *Jane E. Vaicunas*
Sponsoring editor: *Beth Kaufman*
Developmental editors: *Teresa Wise/Kate Scheinman*
Marketing manager: *Daniel M. Loch*
Senior project manager: *Peggy J. Selle*
Senior Production supervisor: *Sandy Ludovissy*
Coordinator of freelance design: *Michelle D. Whitaker*
Cover designer: *Joshua Van Drake*
Cover image: © *Connie Hayes/The Stock Illustration Source, Inc.*
Compositor: *Carlisle Communications, Ltd.*
Typeface: *10/12 Minion*
Printer: *Quebecor Printing Book Group/Fairfield, PA*

Library of Congress Cataloging-in-Publication Data

Weishaar, Mary K.
   Inclusive educational administration : a case study approach / Mary K. Weishaar, John Borsa.—1st ed.
      p. cm.
   Includes bibliographical references and index.
   ISBN 0–07–290531–X (alk. paper)
   1. Special education—United States—Administration—Case studies. 2. Inclusive education—United States—Case studies. 3. Case method. I. Borsa, John. II. Title.

LC3981.W39   2001
371.9'0973—dc21   00–041834
                                                         CIP

www.mhhe.com

Dedication
To Phil, Paul, and Mark Weishaar and
Pat and Joe Konya for their belief in me
and encouragement.
MKW

To Pat, Chris, Brian, Cari, Lane, Tony,
and Libbi Borsa for their support and
encouragement.
JCB

BRIEF CONTENTS

CONTENTS

PREFACE

The belief that regular and special education administrators should work jointly to create and maintain successful special education programs is not new. Nor is the assumption that administrator preparation programs should foster the development of this partnership an inclusive approach. Unfortunately the actual state of a partnership between special education administration and regular education administration has not reached its full potential.

The idea for this book began when we met at an orientation for faculty new to our university. It was by accident that we sat next to each other and discovered similar interests in the relationship, or sometimes lack of relationship, between special education and regular education. Both of us had taught graduate classes and had general and special education responsibilities covering the span pre–PL 94–142 to the present. Our combined experiences include serving as a special education supervisor, special education director, director of a reading clinic, principal, director of curriculum, assistant superintendent, and area superintendent of school districts that range in size from 400 to 25,000 students.

After a few hours of discussion concerning issues we had faced, we concluded that one of the problems that stood in the way of *inclusive administration,* as we coined the concept, was a lack of training in shared problem solving. Other areas of difficulty focused on understanding the systemic nature of school districts and the need to form a community of administrators who would be lifelong learners. A great deal of time was spent reflecting upon the concepts found in the works of Christensen (1987), Newman (1955), Dewey (1933), and Ascham (1570). Each contributed to the development of this text by focusing our thinking on active problem solving.

As we discussed problem solving and the ways our colleagues approached the training of administrators, we decided that a method we had both used successfully—the case study method—was the "glue" that would bind the training of both regular and special education together.

After reviewing various case study texts in administration, we felt that an important aspect was missing from these texts. We decided that we could develop chapters covering areas important to the administration of special education. We believed that by offering concise chapters in these areas, we would help the reader reflect upon issues before reacting to the case studies that follow.

In the highly visible world of school administration, it is important for principals, special education administrators, and superintendents to practice decision making in a classroom context similar to the situations that they will confront in real life. It is also important for aspiring administrators to have the same type of practice.

Inclusive Educational Administration: A Case Study Approach is a book of practice. We believe that the case studies should be thoroughly discussed as part of class. We developed this text to assist aspiring special education and regular education administrators to think, discuss, and review potential solutions, following a case study format. Our text has five primary goals:

1. To introduce the case study method.
2. To review, in a *concise form,* pertinent educational issues in special education.
3. To provoke discussion within a cohort.
4. To assist students to think inclusively.
5. To prepare students to face complex issues.

The case studies presented in this text were taken from actual situations experienced by or related to us by parents, teachers, and administrators. The reader may be dismayed by reactions that particular characters in the case studies had in dealing with situations, even to the point of breaking or bending the law. The case studies presented represent a wide variety of experiences, many complimenting the best of intents, others showing how much further we need to go in assisting "all" children to receive the best education possible.

Although our text concentrates on educating regular and special education administrators, we also recommended that this text be used to train preservice teachers, teachers, administrators, board members, and parents in the use of the case study approach.

We have divided our text into ten chapters: Chapter 1 contains an overview, a semantic map (an organizer), and a case study with associated issues and reflections. Chapters 2 through 10 also each contain an overview, a semantic map, a situation (s), and two or three case studies. Possible answers to questions at the end of the cases are presented in Appendix A, "Questions and Reflections." Appendix B is a matrix specifying primary and secondary issues addressed in the cases. Appendix C is a case study analysis form.

- Chapter 1 presents the case study approach and a template to organize the case study.
- Chapter 2 reviews governance issues.
- Chapter 3 deals with identification and placement issues.
- Chapter 4 focuses on conflict resolution issues.
- Chapter 5 reviews program evaluation.
- Chapter 6 is devoted to fiscal issues.
- Chapter 7 concentrates on human resources issues.
- Chapter 8 reflects on issues dealing with transportation.
- Chapter 9 is devoted to school reform.
- Chapter 10 attends to discipline issues.

This collection of case studies, and the background information provided in each chapter, represents a method for dealing with problem solving in the safety of the classroom. We believe that the case study approach will assist the reader to reflect deeply on the various elements that represent administrative decision-making.

We would like to thank the following reviewers for their helpful comments on our text:

Janet Alleman, Michigan State University
Marvin Gould, Southeast Missouri State University
Jane Huffman, University of North Texas
Thomas Jacobson, University of Nebraska at Kearney
Jack Klotz, University of Southern Mississippi
Robert McCord, University of Nevada, Las Vegas
Mary Alice Obermiller, University of Houston
Winston Pickett, Tennessee Technological University
Mary Kay Zabel, Kansas State University

THE CASE STUDY APPROACH

In this chapter, the case study analysis and the case study approach will be reviewed. After reading the chapter and analyzing the case, you should be able to:

- Discuss the objectives for use of the case study approach.
- Describe the basic format of the case study approach.
- Describe the basic outcomes of cohort learning.
- Describe fundamental principles of the case study method.
- Complete a case study analysis form.
- Successfully complete a case study.

Below is a semantic map detailing Chapter 1.

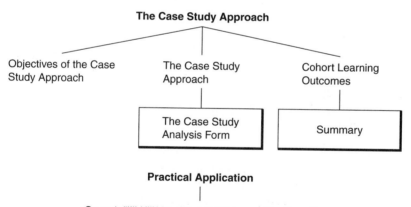

Discussion-oriented, reality-based teaching of the case study approach supports a fundamental objective in this text: to train students in a decision-making process that **focuses upon cohort solutions** to special education issues. The case study approach gives students the opportunity to make judgments in a setting where the consequences of misjudgment are not as great as in an actual situation. Certain outcomes for such a cohort learning experience have been identified by Borsa and Klotz (1998) and revised by the authors of this text to include the following:

1. Experience the opportunity to work collegially as a group.
2. Learn to identify data necessary to address and reach a solution to the presented problem within the context of the case study format.

3. Develop the awareness that administrative problems/issues have some degree of commonality.
4. Develop a sense of the systemic nature of a school district.
5. Evolve into a community of lifelong learners.

In *How We Think* (1933, 15) Dewey stated, "Only by wrestling with the conditions of the problem at hand, seeking and finding his own way out, does he think, . . . if he cannot devise his own solution (not, of course, in isolation but in correspondence with the teacher and other pupils) and find his own way out he will not learn, not even if he can recite some correct answer with one hundred percent accuracy."

Roger Ascham (1570) observed that "learning teacheth more in one year than experience in twenty; and learning teacheth safely, when experience maketh more miserable than wise. He hasardeth sore that waxeth wise by experience . . . . It is costly wisdom that is bought by experience."

Newman (1955, 45) pointed out that students must realize that the case study method cannot include all the variables of a real life situation but ". . . no other method provides a closer approximation to real life situations." Further, Newman indicated that the method also helps to encourage new approaches to problem solving and assists the student to develop speaking and writing skills.

In working with the case study method, the authors found that the judicious use of time is essential. Too little time and the process does not evolve properly. It is important to allow the case to reach its natural conclusion. In real-life situations, a solution that has not been well thought-out could very easily end in litigation. By practicing the case study method, the student, later the practitioner, will develop a method that will assist in making a decision based upon the use of knowledge before action is initiated.

Christensen (1987) reviewed five fundamental principles of the case study method approach. The five fundamental principles, adapted and summarized here are:

1. *The primacy of situational analysis.* Whether someone is an administrator, a student, or an instructor, the situation must be approached as described, not projected to what it might be. "The goal of the case discussion is to help students develop the capacity to deal with the situation-specific, not to deliver commentaries on the general" (Christensen 1987, 30).
2. *The imperative of relating analysis and action.* Marrying the academic's need to know, and the practitioner's need to act is a balance that is important to the success of the case method.
3. *The necessity of student involvement.* The student is offered an opportunity to practice diagnosis and the application of a solution(s) in a safe environment.
4. *A nontraditional instructor role.* The teacher's roles (teacher and practitioner) are that of a promoter of joint discovery. He or she becomes a member of the learning group exploring potential solutions to a specific case.
5. *A balance of substantive and process teaching objectives; the development of an administrative point of view.* The end product of the case study should be the development of an administrative mind set or point of view. Developing an orientation toward action is the ultimate goal of the case approach.

Through trial and error, the authors have found that the case study approach is most successful when the class reacts to each situation as a learning group—each stu-

Case Study Analysis

Primary Issue:

Secondary Issue:

Tertiary Issue:

Audiences:

Decision Makers:

Influential Groups/Individuals:

Inclusive Activities:

Answers to Case Questions:

FIGURE 1.1   *Case Study Analysis*

dent became involved in the case discussion, and the instructor aided the discussion through skillful query.

After using the case study method for a number of semesters, it became apparent that students needed a concise format, a template, to assist them in reviewing each case. The format needed to be simple, yet include the necessary ingredients to form tentative solutions in preparation for class discussion. The process that was developed became known as the *case study analysis* (see Figure 1.1). Before reviewing the case study in class, the student should complete the analysis form (located in Appendix C).

COMPLETING THE CASE STUDY ANALYSIS

The analysis consists of determining: issues, audiences, decision makers, influential groups/individuals, inclusive activities, and answering case questions in preparation for class discussion. The analysis is an organizer, a means of helping the reader to focus upon the important aspects of a decision.

The first step in analyzing the case is to determine the issue that is the source of conflict. A case study may have what appears to be a single issue but upon further reflection the student may find secondary or even tertiary issues. During class discussion of the case, it will become apparent which of the issues are relevant and which are not.

The second step in the analysis is to pinpoint the audience(s) that need to be considered in the development of a solution. An example is in order. A student is believed to have a disability, but has not been referred. The student initiates a fight, ending in serious injuries to another student. During fact-finding and due process the principal realizes that teachers had asked that the student be referred for a special education evaluation. The audiences that might be involved include the staff, students, parents, advocates, attorneys, media, and police. During class discussion the magnitude of various audiences would be determined.

Thirdly, it is important to determine who the decision makers are in the case. Is the decision site-based? Must the decision be made at the district level? Have guidelines been established that indicate what can be decided and at what level a decision can be made? Have training programs been carried out that allow for participants to practice decision making? The answer to these questions has important implications for the successful conclusion of problems that face general and special education.

The fourth step in the case analysis is to determine the influential groups/individuals that influence a decision and decide how to communicate with them. Included in the informal structure might be parent groups (PTO/PTA, booster clubs), civic groups, community action groups, past board of education members, members of the business community, an individual parent or parents, and advocacy groups.

In the fifth step the student or practitioner should develop activities that will include both special education administrators and regular education administrators in the problem-solving process.

In the sixth step, answers to the questions provided are answered. The important part of this step is to remember that any answer may create issues for other parts of the organization. Carefully review the ramifications of an answer on the rest of the school or school district.

Once the student has completed the analysis of the case it is necessary to move to the next step in the case study process—class discussion. To make the case study approach successful, it is important to follow these suggested rules:

1. Each participant should reread the case before each session.
2. Each member should keep a journal of his or her thoughts as the case evolves.
3. Each member should review his or her case study analysis with the group.
4. Under the direction of the instructor the group should brainstorm potential answers to the questions.
5. Conclusions, recommendations, decisions, and implications must be reached and agreed upon through consensus.

An Example

A completed case analysis and case study will be presented in this chapter. The case: "I'll Kill You if You Don't Leave Me Alone," and questions are presented here as an example. Reflections on the answers to "I'll Kill You If You Don't Leave Me Alone" appear at the end of this case. *Please note:* Questions and Reflections and case study analysis for Chapters 2–10 will appear in Appendix A, not at the end of each chapter.

I'LL KILL YOU IF YOU DON'T LEAVE ME ALONE!

Mrs. Cordovan waited patiently in Ms. Weiss's law office. She arrived early as she was anxious to resolve the issue with the school district. After about ten minutes, she was ushered into Ms. Weiss's office. Ms. Weiss immediately got up from her desk to shake Mrs. Cordovan's hand.

"I'm really sorry you had to wait, Mrs. Cordovan," said Ms. Weiss.

"That's OK, I'm just so upset about my son's situation at school. As I told you over the phone, John is back at school today, but he has to have the teacher's aide with him at all times and everyone knows what has happened. I know that kids will make fun of him and avoid him. I'm just so upset! Here is the letter that was sent home to all parents in John's fourth grade class."

Ms. Weiss took the letter from Mrs. Cordovan and read it carefully. It said:

October 22

To the Parents of all Fourth Grade Students:

The intent of this letter is to inform all parents of fourth grade students of a serious situation that occurred two weeks ago and steps the school district is taking to ensure the safety and well-being of all students.

Two weeks ago, a fourth grade student reportedly threatened to kill himself and other students. This incident occurred on the playground and was reported by several students to the principal. The incident was confirmed by the student who made the threats in a conference with the principal.

The student was removed from the classroom, reported to the county juvenile department, and referred for a psychiatric evaluation. The psychiatric referral resulted in the student receiving outpatient treatment. The student has now been cleared by his psychiatrist to return to school. Because the student receives special education services, the school must accommodate the child's educational needs.

Please be assured that the school district is taking appropriate safeguards to ensure the safety and well-being of all students. One of the steps taken to ensure a safe learning environment is that an aide has been employed to be "within arm's distance" of the student every moment the child is at school. The aide will be paid from special education funds.

We feel that every precaution has been addressed and that the school is and will continue to be a safe environment in which to learn. If you have any questions, you may contact the principal, Mr. Wang, at 555-5555.

Sincerely,

Mr. Wang, Principal
Ms. Cato, Superintendent

Ms. Weiss sighed and put the letter in her lap as she asked, "Mrs. Cordovan, did you give written consent to release any information about your son to the school district?"

Mrs. Cordovan said, "No!"

Ms. Weiss began taking notes on her legal pad. She said, "One issue that must be addressed is the breech of confidentiality. Can you tell me what happened?"

Mrs. Cordovan said, "Sure. John is in fourth grade and has been receiving special education services from the resource room teacher for reading since first grade. John has a mild learning disability and has always struggled with reading. He sees the resource teacher an hour a day. His reading has improved, but he really can't keep up with the reading program in fourth grade, so he has continued with special help. John is a very sensitive child. He has had a hard time making friends and sometimes the other kids are pretty mean to him. He really has very few friends. John is really bright and I think that he is sometimes more perceptive than the other children, but he is socially immature. Anyway, a couple of weeks ago, John was having a particularly hard time with some of the boys. One of them had a birthday party and handed out invitations at school and John was the only child not to be invited. The boys were teasing him on the playground and John said something about killing them and himself if they didn't leave him alone. The principal called me and said that John was suspended from school for ten days. She also asked me to attend an IEP meeting. At the meeting, the principal and teachers decided that what John did wasn't related to his learning disability and they referred him for a psychiatric evaluation. I thought I had to go through with the evaluation and I really wanted help for John, so I took him to see the psychiatrist. John now receives counseling weekly. The psychiatrist said part of John's learning disability is that he is socially immature and has a difficult time relating to other children. They didn't

Continue

change his IEP. The day before John returned to school, I received this letter. I don't think this will help John, he already feels bad enough without having an aide follow him around in school."

Ms. Weiss said, "Mrs. Cordovan, what would you like to see happen?"

Mrs. Cordovan replied, "I want John to go back to school without the aide following him. I'm also upset about the letter because every parent knows who John is and what he did. I really think the district overreacted."

Ms. Weiss asked for consent to review John's records and said she would take John's case. The first step was to ask for a due process hearing to insist that the aide be removed. Mrs. Cordovan felt relieved as she left the office.

In three weeks, a due process hearing was convened at the school district office. Ms. Weiss prepared a lengthy case emphasizing the following issues:

- John's disability was related to his comments about killing himself and the other kids, as he was socially immature and was unable to relate to the children in an age-appropriate manner. The psychiatrist's report confirmed this position.
- John's IEP (individual education plan) was not providing a free and appropriate public education because John's social skill deficit was not recognized or addressed as part of his IEP.
- John's placement was inappropriately changed without an IEP meeting. An aide was employed as a related service, which was not part of the IEP.
- The district knowingly engaged in a breech of confidentiality by releasing confidential information about John to other parents without Mrs. Cordovan's consent.

The school district's attorney presented a defense of the district's actions using the following:

- Any time a child makes a threat to kill himself or others, the school district must take extreme measures to ensure the safety and well-being of all students. In this case, the district took appropriate, prudent measures by referring the student to a psychiatrist and employing an aide to closely monitor the student at school.
- The student's disability was appropriately addressed in his current IEP.
- The letter sent to parents of students in the fourth grade was meant to ease parents' fears after rumors had been rampant.

Three weeks later, Mrs. Cordovan received the decision of the hearing officer. It read, in part:

- The district will immediately remove the aide from her current assignment of monitoring John at school.
- The district will conduct a reevaluation of John, to be completed fifteen days from receipt of this order. The reevaluation will also include a functional behavior assessment and consider the psychiatric report recently conducted.
- Based on results of the reevaluation, the district will convene an IEP meeting with the purpose of addressing all of John's special needs, including, if appropriate, social skills deficits. In addition, the IEP will include an appropriate behavioral management plan based on the results of the reevaluation.
- The district is ordered to request from the State Board of Education an inservice of at least three hours in duration on confidentiality and records for all district administrators. Based on this inservice, the district shall review its records policy, disseminate the policy to all staff, and inservice all school staff on the policy.

Although district administrators and board members were unhappy with the outcome of the due process hearing, they did not appeal the decision and they reluctantly complied.

Mrs. Cordovan, through her attorney, requested and received attorneys' fees. Although John continued to experience difficulty in school, he matriculated from eighth grade and continued his education at the local high school.

Note to the reader: You will now be asked questions about the case (see below). Before you read the Questions and Reflections section at the end of the chapter you should fill out the case study analysis (refer back to Figure 1.1), then answer the questions and share your ideas with the class.

Questions

1. In the IEP meeting following the incident, what should have been determined for the district to find that John's disability was not related to his behavior during the incident? Do you agree with the determination reached? Why or Why not?
2. Why did the hearing officer order the district to immediately remove the aide from her current assignment of monitoring John at school?
3. Should a letter informing parents of the situation have been sent? Why or why not?

CASE STUDY ANALYSIS

Before you read the authors' reflections on the above questions finalize your answers keeping in mind the variables of the various audiences, decision makers, and influential groups/individuals that may contribute to the success of your solutions.

- Primary issue: Appropriateness of the IEP, placement
- Secondary issue: Confidentiality of information
- Tertiary issue: Human relations
- Audiences: The staff, students, parents, the board of education, and the community in general
- Decision makers: Board of education
- Influential groups/individuals: Parent groups (PTO/PTA), teacher's association, community groups, advocates, legal counsel
- Inclusive activities: In each case discuss how special and regular education can work together to carry out a mock IEP meeting for this case, review manifestation determination, review the process a hearing officer follows in rendering a decision, review the Family Educational Rights and Privacy Act, review district guidelines for communications dealing with dangerous situations.

Questions and Reflections

Note: In Chapters 2–10, Questions and Reflections will appear in Appendix A.

Question 1: In the IEP meeting following their incident, what should have been determined for the district to find that John's disability was not related to his behavior during the incident? Do you agree with the determination reached? Why or Why not?

Answer: To find that no relationship existed between John's disability and the incident, the IEP team should have conducted a manifestation determination. The team should have considered all relevant evaluation data, observation of the student, and the student's IEP and placement. For the IEP team to make the decision, the following questions should have been addressed:

- Was the IEP appropriate?
- Did the disability impair the student's ability to understand the impact and consequences of the behavior?
- Did the disability impair the student's ability to control the behavior?

If the above were not met, the behavior was a manifestation of the disability.

It was questionable whether the IEP was appropriate given the history of John's behavior in school and the psychiatrist's input. John was known to have difficulty with social skills and this was never addressed in the IEP. In addition, it was possible that part of his disability was a social skill deficit. Therefore, he may not have fully understood the impact and consequences of his behavior. If the IEP was not appropriate or if he didn't understand the consequences of his behavior, the team would have found a relationship between John's disability and the incident.

Question 2: Why did the hearing officer order the district to immediately remove the aide from her current assignment of monitoring John at school?

Answer: The hearing officer agreed with the parent that the aide was a related service that was added to John's IEP outside of an IEP meeting. Information in this case suggests that the aide was not discussed at the IEP meeting.

Question 3: Should a letter informing parents of the situation have been sent? Why or Why not?

Answer: Confidential information about a child with a disability should not be released to anyone without the parent's consent unless the information is released to a staff member with an educational interest in the information (see Family Educational Rights and Privacy Act). Although the letter did not specify the child's name, there was enough information for parents to identify the child involved. This was a breech of confidentiality and should not have occurred.

Letters to inform parents of dangerous situations should be careful not to reveal information about any particular child and should be general in nature. One must carefully consider the purpose of such a letter prior to sending it to anyone. Once a letter is sent, it is essentially public information. Although there are times when letters should be sent to dispel rumors, it is questionable that this situation is one that warranted such a letter. The letter sent by the principal and the superintendent created a human relation's issue that will be difficult to overcome.

SUMMARY

Learning to work as a cohort/team, in the real world of administration, is not easily learned. Some decisions are fairly simple while some decisions have systemic implications that ripple through the entire organization. It is essential that decision making be taught, not left to the inconsistencies of learning through experience.

This chapter reviewed: the objectives of the case study approach, the basic format of the case study, and introduced the case study analysis form. In addition the reader was given an example of how to approach a case study. A completed case study analysis, questions, and reflections were also provided to assist the student in understanding the process.

Inclusive School Governance and Special Education

In this chapter, the reader is provided with an overview of how special education is organized and to the concept of inclusive school governance. After reading the chapter and analyzing the cases, you should be able to:

- Discuss factors affecting how special education is organized.
- Discuss the types of organizational structure in special education.
- Define the concept of inclusive school governance.
- Discuss factors that could bring about inclusive school governance.

Below is a semantic map detailing Chapter 2.

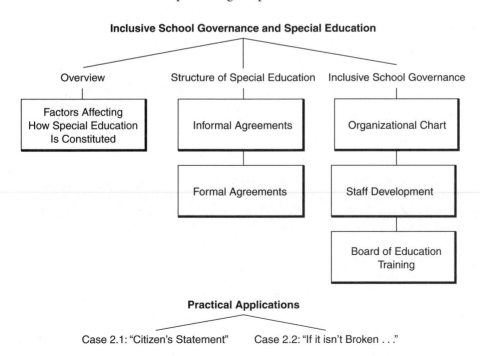

Inclusive School Governance and Special Education

Overview | Structure of Special Education | Inclusive School Governance

Factors Affecting How Special Education Is Constituted | Informal Agreements | Organizational Chart

Formal Agreements | Staff Development

Board of Education Training

Practical Applications

Case 2.1: "Citizen's Statement"   Case 2.2: "If it isn't Broken . . ."

OVERVIEW

Historically, special education and regular education have developed into a dual system of governance and practice. For example, special education has specific financing that regular education does not have, students in special education must receive education even if they are expelled from school (in contrast to students in regular education), and students in special education have access to specialized instruction that is not available to students in regular education. Although this system has evolved to provide equal access to, and appropriate education for students with disabilities, criticism has often been expressed that the dual system is unfair.

To illustrate some of the problems of a dual system, consider the following scenarios.

1. Bonita Wells, a fourth grade teacher, was extremely frustrated. She had expressed her concerns to her building principal, special education director, and assistant superintendent, all to no avail. Bonita was upset about the large number of students in special education who were assigned to her class. Her classes averaged 28 students with 8 or 9 of the children eligible for special education. She expressed to the assistant superintendent, "I teach fifth grade at Park School. I was never trained to work with special education students, yet many of my students have special needs. Why can't the special education teacher take greater responsibility for teaching her kids? Most of my problems come from dealing with the parents of her kids. They want me to spend all day trying to teach children who will never learn how to do all that is expected by the new state assessment test or to meet parent expectations. I am tired of having more children in special education than the other teachers."

2. Because there was no local program within the school district or region to meet Billy's special needs, the IEP team recommended an out-of-state residential facility. The superintendent, relying upon the recommendation from the special education director, communicated an overview of the situation to the board of education. The superintendent recommended the placement, even though the placement was costly ($90,000 annually). The board president was upset, saying, "Where are we going to get the money? You know that I have been promising the voters that we would have an expanded gifted program. This will stop my plans cold."

Each of the scenarios deal with organization and governance issues of the school district. In the first scenario, Bonita views the students in special education as the special education teacher's responsibility. She is clearly frustrated, perhaps due to the lack of support and availability of services. In addition, she has communicated her frustration with other administrators, but doesn't feel that anything is changing. To help resolve the issue, the special education administrator might listen actively to Bonita's concerns, review the staff development needs of teachers, and prepare a review of the number of special education students in each class for the past five years.

In the second scenario, the organization is faced with what the board of education thinks are competing issues. The superintendent must deal with two problems—lack of funding and insufficient knowledge of special education law on the part of the board of education. If you were the superintendent, would you force the issue of the special education placement with the board president? If you were the special education director, how would you justify the cost of the placement?

Are there simple solutions to each of the scenarios? At the root of each of these situations is a common assumption that an issue is isolated and has little relationship to the larger organization. The systemic nature of most organizational problems is often overlooked or misunderstood. The challenge is to survey the reasons that bring about the problem and then make adjustments to the organization so that a long lasting solution can be put into place. It is not enough to develop a solution to an individual problem.

WHAT FACTORS AFFECT HOW SPECIAL EDUCATION IS CONSTITUTED?

Sage and Burrello (1994) suggest that the configuration of special education in a particular school district is the result of six factors. These factors are part of the system that define special education at any one place at any one time.

The first factor, *terminology,* deals with how we define who has a disability and who requires special education services. For example, one school district might evaluate and make eligible for learning disabilities a first grader who was having difficulty learning to read in December. In contrast, another school district might not evaluate the same child, but provide extra support from the regular classroom teacher.

The second factor focuses on *philosophical issues within the system.* The philosophy of one school faculty, for example, might be to work with all children within the regular classroom, regardless of ability. The special education teacher might team teach with regular education faculty, consult with teachers, and provide support for individual children. Special education might be viewed as a last resort in helping children in this school. In contrast, the philosophy of another school faculty might be that any child who deviates from the norm requires special education assistance outside of the regular classroom. This faculty might look to special education as a first choice for assistance when a child has difficulty learning.

The third factor is the *history of the organization* and how that history affects the definition of special education. Historically, children with disabilities were segregated into special schools or denied access to the public schools. Since that time, schools have opened their doors to all children, regardless of ability. The history of special education provides a context that helps define where we are today. The context has been influenced by many factors, e.g., parents, case law, statutory law.

The fourth factor focuses on *local traditions within the school district.* Most school districts have been and continue to be under local control by the community via the elected board of education. For example, if a local board member had a child with a severe disability and requested that the child remain in a regular classroom, this person may have exerted influence on the school district's organization of special education services.

The fifth factor are the *legal foundations of special education,* including case law and statutory law. Since federal legislation in the mid 1970s (i.e., Public Law 94–142 and its current version, the IDEA), public schools have opened the doors of appropriate education to all students with disabilities. Case law in special education has helped to define who receives special education, the concept of appropriate placement, discipline of students with disabilities, etc. For example, ten years ago, it would have been unusual for a regular first grade classroom to include a child with severe disabilities. Today, partly due to case law, it is not unusual for this type of placement to occur.

The last factor, *fiscal constraints*, helps to define special education. Although it is illegal to formally define a student's placement in special education by the school district's financial status, the types of funding formulas that states and the federal government use to distribute funds for special education can influence particular placements. For example, if a state provides funding for each child eligible for special education with an IEP (individual education plan), there is an incentive to identify more children with disabilities. If the state provides funding based on a general census of all students, the incentive to identify more students for special education is removed. This issue is discussed in more detail in Chapter 6.

CURRENT STRUCTURE OF SPECIAL EDUCATION

The organizational structure of special education varies widely from school district to school district and from state to state. The structure may be established as a product of careful planning where a mission and goals are established. However, the structure is sometimes a reflection of traditional patterns, following the path of least resistance.

The primary consideration of any special education organizational structure is how well it gets the job done. Special education organizations typically operate along a continuum as centralized systems or decentralized systems. At one end of the continuum is a centralized system, where the local school district has little control over special education. In this case, the special education organization takes total control over the employment of special education personnel and the provision of services to students with disabilities. At the other end of the continuum is a decentralized system, where the local school district maintains control over special education. In this case, the local school district might employ all or most special education personnel and provide services to students with disabilities. The special education organization only provides support services, e.g., occupational and physical therapy, administrative services, evaluation services.

There are two basic types of special education organizational structure: informal agreements and formal agreements.

Informal agreements are often established between two school districts to assure that children receive appropriate services. For example, a large school district may establish a program for students with moderate mental impairment at the high school level. A smaller school district with one high school student with moderate mental impairment might not have this type of program due to the small number of eligible students. To provide an appropriate education to the student, the small district might establish an informal agreement to transport the student to the larger district's program and pay tuition. This type of agreement is often not written or formalized. Informal agreements are examples of decentralized systems, where local districts maintain control over special education services.

A second type of organizational structure in special education is a *formal agreement* between school districts. The driving force behind formal agreements is to assure appropriate special education services, while maintaining some degree of local school district control. Formal agreements can be centralized or decentralized depending upon the nature of the agreement. Formal agreements recognized by the state education agency take many shapes, such as cooperative agencies, regional agencies, and special school districts. These three types of formal agreements are described below.

In a *special education cooperative*, formal agreements among smaller school districts are established to provide special education services to member districts. For example, ten small school districts pool funds to provide special education administration, evaluations, and related services such as services for the visually impaired or occupational therapy. One single school district would be financially unable to provide these services to the few students within its district, but together several districts can provide the services in a fiscally responsible manner. The cooperative board is often comprised of the school district superintendents and possibly lay board members who recommend the employment of personnel and essentially make programmatic decisions. In a special education cooperative, special education services are the responsibility of both the cooperative and the local school district. Figure 2.1 summarizes the roles and responsibilities of the special education cooperative relative to the local school district using an example.

If a school district is large enough to provide all special education services to children within the district, it may not become part of a larger cooperative. A larger school district may be able to provide all special education services on its own.

In another type of formal special education organizational structure, *regional programs* are established, often to provide special education services to cooperatives and school districts that cannot be provided within the cooperative or district. In a regional program, formal agreement is established between special education cooperatives to provide services to a larger geographical area. For example, four special education cooperatives, each consisting of five school districts, have a common need for services for the visually impaired. Each cooperative has one child in need of the services and it would be fiscally difficult for each cooperative to employ someone to fill this role. The cooperatives join together in a regional program to employ a teacher for the visually impaired. This teacher would travel to each cooperative to provide services to children in need of the service.

Problems have been associated with regional programs and special education cooperatives. For example, the cooperatives often pay an overhead cost to be a member of the regional program, but a cooperative may not need services from the regional program in a given year. Therefore, the cooperative pays a cost to the regional program, but doesn't get direct benefit. This situation may change year-to-year as cooperatives' needs change. The cost paid to become a member of a regional program ensures services in the event that the cooperative may need the specialized services of the regional program. The same situation may occur in a special education cooperative and its member districts.

The last type of organization in special education, a *special school district,* is infrequently used. The special school district is a legally constituted unit of school governance, much like a separate school district. A special school district can levy taxes, unlike the special education cooperative or regional program. The purpose of the

---

Special Education Cooperative – 10 School Districts – Formal Agreement – Decentralized

Governance:	Board may consist of 10 member school district superintendents.
Administration:	Governing board employs special education director who makes recommendations regarding finance, personnel, program, and services within the local districts.
Personnel:	Board might employ (in addition to director) special education supervisors, secretarial staff, psychologists, social workers, occupational therapists, and physical therapists.
Finance:	Member districts pool federal and state special education resources for cooperative expenses.
Role:	Provide special education support services (as defined in agreement) to member districts.

Local School Districts Who Are Members of the Cooperative

Governance:	Board consists of locally elected school board members.
Administration:	School board employs superintendent who makes recommendations regarding finance, personnel, program, and services for the school district; superintendent sits on governing board of special education cooperative.
Personnel:	Board might employ (in addition to superintendent) assistant superintendent, special and regular education coordinators, building principals, secretarial staff, support staff, regular and special education teachers and paraprofessionals.
Finance:	Local school district finances, primarily through local taxes, services for all children in the district. Some state and federal special education monies are given to the special education cooperative.
Role:	Ensure an education for all children residing in the local school district with the help of the special education cooperative; maintains local control over special education services in the school district.

FIGURE 2.1 *Example: Roles and Responsibilities for Special Education Cooperative and Local School District*

special school district is to provide all special education personnel and services to local school districts within its boundaries. This type of organization is the ultimate in centralized and separate governance and local school districts have little control over special education in their districts.

In all forms of special education organizational structure, a dual system in special and regular education has formed to a greater or lesser extent. Separate administration, separate employers, separate fiscal sources, and separate governing boards contribute to the dual system.

Inclusive School Governance

School governance is a complex and oftentimes difficult concept to successfully put into practice. This is especially true when emphasis is placed on providing equal educational opportunities for all children in an inclusive setting. Mayer (1982, xi) described the situation in this manner:

> "Every minute of every school day in thousands of schools throughout the nation, school administrators are faced with opportunities and obligations to provide special programs for handicapped and gifted students. Decisions are made, activities are initiated, parent conferences are held, and students are taught in the school buildings and in the district offices of thousands of local education agencies. At the same time, legislatures, courts, school boards, and numerous federal, state, and local agencies are busy writing, adopting, and implementing new laws, regulations, and policies for operation of school programs."

What is inclusive school governance? The term refers to a school organization that focuses its governance on providing a seamless, instructional format that assists all educators to work effectively with children displaying a wide range of abilities and disabilities. Basically, if a child needs assistance, the child would receive assistance without the complicated system of singling out certain children (providing an evaluation often not connected to instruction but connected to a particular label), labeling children, and separating them out to provide special services. Inclusive school governance requires a district to think about its strategic planning in relationship to all students, provide the necessary funds and training needed for all stakeholders to understand the process, and put into place a system that does not propagate differences. Of course, this is easier said than done.

Stakes and Hornby (1997) cite seven issues that act as controlling factors in moving towards an inclusive educational setting. The first factor deals with the integration of students with disabilities into the regular education program. Although inclusive education has been an issue for many years, it continues to be a major and unsettled concept for many educators.

The second factor deals with problems generated when a resource-based budget comes into conflict with demand-led special education needs. Parents have become well educated in terms of new and more effective programs and the use of technology. When districts indicate a reluctance to fund these innovations because resources are not available, parents move toward legal solutions.

A third factor deals with political activity. Initially, compulsory education did not include programming for students with disabilities. Currently, federal and state legislation focuses upon special education. Unfortunately, special education needs come into conflict with what regular education perceives to be best for all children.

The fourth issue deals with social factors. For the most part, there has been a positive change in societies' attitude toward education and toward people with disabilities.

Curriculum is the fifth factor. With a movement towards a "curriculum for all," pressures have been placed on assessment and on more academic subjects and appropriate curricula for students with disabilities.

The sixth factor deals with professional development. School districts have had difficulty in funding as well as finding the time to offer staff development.

The last factor deals with management. Management has had difficulty in coordinating planning for regular education and special education. This lack of coordination continues to create issues dealing with funding, curriculum, and staff development.

Stainback, Stainback, and Bray (1996) summarize seven factors that are necessary for inclusion to be successful. These factors are:

1. Visionary leadership;
2. Collaboration;
3. Refocused use of assessment;
4. Supports for staff and students;
5. Funding;
6. Effective parental involvement; and
7. Curricula adaptation and adopting of effective instructional practices.

In the report, *Winners All: A Call for Inclusive Schools* (NASBE 1992), criticism was leveled at systems that continued to allow for lower instructional expectations for students with disabilities and allow children to be pulled out of the regular classroom just because of their disabilities. The criticisms that the report focused upon in 1992 continue to be a source of weakness in our nation's schools.

To further complicate inclusive governance, administrators are given little cross-training in special education. Sage and Burrello (1994) point out the need for administrators to develop the skills that will assist them in carrying out their responsibilities to special education.

The factors listed above have contributed to school governance that has continued to separate regular and special education. What could a district do to blur the line between regular education and special education, in effect putting into place inclusive school governance?

Inclusive school governance could be promoted if the following areas were addressed:

1. Developing an organizational chart that would promote inclusive administration;
2. Implementing a staff/administrative development program that promotes special education in a planning training cycle; and
3. Providing the local school district board of education with training, which would assist them in understanding the importance of inclusive school governance.

The Organizational Chart

Understanding a district's educational system may be enhanced or diminished by the organizational chart. The more complex the chart, the more inefficient it is generally perceived to be. Most communication problems within an educational organization can be attributed to a district's official reporting sequence and the timeliness of the decision-making process as related to the organizational chart.

It is important, as a first step, to review a district's organizational chart for complexity and decision-making ease. If, for example, a student with an IEP needs to have a special text for a social studies class and the decision to purchase the text must go through the coordinator for special education, the director of special services, and the assistant superintendent, the reporting sequence and decision-making sequence are too cumbersome.

An organizational chart does not make successful school district or successful programs, but to be successful a district must deliver needed services and materials in a timely manner. Timeliness can be best accomplished by making decisions as close to the problem as possible. The organizational chart and decision-making philosophy should adhere to the concept of simplicity and balance of power if special education is to take its place as an equal partner in the educational process.

Placement on the organizational chart is very important. If a balance of power is to be attained, it is essential that someone with special education responsibility be part of the district's decision-making group.

Students training to become regular or special education administrators would gain a great deal of knowledge by reviewing various organizational charts. Students interested in special education and regular education, but not in administration, would also learn a great deal by reviewing organizational charts. It is also useful to review small and large, rural, urban, and suburban school district organizational charts. When reviewing the organizational charts, it is helpful to ask the following questions:

1. How many faculty and staff report to each of the upper level administrators (coordinators, assistant/associate superintendent)?
2. How many administrators must be part of a decision dealing with a student in special education?
3. Is there an individual responsible for special education?
4. Is the individual responsible for special education an assistant superintendent?
5. Are special education and regular education treated equally on the chart?

Staff Development

Staff development is an area of concern for most school districts. Time, funding, and area of staff development concentration continues to present district administrators and teachers with difficult choices. With sparse amounts of time, funding, and an unlimited number of potential issues to cover, districts often lose sight of the problems associated with special education.

Upon review of a school district's staff development plan, two trends emerge in most districts. The first trend tends to focus upon a current "topic du jour." Frequently, districts spend a great deal of attention on what has been selected as its most important thrust for the year, often following national trends. Unfortunately, the trend changes from year to year, never to be seen again.

The second trend deals with historically important staff development needs. Districts tend to have areas that receive attention just because "it has always been that way."

To learn more about a district's staff development plan, it is useful to review the plan for the past five years. Does the district have continued emphasis on special education for both special education teachers/administrators and regular education teachers/administrators? A staff development plan can be broken down into topics that are current and those that have an ongoing focus. An example of a current topic might be authentic assessment or the state assessment plan. An ongoing focus might be techniques for working with classroom discipline. How many staff development programs dealt with special education over the five-year periods? How did this compare with more general topics for staff development?

Board of Education Training

The importance of local school district board of education training cannot be underestimated. Board members are typically elected by community members and they are responsible for making costly and important decisions about the education of all children in the community. Typically, a board of education member is trained under two formats. The first formal deals with the state mandatory training program for new and tenured board members. These programs are routinely developed around fiscal, legal, and curricular issues. The second form of training is situational. Here, the board member learns by experiencing a wide range of problems during his or her time on the board. Both types of training are important, but a third, district-initiated board development program should be in place for new and experienced board members.

An ideal setting for this training would be during a board of education work session. These sessions provide an invaluable opportunity for board members and staff to work together and still meet the open meetings provisions that must be followed.

Special Education and Regular Education

Many of today's classroom issues did not exist, in their present numbers, just a few years ago. Many teachers currently began their careers when families were fairly stable, the job market was predictable, discipline was easily maintained, and there was a sense of direction.

As a large number of the teaching workforce reaches retirement age, they see that the training they received in preparation to teach or during inservice development was not enough to meet the needs, in one classroom, of the student with average abilities, the student who is gifted, the student requiring special education services, or the student who is at-risk of academic failure.

Constant criticism and pressure are the mainstay of the school administration. Many educational problems are systemic and can be related to the need to change. But how do systems change when the universities that do the training still follow, for the most part, separate special education and regular education training? This dilemma can best be summarized by the following:

> "Most administrators spend the bulk of their time reacting to problems: due process actions brought by parents, complaints from the state department on the completeness of pupil records, pressure from the superintendent regarding the need to limit expenditures to budgeted amounts. First, it leaves the staff with distressing but accurate perceptions that their lives are being controlled by external events; priorities change from one crisis to the next, and stability never seems to arrive. Second, it leaves little time for other important administrative responsibilities, such as improving existing programs. Finally, it creates a vicious cycle; the more time spent reacting to crises, the less time for taking preventive measures" (Mayer 1994, 34).

In the epilogue to their book, *Effective Management of Special Education Programs,* the authors look to the future, ". . . when special education will not be delineated from regular education" (Osborne, DiMattia, and Curran 1993, 4). This is the task that faces our profession as we move to an inclusive form of school governance, one that does not look at students and programs as separate, but rather one that includes "all."

You will now be presented with case studies dealing with special education governance and organization. These cases will assist you in solving real-life problems in these areas. As you read the cases, keep in mind the concept of inclusive school governance.

CASE 2.1: "THE CITIZEN'S STATEMENT"

Dr. Maria Gonzalez-Lane had been the superintendent of the Pleasant View School District for eleven months. She was recruited for the position because of her ability to deal with difficult situations, and her knowledge of curriculum. The Pleasant View School District was twice the size of her former district and seemed to have ten times the problems. In the last eleven months she and her staff had faced issues dealing with contract negotiations, difficulty getting each of the board members to agree to a tax referendum, problems with the zero tolerance policy, and two harassment charges against a middle school teacher.

Dr. Gonzalez-Lane's mind drifted as she readied for the board meeting to begin. "This has been a long, difficult eleven months; seems like I have been here for two years. What is Jack Petrocelli doing here? I hope he isn't going to bring up sex education again. There is Mrs. Fox. What would we do without her positive comments at each board meeting?"

With the exception of those board meetings that had controversial issues, the last being sex education, board of education meeting attendance had been sparse. This meeting was no different. There were fifteen parents and administrators in the audience.

The agenda for this evening dealt with consensus items, hiring principals for next year, a curriculum report, a report from the Human Resources Department on problems in retaining substitute teachers and a report on finding replacements for retiring special education teachers. Since this was the last meeting of the school year, she had hoped that the meeting would go smoothly. But, this was a board meeting and anything could happen.

Five minutes before the meeting was to begin, Lester Finkelstein, the board president walked over to Dr. Lane and said, "I am sorry I couldn't finish our conversation this afternoon about Mrs. Taylor, but I had a long distance phone call." Earlier that day he had called Dr. Lane to inform her that there would be a citizen's statement. The citizen, Mrs. Taylor, said that the subject of the statement would be special education.

Dr. Lane tried to call Bill McAdams, director of special education, but he was at a meeting out of the district and would not be back until the board meeting.

At 7:00 P.M. Mr. Finkelstein brought the meeting to order by saying, "Let us please rise and recite the Pledge of Allegiance to the Flag." After the pledge Mr. Finkelstein reviewed the agenda for the board and the audience. "This afternoon I received a call from Mrs. Pat Taylor. Mrs. Taylor requested that she be given an opportunity to address the board of education about problems in the special education program. She also asked if the board would give her additional time to speak beyond the five-minute maximum per statement."

As the board president spoke, Dr. Lane looked around the room and saw the reporter from the *Dispatch.* For some reason, unknown to her, the *Dispatch* always seemed to be very hard on the district and its programs. She also saw Bill McAdams walk into the room; he focused on Mrs. Taylor, and shook his head as if to say, "I don't know why she is here or what she is going to say."

Mr. Finkelstein looked at each board member and said, "Do I have consensus to extend the time limit for Mrs. Taylor? Thank you. Mrs. Taylor, you have the

(Continue)

CASE 2.1: "THE CITIZEN'S STATEMENT" (CONTINUED)

additional time, if you need it. As you may know, the board does not generally indulge in discussions with the person giving a citizen's statement. Our procedure is to listen to you, then, later this week I will send a letter to you reviewing the board's reaction to your statement."

Mrs. Taylor stood up and walked to the front of the room. She gave a written copy of her statement to the board secretary, stepped up to the microphone and said:

"Thank you Mr. Finkelstein, board members, and Dr. Lane for giving me the opportunity to speak at this, the last board meeting of the school year. I am very nervous so I have prepared this statement to read to you, if you don't mind. My name is Pat Taylor. I live at Number 1 Shaw Avenue. I am very involved in the PTO and the Citizen's Advisory Council. I am also a volunteer at my daughter's school.

Some of you may know that I have a daughter in the district's special education program. Julie, as I said, has special needs. When she was six months old she contracted meningitis, which caused severe brain damage and subsequent seizures. Julie has never been able to play or do the things that nondisabled children can do.

When I moved here, two years ago, I had hoped that I would find a district that would work with me. That has not happened. It is impossible for you, as board members, to understand the complexities of every program that the district offers. But I plead with you to spend time learning about the needs of the students in your special education program.

You already know that you have a wonderful staff. They are kind and do a great job of working with the students in the regular education program. But for children like Julie, they and the district's administrators do not have the training that is needed to establish and follow through with classroom accommodations. I do not mean to be contentious, but as a board you also do not have the knowledge to make the differences that are needed.

Since this is the third district and the third state I have lived in over the past six years, I think that I have become an expert on the problems that face the parents and children in special education programs. Now, if you will bear with me, I have a number of thoughts that I would like to share with you.

- I have a sense that special education takes a back seat to regular education in this district. I have reviewed the staff development offerings for this current school year and noted that there is only one special education offering, and that was for special education teachers only.
- There were no special education staff development offerings for regular education teachers. I asked the person in charge of staff development if there were any plans for special education topics to be presented to the administration; I was told no.
- I believe that the district is not proactive when it comes to the needs and wishes of the parents of students in your special education program. As an example, when I moved here I had hoped that a district representative would meet with me to discuss the total special education program, from kindergarten through transition. I had to call three numbers before I could find out who was in charge of the program—not very good human relations.
- I know that there are teachers who have not read the IEP for special education students in their classes.
- I have noticed that special education staff and the regular education staff don't seem to interact with each other. It seems that the district has two different organizations—regular education and special education.

This, the last item may be just as important as all the others combined.

- When someone tries to get a decision about special education they must go through a maze. There doesn't seem to be anyone with decision making below the superintendent. You must go through the special education teacher, the principal, the director of special education, the assistant superintendent, and the superintendent.

(Continue)

CASE 2.1: "THE CITIZEN'S STATEMENT" (CONTINUED)

I have finished my list, but one more comment please. I came here tonight to tell you that I have almost given up on public schools. I have even thought about starting a charter school. Julie has shown very little progress in your special education program. I don't know what to do. Please help Julie. Please help all the students in your special education program. Thank you for letting me speak tonight."

The board president made eye contact with Mrs. Taylor and said, "Mrs. Taylor, the board of education thanks you for your comments. I can assure you that we want to promote and implement a sound education for every student in this district. I will meet with the superintendent to review your comments."

The board meeting moved into the agenda. The board president leaned over and said, "Dr. Lane, I know that you have discussed changes to the special education program. Do you think that Mrs. Taylor's statements are on target?" Dr. Lane looked at him and nodded yes.

Dr. Lane woke up the next morning and opened the *Dispatch.* On the second page was the following article:

Parent Criticizes the District's Special Education Program

Mrs. Pat Taylor addressed the board of education last evening. Mrs. Taylor's daughter is a special education student attending Herrin Middle School. Mrs. Taylor summarized her disappointment with the district's special education program. She listed a series of problems that have not been addressed, even after she brought the issues to the attention of the administration. "I am not a rebel, I generally don't cause problems, but in this case something has to be done." She said after the meeting.

The board of education president, Mr. Finkelstein, commented, "I will meet with the superintendent to discuss the issues that Mrs. Taylor raised. It is my understanding that special education is an area that most school districts need to pay more attention to. I have all the confidence in the world in our administration to make a difference in correcting any problem that may exist."

"Why did this happen as the district prepares for a tax referendum? What should I do next?" wondered Dr. Lane.

Note to readers: You will now be asked questions about this case. Before you read the Questions and Reflections section at the end of the book (Appendix A), you should fill out a case study analysis (refer back to Figure 1.1), then answer the questions and share your ideas with the class.

Questions

1. What are Mrs. Taylor's concerns?
2. What are the special education issues confronting the district?
3. Is it unusual for a parent to be so well versed in the issues related to special education?
4. If you were the director of special education how would you approach the problem? Should you approach Mrs. Taylor immediately after the board of education meeting to defend the program?
5. If you were the director of special education and was asked to meet with the reporter, what would you do?
6. If you were superintendent, how would you approach the issue?
7. Can this situation be salvaged?

CASE 2.2 "IF IT ISN'T BROKEN . . ."

Richard Elliott felt very fortunate to be chosen as the director of Pupil Personnel Services for the Lincoln School District. He had just received his doctorate and was anxious to become a central office administrator. Richard had served as the high school principal in a district two hundred miles from Lincoln.

On his first day at the central office, Adele Washington, the Assistant Superintendent for Administrative Services for the Lincoln School District called Richard into her office. "Richard, good to see you again. We are all very happy that you accepted the position. I am especially pleased that we will be working together."

As they sat down Adele said, "Lincoln is a very traditional school district, some would say too traditional. When other school districts are implementing the newest educational innovations we sit back and let the dust settle. It takes a great deal of time before we accept any new programming. I wanted to tell you this before you begin thinking about your area of responsibility."

"Now that I have said that, there is one area that the board wants to have in place within the next two years. They are interested in creating an alternative high school program. You and I will be responsible for developing the proposal. Look at your calendar and see if you can meet with me next Thursday to develop a timeline for the project."

"Now, let me tell you about a pressing issue that you will need to deal with today. For the past few weeks the superintendent and I have been dealing with a family new to our district. The Steiv family moved into the Fern Meadow Elementary attendance area recently. Before I go into the Steiv issue I need to review the personal history of the principal of Fern Meadow. Randy Bell is a legend in the district, a bit eccentric, but very popular. This is his thirty-fifth year in the district. Most of the board members and business people were either taught by him or went to school when he was the principal. He doesn't exactly work within the rules, but he is highly effective." Adele took a sip of coffee and looked out the window. She continued, "You will find him to be very easy to get along with, but remember that will continue as long as he gets his way."

"Now to the Steiv family. As I said, they had moved into the district recently. Mr. Steiv visited Fern Meadow and immediately had an argument with Randy Bell. Mr. Steiv wanted to know why the school was not following

his son Jim's IEP. Randy said that he had a policy of letting the teachers work with a student for a few weeks before following the IEP. They got into a yelling match and Randy asked Mr. Steiv to leave. Now it is your job to work with Randy and Mr. Steiv to resolve the issues. I can tell you right now you probably won't get very far with Randy."

"I can't wait to meet him, Adele. I know that every issue has two sides but as you have explained it, Mr. Randy Bell is breaking the law. I will call you about next week's meeting. I will also call Randy and set up a meeting before I talk to Mr. Steiv," said Richard.

That afternoon Richard's secretary brought in his mail. The first envelope he opened was from Mr. Steiv. There was a letter and a copy of his son's IEP. The letter was concise. Mr. Steiv wanted to speak to someone at the central office before he sought legal assistance. He wanted to know what district policy allowed Mr. Bell to change an IEP.

The IEP indicated that James had a severe learning disability. His IEP was to be carried out in a regular education classroom with a number of modifications. According to additional information, James was showing very good progress. "How could Randy refuse the IEP placement?" wondered Richard. He reached for his phone and called Fern Meadow to set up an appointment with Randy Bell.

The next day Richard drove to Fern Meadow. He went to the office, introduced himself and asked to see Mr. Bell. The secretary looked up from her computer and said, "Dr. Wilson can't see you right now. He is busy. Why don't you have a seat." Thirty minutes later Randy Bell opened his door and said, "Come in, sit down. So you are the new guy on the block. Good to meet you, I think. I was wondering how long it would take you to come to see me. I know one of the first things that you will want to discuss is the Steiv issue."

Randy was becoming angry but he kept calm and said, "Yes, that is why I am here, to meet you and hear your side of the story. Also, Randy, I am not particularly happy that you had me sit in your office for a half-hour when we had an appointment."

Randy looked at Richard and said, "Let me make myself perfectly clear. You are new. Remember that I have been working with children longer than you have been alive. Most people around here would say that I

(Continue)

CASE 2.2 "IF IT ISN'T BROKEN . . ." (CONTINUED)

have forgotten more about education than they know. I treat all my kids the same way, with respect and the understanding that it is my responsibility to give them the best possible education. Now I know what Steiv has been yelling about. He is saying that I won't put his son into a regular education class, that I won't follow the IEP. Is that right?"

"Yes you summed up his concerns. What I don't understand, after reading the IEP, is why you won't let your teaching staff follow the program established for James Steiv?" questioned Richard.

"You know, Rich, it is easy to get along around here if you don't create too many problems. I am very successful with all my kids, the brightest as well as those that need special help. I know you don't agree with me but I don't believe that these IEPs are always right. That is why I don't want to put the Steiv youngster in a regular education classroom."

"Well, Randy, it doesn't seem that we are getting off to a very good start, does it? I have been a principal also. I do know that it is essential for everyone to follow the same rules or there is chaos. If you don't mind I will set an appointment to come back to Fern Meadow tomorrow to observe James Steiv. I would also like to talk to you tomorrow and go over the rules and regulations that govern special education," said Richard as he got up and walked toward the door.

The next day the superintendent came into Richard's office. "Richard, I understand that you had a bit of a run-in with Randy yesterday. There is an old saying, 'Don't fix something that isn't broken.' I think that if I had a problem with Randy the board might ask me to leave before they would let him go. Randy is a rare one. He can get you angry but he gets results. I think that the Steiv complaint is the first I have had about him in the past ten years."

Richard looked at the superintendent and replied, "I am new here, but I do know that Randy is doing a great deal of harm to the special education program and is breaking the law concerning James Steiv. I must be frank with you. It is only a matter of time before the district is faced with a law suit."

Note to readers: You will now be asked questions about this case. Before you read the Questions and Reflections section at the end of the book (Appendix A), you should fill out a case study analysis (refer back to Figure 1.1), then answer the questions and share your ideas with the class.

Questions

1. What problems face Richard as he works through the Steivs' complaint?

2. Is the district responsible for Randy's actions?

3. What recourse does the Steiv family have in dealing with the district's approach to their son's IEP?

CHAPTER 3

IDENTIFICATION AND PLACEMENT ISSUES IN SPECIAL EDUCATION

In this chapter, the basic principles of the identification and placement process in special education will be reviewed, along with the Individuals with Disabilities Education Act (IDEA). After reading the chapter and analyzing the cases, you should be able to:

- Describe six basic principles of the IDEA.
- Describe the steps involved in the identification and placement process.
- Analyze and describe connections that exist between the activities that result in a child's placement in special education.
- Analyze common pitfalls for administrators in the identification and placement process that could result in denial of a free appropriate public education (FAPE) and unnecessary conflict.
- Discuss how inclusion can be viewed as an issue of placement.
- Discuss how administrators can be proactive in planning for inclusion.

See semantic map detailing Chapter 3 on page 25.

WHAT DO ADMINISTRATORS NEED TO KNOW?

Consider the following real-life examples involving the identification, evaluation, and placement of children with disabilities in special education programs.

1. In a parent-teacher conference in September, Robin's mother verbally requested that Robin be referred for a special education evaluation. It is now February and Robin has not been evaluated nor has her mother been asked to sign a consent for evaluation. Upon further investigation, it was noted that Robin's teacher thought that only teachers could make referrals and she felt that Robin needed more time in school before a decision about the referral was made. Should Robin's teacher have made the referral even though she did not think it was appropriate or should the request from Robin's mother have been considered a referral?

2. Mrs. King, an elementary building principal, told her teachers at a faculty meeting in August that students in Mrs. White's primary special education class would be scheduled to eat lunch together at 11:00 A.M. before other

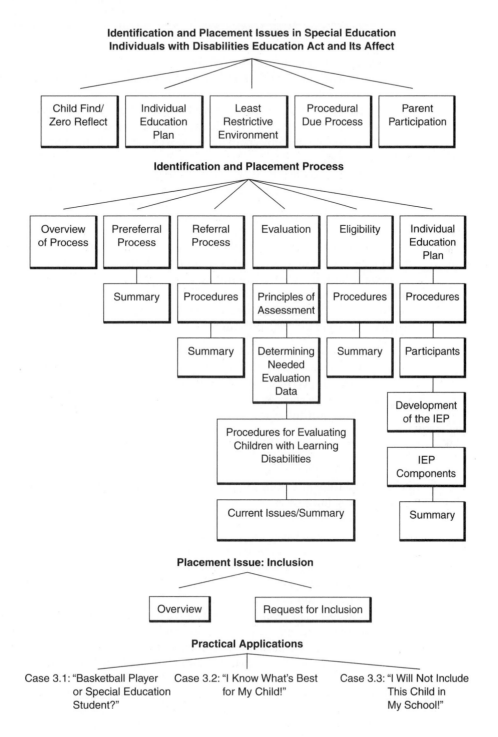

Identification and Placement Issues in Special Education Individuals with Disabilities Education Act and Its Affect

- Child Find/ Zero Reflect
- Individual Education Plan
- Least Restrictive Environment
- Procedural Due Process
- Parent Participation

Identification and Placement Process

- Overview of Process
- Prereferral Process
  - Summary
- Referral Process
  - Procedures
    - Summary
- Evaluation
  - Principles of Assessment
    - Determining Needed Evaluation Data
      - Procedures for Evaluating Children with Learning Disabilities
        - Current Issues/Summary
- Eligibility
  - Procedures
    - Summary
- Individual Education Plan
  - Procedures
    - Participants
      - Development of the IEP
        - IEP Components
          - Summary

Placement Issue: Inclusion

- Overview
- Request for Inclusion

Practical Applications

Case 3.1: "Basketball Player or Special Education Student?"

Case 3.2: "I Know What's Best for My Child!"

Case 3.3: "I Will Not Include This Child in My School!"

primary children entered the cafeteria at 11:30 A.M. When asked why, she said that the scheduling of lunch periods was tight this year and it was convenient to schedule the "special education students" first. Mrs. White was upset as most of her students were to be integrated with nondisabled children during lunch. Mrs. White was told to "change the IEPs." Is it appropriate for Mrs. White to change her childrens' IEPs to accommodate the schedule change?

3. Jamie, a high school student with a behavior disorder, was suspended from school for ten days. When Jamie's attorney reviewed her IEP, it was noted that the only goals and objectives for Jamie were written in the area of mathematics.

   When questioned, the special education mathematics teacher stated that he taught math and, therefore, goals and objectives for all students in his class reflected content in math, not behavior. Should IEP objectives reflect curriculum or the student's needs?

Any of these situations could result in conflict, due process, or litigation. The major issue in each situation centers around the identification and placement process in special education. One might question why these situations still occur, since the prominent law governing special education, i.e., the Individuals with Disabilities Education Act (IDEA) and its predecessor, the Education for All Handicapped Children Act, has been in place since 1975. Contributing factors might include:

1. Lack of knowledge about the statutory law, i.e., the IDEA.
2. Lack of knowledge about local procedures used to identify, evaluate, and place children in special education programs.
3. Lack of knowledge about the connections between each major stage of the identification and placement process.

Special education administrators must develop a shared responsibility with regular education administrators to communicate knowledge, procedures, and connections between these important concepts to teachers and parents. They must do this not only to ensure that children are properly identified, evaluated, and receive appropriate services, but also to avoid costly conflict.

In addition, it would be helpful if regular educators were trained in special education, beyond the usual survey undergraduate course often required for teacher certification. If regular educators and special educators received some common training, special education administrators would develop a shared responsibility with all educators in ensuring that children would be properly identified, evaluated, and would receive appropriate placements.

The focus of this chapter will be to answer the question, "What do administrators need to know about the identification and placement process in special education?" Each important concept in the process will be highlighted and the importance of the connections between each concept will be emphasized. Important issues will be summarized and a brief overview of the IDEA will be included. Because the IDEA forms the basis of information concerning the identification and placement process, foundations of the IDEA will first be reviewed.

INDIVIDUALS WITH DISABILITIES EDUCATION ACT (IDEA) AND ITS EFFECT

The IDEA provides federal monies to states and local education agencies if they agree to comply with certain conditions specified in the law and regulations. The IDEA has had a profound effect on the education of children with disabilities. Its purpose is to assure that children with disabilities receive a free appropriate public education (FAPE) and are not discriminated against in or by any public agency providing special education services. Six building blocks or principles form the foundation of the IDEA (Figure 3.1).

Child Find/Zero Reject

The principle of zero reject means that a local education agency (LEA) can no longer exclude a student with disabilities from the public school due to the nature and/or degree of his/her disability. In other words, all students with disabilities must be provided with a free appropriate public education. The principle of child find says that states are also required to implement procedures to locate children with disabilities who are not being served and inform parents or guardians of programs available.

Nondiscriminatory Assessment

The second principle is nondiscriminatory assessment. Tools used in assessment must be free from racial and cultural bias and must not discriminate on the basis of disability. If the student's native language is not English, the LEA (local education agency) must make an effort to provide an assessment in the student's native language. Assessments must focus on the child's educational needs resulting from the

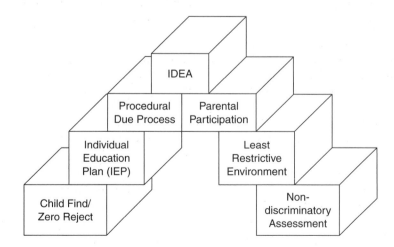

FIGURE 3.1   *Building Blocks of Idea*

disability. Assessment must also be comprehensive and multidisciplinary. Several sources of information should assess all areas of performance. A single measure should never be used as the basis for placement in special education and the evaluation team must consist of persons representing several disciplines with one person knowledgeable about the child's suspected disability. Assessment tools must be technically adequate and administered by trained professionals. In addition, the rights of students and their parents must be protected during evaluation.

Individual Education Plan (IEP)

The third principle is the development of individual education plans (IEPs) for children eligible for special education services. The IEP is child-centered and driven by student needs resulting from the disability. It is essentially a blueprint of special education services needed by the student and goals for the student so he or she can be provided with an appropriate education. Special education services could include specialized instruction, related services like physical therapy or transportation, supplementary aids and services provided to the child, or program modifications or supports for school personnel that will be provided. The IEP is developed by a team, including the child's parents and other professionals.

Least Restrictive Environment (LRE)

The fourth principle of the IDEA is least restrictive environment (LRE). To the maximum extent appropriate, students with disabilities should be educated with children who are not disabled. A continuum of alternative placements must be available to meet the needs of children with disabilities. A continuum of placements can be viewed as having several logical benchmark placements (e.g., resource, self-contained) from least restrictive to more restrictive. In between the benchmarks are a multitude of placements and configurations of services determined by the IEP team.

Procedural Due Process

A fifth principle is the concept of procedural due process. This means that childrens' educational interests are protected and parents are afforded rights to ensure that they are equal partners in the educational process. Examples of procedural rights include the following:

- Parents are to give informed consent for evaluation and initial placement of the child in special education.
- Parents are to be fully informed of all decisions regarding the child in language understandable to the general public and in the native language of the parents.
- If parents disagree with the local education agency's (LEA) decision regarding the child (i.e., placement or evaluation), the parent or LEA may request mediation and/or an impartial due process hearing to resolve the disagreement.

Parent Participation

The sixth principle, parent participation, ensures that parents will be full partners in the education of the child. Parents will be appropriately notified of meetings about the child and will be afforded the opportunity to be full participants in decisions regarding the child's education.

Overview of the Identification and Placement Process

It is essential that all administrators understand the connections between every stage of the identification and placement process in special education (Figure 3.2). The pre-referral process is a way of demonstrating and documenting that valid attempts have been made to assist the child within the regular education setting. If those attempts are unsuccessful, a referral for special education may be made. The documented attempts to maintain the child in the regular classroom will become part of the rationale for the referral and will guide the evaluation team in planning appropriate and efficient assessments. The evaluation team will then gather pertinent data about the child in every area of suspected disability. This information will be used to determine, in the eligibility conference, if the child has a disability, if the disability interferes with learning and the specific needs the child has as a result of the disability. These specific special needs are then used as a foundation for the IEP. The IEP focuses on what special education goals are appropriate to meet the special needs interfering with the child's learning that prevent him/her from success in the regular classroom. In addition, special education services, related services, program modifications and/or support services needed are designated to assist the child in meeting goals and to be involved and progress in the regular education curriculum. Each piece of the identification and placement process will be discussed in detail later in this chapter. However, it is helpful to develop a perspective of the entire process.

Each stage of the identification and placement process is dependent upon the other. Sometimes administrators think that one stage of the process stands in isolation. Consider, for example, the IEP process. An administrator might think that if he or she has an IEP on each child, the child's education is appropriate. However, it is essential that the administrator understand that the foundation for the IEP originates with information from the eligibility conference, i.e., special needs resulting from the disability, the evaluation, the referral, and the prereferral process. If information from one stage is incomplete or incorrect, it is possible that the child's IEP could be affected and appropriate education compromised.

An important role of the special education administrator (and all administrators) is to assure that children are properly identified and receive an appropriate education if a disability is present. In order to fulfill that role, the administrator must draft procedures to operationalize the law in his/her LEA. The procedures should follow federal law and regulations, follow state law and regulations, and be board-approved (both cooperative board, if appropriate, and LEA board). It is essential that the procedures be communicated to all professionals in each LEA and that all personnel follow the procedures. It is embarrassing in a due process hearing when a regular education teacher is testifying

Prereferral → Referral → Evaluation → Determine Eligibility → IEP Process**

Prereferral

Intervention provided by regular education teacher

Referral

Parent
Teacher
Other

Evaluation

Specific assessments (as appropriate)

Parent consultation

Social or cultural assessment

Adaptive behavior assessment

Health, vision, hearing assessment

Social and emotional assessment

General intelligence

Academic performance

Communicative status

For suspected LD, observation of child in regular classroom

Determine Eligibility

Indicate deficits found during evaluation process (i.e., does the child have a disability).

Define special needs (deficit areas) that adversely affect child's learning.

If not eligible for special education, process stops.

If eligible, IEP meeting is conducted.

IEP Process**

Current Performance Levels

Summarize specific areas of need as specified at eligibility meeting. Include current performance level and how disability affects involvement and progress in general curriculum.

Develop Goals and Objectives

Must be based on current performance levels and areas of need as specified at eligibility meeting. Objectives could be related to child's needs to enable him/her to be involved in general curriculum and each other's needs resulting from disability. Describe how child's progress toward goals will be measured, how parents will regularly be informed, and progress made by child.

Determine Services Needed

For each performance level (i.e., area of deficit), list needed special education and related services.

Also list program modifications or support services needed for child to be educated with nondisabled children. Address extent to which child will participate, with/without modifications, in district or state assessments.

Other Services

Include other services needed (i.e., behavioral intervention plan, language needs of limited English proficient children, Braille instructions, communication needs of child, assistive technology, transition, transportation).

Educational Setting Placements

Determine placement. Include explanation of extent to which child will not participate in general education.

**Regular educator shall participate.

FIGURE 3.2 *Identification and Placement Process in Special Education*

about her involvement with a particular child who may have a disability and the teacher states that she does not have knowledge about the LEA's referral process.

PREREFERRAL PROCESS

One trend affecting special education is a concept known as the *prereferral process*. It is viewed as a process to provide a regular education teacher experiencing difficulty with a particular child with interventions to assist that child. Prereferral activities refer to any activity regarding a specific child that occurs prior to formal referral for a special education evaluation. Prereferral interventions can be defined as "individualized accommodations and adaptations made in the general classroom, with the goal of avoiding referral to special education" (Hocutt 1996, 92). Generally, prereferral intervention teams are building-based teams comprised of regular educators whose job it is to assist teachers in generating effective interventions for children experiencing difficulty within the regular education classroom. The prereferral process is not mandated by federal law. However, it is considered best practice.

Prereferral intervention teams have been viewed as a way to reduce referrals to special education and to serve at-risk students within the regular classroom. The teams have had many names since the 1970s, although Graden, Casey, and Christenson (1985) coined the term "prereferral intervention" in special education. Other names include teacher assistance teams (Chalfant, Pysh, and Moultrie 1979), peer intervention teams (Saver and Downes 1991), student study teams (Male 1991), student program planning teams (LRE Project 1990), and child study teams (Laycock, Bable, and Korinek 1991).

The IDEA does not reference the process of prereferral intervention, so it is not a mandatory process. However, the concept has become widely accepted. By 1989, 23 states required and 11 states recommended some form of prereferral intervention (Carter and Sugai 1989). The concept was widely introduced in 1986 by a U.S. Department of Education task force (Will 1986). The task force suggested that schools establish support systems for teachers to assist in helping children experiencing difficulties within the regular education classroom. "The ability of regular education teachers to serve students with learning problems can be greatly enhanced by establishing building level support teams" (Will 1986, 12). These recommendations may also have been a reflection that too many children were being referred for special education, that students were being misclassified, and costs in special education were rising. The purpose in establishing the teams was so that students experiencing learning difficulties could be effectively served within the regular classroom.

In general, teams progress through four stages. First, teams define and clarify the nature of the problem. This stage may include gathering data. Second, teams determine interventions that can be implemented. Third, the interventions are carried out within the classroom. Fourth, the team evaluates the effectiveness of the interventions. Forms are often used to track and document the progress of the team (see Figures 3.3 and 3.4).

Research data on the effectiveness of prereferral intervention teams has been generally supportive of the process. Teachers perceive that students progress toward goals established, fewer students are referred for special education evaluations, and

Student Name: _____   Date of Birth: _____

Teacher Name: _____   Grade: _____   Race: _____

1. Reason for referral. (Briefly describe the problem including adverse effects on the child's education.)

_____

_____

_____

_____

2. Describe any interventions you have tried to remediate the problem.

_____

_____

_____

3. Does this child receive any specialized services? (special education, speech/language, Title I)

_____

_____

_____

4. Does this child have any medical, social, emotional problems that might influence his/her progress?

_____

_____

_____

5. What question/concerns would you like addressed by the consultation team?

_____

_____

_____

(Please bring any work samples and/or documentation that reflect this child's problem.)

FIGURE 3.3   *Example: Consultation Team Request for Consultation*

Student Name: _____ DOB: _____

Teacher Name: _____ Grade: _____

Date of Consultation Meeting: _____

Target Deficits/Behaviors:

1. _____

2. _____

Intervention (strategies, techniques, adaptations):

_____

_____

_____

_____

_____

_____

_____

_____

_____

Scheduled Review Date: _____
Intervention Review:

_____

_____

_____

_____

_____

_____

_____

_____

Participants: _____

FIGURE 3.4   *Example: Consultation Team Intervention Plan*

teachers increase skills in working with students who have learning and behavioral problems (Bay, Bryan, and O'Conner 1994; Chalfant and Van Dusen Pysh 1989; Gutkin, Henning-Stout, and Piersel 1988; Nelson et al. 1991; Slavin, Karweit, and Madden 1989). It is important to also note that improved quality of interventions led to more successful outcomes for students (Flugum and Reschly 1994).

Summary

It is likely that educators in the future will continue to see an emphasis on the prereferral intervention process. The process focuses on prevention of learning and behavioral problems and serving as many children as appropriate within the regular classroom. In the past, educators often engaged in an immediate reaction of referral to special education when faced with learning and behavioral problems in the classroom setting. Where prereferral teams are functional, this is no longer the situation. If prereferral interventions are not successful, a referral to special education would be appropriate. Data gathered about the child and the interventions used in the prereferral process (e.g., authentic assessments) could be useful in the referral to special education and possible placement of the child in special education.

REFERRAL PROCESS

When a child is not successful in the regular education classroom despite the best efforts of the teacher and prereferral team to implement successful strategies, the teacher or parent might initiate a formal referral for an evaluation to determine if the child has a disability. Salvia and Ysseldyke (1995) define referral as a " . . . formal process involving the completion of a referral form and a request for a team of professionals to decide whether a student's academic, behavioral, or physical development warrants the provision of special education services" (p. 12).

Referrals are an important piece of the identification and placement process as most children who are referred are evaluated and found eligible for special education services. Research has shown that 3 to 5 percent of students in public schools are referred for evaluations, 92 percent of those referred are tested, and 73 percent of those tested are found eligible for special education (Algozzine, Christenson, and Ysseldyke 1982). This data has not changed significantly since the original study was conducted in 1982 (Ysseldyke, Vanderwood, and Shriner 1997).

Procedures

After a referral is made, the regular education teacher usually completes a referral form. The referral form is forwarded to a child study team who makes a determination on whether the referral is warranted. In most cases, referrals proceed to an evaluation and parents must be fully informed of the decision to accept or reject the referral for an evaluation. The specific content of a referral form will differ depending on the LEA procedures. An example of a referral form is detailed in Figure 3.5.

Referrals are not subject to federal law. Federal law states that the LEA must conduct a full and individual initial evaluation to determine if the child has a disability and to determine the educational needs of the child. It is generally accepted that the

REFERRAL FOR EVALUATION

Student's Name _____ Birthdate _____ CA _____ Sex _____ Grade _____
Parent/Guardian _____ School _____
Address _____ Home Phone _____ Work Phone _____
Language Spoken in Home _____ Language Used by Child _____
Principal's Signature _____ Person Requesting Evaluation _____
Classroom Teacher _____

1. Is there any reason to believe the child has any of the following handicaps?

_____Visual _____Orthopedic _____Other _____Speech _____Hearing

Describe:

2. Reason for referral. Student has difficulty in the following areas:

_____Reading   _____Math
_____Spoken language   _____Written language (includes spelling)
_____Fine motor (i.e., handwriting) _____Gross motor
_____Social skills   _____Classroom behavior
_____Emotional status   _____Attention/on-task behavior
_____Other (describe):

3. Describe in detail your concerns about the areas marked. Use reverse side if needed.

4. Attach *copies* of transcripts (current year & 1 page cumulative grade sheet) and
   achievement test scores (i.e., SRA, Chapter 1, etc.).

5. Mode of communication:

_____Spoken language   _____Gestures
_____Signing   _____Unstructured sounds
_____Other, please explain: _____
_____

6. Cultural background (i.e., urban, rural, etc.):

7. Present instructional levels:

Subject	Current grades (i.e., A, B, S, M/C, etc.)	Teacher Estimate of Child's Skill Level (i.e., beginning 4th grade level)
Reading		
Spelling		
Arithmetic		
Written language		
Other		
Other		

FIGURE 3.5 *Example: Referral Form (continued)*

8. Interventions tried:	Effective	Not Effective	Comments About Interventions
a. Consultation with parents			
b. Clarification of classroom rules			
c. High interest, low-level materials			
d. Use of peer tutors			
e. 1–1 teacher time			
f. Counselor conference			
g. Repeat/reteach (direction)			
h. Remedial classes			
i. Varied use of learning or modes (i.e., groups, individuals)			
j. Breakdown of tasks into smaller increments, modify/shorten assignments			
k. Use of different learning approaches (visual auditory, multisensory, kinesthetic)			
l. Modification of schedule or school day			
m. Use of work on behavior contracts			
n. Use of instructional aides			
o. Brief student on key points before starting assignments			
p. Frequent feedback/reinforcement re: work/behavior			
q. Oral exams or reports			
r. Modify the physical environment (change seating, grouping, carrels)			
s. Reduce the reading level of assignments			
t. Allow more time for assignments/tests			
u. Other(s); please list			
v. Interventions implemented as part of the prereferral consultation team. If yes, please attach request for consultation and intervention plan.			

Date Form Completed _____

Date of Referral _____

FIGURE 3.5 *Example: Referral Form (continued)*

REFERRAL STATUS (to be completed by psychologist):

CONSULTATION WITH TEACHER:

Referral is:

_____ Accepted _____

_____ Rejected _____

Special referral questions to be answered:

1. _____

   _____

2. _____

   _____

3. _____

   _____

FIGURE 3.5   *Example: Referral Form (continued)*

referral date is the date when the request is made for an evaluation, either verbally or in writing. In the case of Robin, summarized at the beginning of this chapter, the parent verbally made a request for an evaluation in September. Because the teacher felt that Robin needed more time in school to make a referral request, the referral was never made. Robin's teacher should have formalized a referral based on the parent's request as this verbal request should have been considered a referral. If the LEA had written policy and procedures to detail the referral process, the teacher might have pursued a different action, i.e., a referral.

Summary

It is important that a connection be made between what happened prior to the referral and the formal referral for an evaluation. A referral should summarize information from prereferral teams (i.e., what was successful with the child, what was not successful with the child). A referral should not be a quick reaction to a child experiencing difficulty in school. Rather, it should be the next carefully thought-out step in a process to help all children succeed. Figure 3.6 shows a conceptualization of how referrals for evaluation can be viewed within this context. As indicated, most children will never require any special interventions to be successful in the regular classroom. A smaller number of children will need different interventions determined by the classroom teacher to be successful. Of this group, a smaller number of children

FIGURE 3.6   *Referral Process*

will be the subjects of prereferral intervention teams. Still a smaller number of students will be referred for a full evaluation to determine if a disability is present as all levels of intervention were unsuccessful.

It is essential that the formal referral process be delineated and communicated to all professionals within the LEA. If a parent makes a request, however informal, that a particular child needs to be evaluated for special education, the regular education teacher would know that this is a referral and the formal referral process should immediately begin. Likewise, if a regular education teacher verbalizes that a child should be evaluated, the formal referral process should proceed. This procedure does not prevent the child study team from determining that the referral should be rejected, but ensures that action will be taken on each and every referral for an evaluation, however informal the request. An administrator would not want a child to be identified as having a disability in the sixth grade only to find out that every teacher from kindergarten through fifth grade noted concerns about the child's progress.

EVALUATION

After a child has been referred for an evaluation, a child study team conducts an assessment or evaluation of the child. Assessment can be defined as "the process of collecting data for the purpose of (1) specifying and verifying problems and (2) making decisions about students" (Salvia and Ysseldyke 1995, 741).

The IDEA provides specific procedures for assessing a child so that each child referred receives a full and individual evaluation, if appropriate. The purpose of the assessment or evaluation is to determine if the child has a disability and to determine the educational needs of the child. Specific procedures concerning evaluation include the five principles that follow.

Assessment Is Nondiscriminatory

Assessment must be nondiscriminatory. Tools used should be free from racial and cultural bias. If the student's native language is not English, every effort must be made to provide the assessment in the student's native language to prevent a child from being labeled as having a disability when the child's native language is the issue of concern. In addition, tools must not discriminate on the basis of disability. For example, if a child is blind, the examiner would not want to use a visual test to assess reading. If assessment is discriminatory, children could be inappropriately labeled as disabled.

Assessment Focuses on Educational Needs

An assessment must determine the educational needs resulting from the child's disability. It is not enough to determine that a child has a disability. For example, a child may have cerebral palsy and be confined to a wheelchair. However, the child may not have special needs resulting from the disability that prevent him/her from success in the regular classroom. According to the IDEA, this child would not be eligible for special education services based on the lack of special needs resulting from the disability. It can be noted that this child would be protected from discrimination by other federal laws (i.e., Americans with Disabilities Act, Section 504 of the Rehabilitation Act of 1973).

Assessment Is Comprehensive and Multidisciplinary

All areas of suspected disability should be assessed including, if appropriate, health, vision, hearing, social and emotional status, general intelligence, academic performance, communicative status, and motor abilities. Information gathered by the assessment should be functional and developmental. Areas assessed should use several sources of information. No single measure can be used as the basis for eligibility and placement in special education. The child study team assessing a child must consist of persons representing several different disciplines with at least one person knowledgeable about the child's suspected disability. Comprehensive and multidisciplinary assessment is one way to prevent bias and discrimination in assessment and placement.

Assessment Tools Are Technically Adequate and Administered by Trained Professionals

Tools used to assess a child must be validated for the specific purpose for which they are used. Tests and other evaluation materials must be administered by trained personnel. For example, if a 14-year-old is assessed in the area of expressive language with a test normed for three- to seven-year-olds, the test would not be valid for the 14-year-old.

The Rights of Students Must Be Protected

A basic tenet of the IDEA is that parents and professionals participate in shared decision making in regard to the child's education. Parents, therefore, exercise specific rights on behalf of the child. Rights of parents with respect to evaluation are summarized below.

- Parents must receive written notice prior to initiating or changing the identification, evaluation, or educational placement of the child.
- Parents must give written informed consent prior to:
  1. an initial evaluation,
  2. a reevaluation, and
  3. an initial placement.
- If parents refuse to give consent, the LEA may:
  1. request mediation, and/or
  2. request a due process hearing.
- Parents have the right to:
  1. inspect and review records, and
  2. obtain copies of records at no cost, depending upon ability to pay.
- Parents have the right to:
  1. an independent evaluation, and
  2. have the LEA pay for the independent evaluation if it is determined at a due process hearing that the LEA evaluation was not appropriate.

Determining Needed Evaluation Data

An IEP team may determine needed evaluation data for initial evaluations, as appropriate, or reevaluations. If available, teams may review existing evaluation data on the child including information provided by the parent and classroom-based assessments (including observations). On the basis of that data, the team will decide what additional data, if any, are needed to determine if the child has a disability or continues to have a disability. If the team determines that additional data are needed, the LEA will administer tests and other evaluations as necessary. For example, a parent of a child with a learning disability may submit a psychological evaluation completed by a local teaching hospital. The IEP team might decide, in completing a reevaluation, that an additional psychological evaluation completed by school staff would be redundant. The team might decide to include the hospital's psychological evaluation and gather achievement data, speech and language assessment data, and an assessment of the learning environment.

Additional Procedures for Evaluating Children with Learning Disabilities

If it is suspected that a child being evaluated may have a learning disability, the IDEA requires additional procedures. To identify a child as learning disabled, the following procedures apply.

- Team members are expanded to include:
  1. the child's regular teacher, and
  2. at least one person qualified to conduct an individual diagnostic evaluation of children (e.g., school psychologist, remedial reading teacher).
- One team member, other than the child's teacher, must observe the child in the regular classroom.
- A written report of the team's findings must include:
  1. statements of whether the child has a learning disability,
  2. the basis for this decision,
  3. behavior noted during the classroom observation,
  4. the relationship of the behavior to academic functioning,
  5. relevant medical findings,
  6. whether there is a severe discrepancy between achievement and ability not correctable without special education services, and
  7. any impact of environmental, cultural, or economic disadvantage.

Current Issues/Summary

The identification process and assessment practices have been criticized in recent years. There have been reported problems with current assessment practices related not only to methods and technical quality (Christenson and Ysseldyke 1989; Reschly 1980; Salvia and Ysseldyke 1995; Witt 1986), but to the context and purpose for which methods were used. Other concerns included a lack of connection between assessment and student needs (Reschly 1996).

The formal assessment of children to determine who is or who is not eligible for special education has been viewed as a gatekeeping function, with little connection to the prereferral and referral processes or to the planning and instruction process. Once a child had failed to succeed in the regular classroom and a referral made, the assessment process often consisted of a "standard battery" of tests, often administered by a school psychologist. Educational tests administered by the school psychologist (and other specialists) often were administered in a separate room isolated from the child's natural environments. There often was little connection between a psychologist's formal test scores and formulating a plan for instruction.

In a position paper written by the National Association of School Psychologists (NASP/NASDE/OSEP 1994), sweeping changes in the identification and assessment process in special education were recommended. The first step recommended was to change the categorical classification system and fund services needed by children without disability categories. Second, it was recommended that a comprehensive problem-solving approach be promoted that would be used to determine eligibility for special services, to organize and provide those services, to monitor progress, and to evaluate outcomes. Specific assessment changes resulting from these recommendations would include a focus more on intervention—that is, what can be changed in environments to produce improved learning, and a focus on gathering information in natural environments with direct measures of behavior instead of the standard battery of formal tests (e.g., intelligence tests, achievement tests). These measures would then be used to define problems, establish interventions, monitor progress, and evaluate outcomes as well as be used as a basis for classification of students as eligible for more intensive programs.

The traditional role of the school psychologist as "testing and placing" children in special education is evolving and changing. More emphasis is placed on consultation, prevention, and problem-solving functions. The old paradigm of the school psychologist as primarily administering standardized tests is slowly being supplemented by a new role where psychologists assist teachers in developing effective interventions in regular classrooms and possibly participate in school-based prereferral teams.

An example of a statewide initiative began in 1987 in Iowa (Tilly, Flugum, and Reschly 1996). Stakeholders in special education met and determined several areas of concern in special education. The major issues of concern included the following areas:

1. There was a perception of overreferral of students for evaluations and the overidentification of students to be placed in special education.
2. There was a perception of overemphasis on standardized assessment techniques utilized primarily to determine if a student is eligible for special education.
3. Evaluation of special education activities has been based too much on programs rather than student outcomes.

Out of these concerns grew an educational reform movement titled the Iowa Renewed Service Delivery System (RSDS). After changes were piloted in trial sites, the reform includes over 90 percent of all school-age students in Iowa. The purpose of these reforms was to increase the availability of effective educational programs and to more clearly document the effectiveness of educational programs to students. Some of the principles underlying RSDS included:

1. Better integration of special and regular education services for students with disabilities and at risk for school failure;
2. Reduced reliance on teaching children with special needs in separate settings;
3. Greater emphasis on meaningful assessment procedures, e.g., curriculum-based measurement;
4. Measuring student performance frequently and changing programs when students weren't successful;
5. Prevention of and early intervention through prereferral activities.

In many schools, changes were made in established educational practices in both special and regular education to better meet the needs of all students. Initial evaluations of the statewide project have been encouraging (Tilly, Flugum, and Reschly 1996; Tilly et al. 1992). This unique plan was collaboratively sponsored by the Iowa Department of Education, Area Education Agencies and local school districts.

Other statewide and local educational agency changes in assessment practices are occurring throughout the country. These innovative projects often give priority to connecting the evaluation process with instruction or developing meaningful interventions to directly assist a child succeed. Given support and careful planning, these innovative programs may change the way we assess children and provide services.

ELIGIBILITY

Upon completion of an evaluation, it must be determined if the child has a disability. In addition, special needs of the child must be specified. Prior to the passage of Public Law 94-142, these decisions were sometimes made unilaterally by teachers or administrators using little data without parental input. After 1975, the decisions were required to be made by a team of professionals, including the parents, using various sources of information. In making these decisions, teams must do more than determine that a child has a disability. Some students can be disabled and not require special education, that is, not have special needs.

The IDEA has designated thirteen categories of disability and they include: mental retardation, deafness, deaf-blindness, hearing impairment, speech or language impairment, visual impairment, emotional disturbance, orthopedic impairment, autism, traumatic brain injury, other health impairment, multiple disabilities, or specific learning disability. State definitions of disabilities must be consistent with federal law, but may vary. For example, a state may opt to categorize children with disabilities, ages 3 through 9, as having a "developmental delay," or a state may use the term "behavior disorder" rather than "serious emotional disturbance."

Procedures

Based upon the evaluation, a team of qualified professionals and the parent (i.e., child study team) must determine if the child has a disability and specify the special needs of the child, if any exist. In making these decisions, the team will draw upon information from several sources, including aptitude and achievement tests, teacher input, physical status of the child, cultural background of the child, and adaptive behavior of the child. All information considered must be documented and the LEA must provide a copy of the evaluation report and documentation of eligibility to the parent.

Summary

Making an eligibility determination is very important because the child's program and placement are built upon this information. Therefore, it is essential that evaluations contain valid data upon which the team can make sound decisions about eligibility and special needs so that appropriate instructional planning can occur. It is when these pieces are disconnected that problems occur. Consider, for example, the scenario at the beginning of this chapter about Jamie. Jamie's IEP only had goals and objectives in the area of mathematics, presumably his only class in special education. One may also assume that Jamie was labeled behavior disordered because he had special needs resulting from this disability that interfered with success in the regular classroom. It is these needs that should have been addressed in Jamie's IEP, not the curriculum content of mathematics. The process appeared to break down between the assessment phase, the eligibility phase, and the planning phase. The reason this occurred could have many possibilities. Perhaps the child study team who determined Jamie's eligibility for special education did not clearly specify special needs resulting from the disability, making it difficult to write appropriate goals and objectives. Maybe, due to lack of information, the special education mathematics teacher did not know that IEPs should be written addressing special needs determined at the eligibility stage. Whatever the reason, errors like this occur more often than most administrators would like to admit. It is these seemingly small errors that contribute to inappropriate placements and the growing body of litigation. It is clearly important that the team making eligibility decisions be well informed about how to make these decisions—that is, that eligibility should be consistent with state and federal law and that special needs resulting from the disability should be detailed enough so that appropriate placements can be built upon the information.

INDIVIDUAL EDUCATION PLAN (IEP)

As defined by the IDEA, an IEP is "a written statement for a child with a disability that is developed and implemented in accordance with (the IDEA)" (IDEA, 20 U.S.C. § 1401 (a)(20)). Essentially, the IEP is the "heart" of the law. Without an IEP, students with disabilities would be dependent upon the good will of the school districts to provide services. An effective IEP is:

1. A communication vehicle between parents and LEA personnel so that services can be collaboratively determined;
2. An opportunity for resolving differences;
3. A commitment of resources from the LEA to ensure appropriate services;
4. A management tool for the LEA;
5. A compliance document for state and federal compliance agencies;
6. An evaluation device to assess student progress toward goals and objectives.

The IEP provides a blueprint for instruction and a planning tool. It picks up where the eligibility decision ended and provides the link between evaluation and instruction (Figure 3.7). Areas of special need as specified in the eligibility conference should be directly addressed in the IEP goals, objectives, and services provided. The local education agency or school district (LEA) must provide all services detailed in

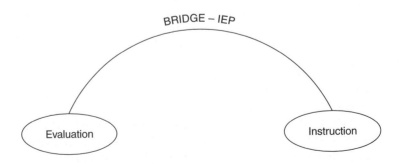

FIGURE 3.7 *Connection Between Evaluation and Instruction*

the IEP; however, the LEA is not legally accountable if the child does not reach goals and objectives. The LEA must make a good faith effort to assist each child in reaching goals and objectives.

There are two parts to the IEP. The first part is the IEP meeting and the second part is the document produced (i.e., the IEP) at the meeting. The IEP document becomes a written record of decisions reached at the meeting.

Procedures

The IDEA mandates strict procedures for developing an IEP. If there are numerous or serious violations in the IEP it could be inappropriate, denying the child a free appropriate public education—FAPE, which is a foundation of the federal law. For example, if an IEP was written without notifying the parents of the IEP meeting, the parents would have had no input into the IEP. This procedural error could render the IEP inappropriate. As another example, if a child was supposed to receive speech therapy for 60 minutes per week and only received therapy 15 minutes per week, the LEA would be at fault for committing services and not providing the services. The child's access to a free and appropriate education would be compromised.

The specific format of forms used to develop an IEP are not addressed in the IDEA and are left to the discretion of states and LEAs. Some states have developed mandated forms and others have developed recommended forms.

Participants

The IEP team could consist of eight persons including the following:

1. The child's parent or guardian;
2. The child's regular education teacher, if the child is or may be participating in regular education;
3. The special education teacher who is or may be providing services;
4. An LEA representative who is qualified to provide or supervise special curriculum, and who is knowledgeable about resource availability in the LEA;
5. A professional who can interpret the instructional implications of the evaluation results;
6. Other persons, at the discretion of the parent or LEA;
7. The child, if appropriate (required for transition IEP);
8. Transition services providers if it is likely that they might be responsible for providing or paying for transition services.

The 1997 amendments to the IDEA include the following changes with respect to participants:

- The regular education teacher must be present if the child may be or is placed in regular education.
- The regular education teacher must participate in the development of positive behavioral interventions, if appropriate, and the determination of supplementary aids and services, program modifications, and supports for the child.

- There is an emphasis on the attendance of the parent:
    1. Meetings may be conducted without a parent if the LEA is unable, by documented attempts, to convince the parent to attend.
    2. Although the IDEA does not specify the specific number of times a parent must be contacted, it does give examples of the types of contact the LEA must make. Documented attempts should include records indicating the meeting was scheduled at a mutually convenient time and place, records of telephone calls to reach the parent, and records of home visits or visits to the parent's place of employment. Parents must be properly notified in advance of the meeting by written notice.

Development of the IEP

The IEP team must review an IEP at least annually and any other time significant changes are anticipated in the child's program. After conducting an IEP meeting, it is good practice to document on the IEP form and date any and all changes in the child's program. When in doubt of whether or not to hold an IEP meeting, it is better to err on the side of holding a meeting. As an administrator, it is easy to understand the evolution of a child's program if changes and dates of those changes are clearly noted on the IEP form.

When developing or revising an IEP, the team must consider the strengths of the child, parental concerns, and results of the child's most recent evaluation. Depending upon the child, the team must also make five special considerations. First, if the child's behavior impedes his/her learning or the learning of others, the team must consider positive behavioral strategies and supports to address the behavior. For example, if a third grade child with learning disabilities fights with other children on the playground, the IEP team should consider strategies and supports for the child. Second, if the child is limited in English proficiency, the team must consider the language needs of the child as they relate to the child's IEP. For example, if the child is from a Spanish-speaking home and is limited in speaking English, the IEP team might consider providing an interpreter in some situations. Third, if the child is blind or visually impaired, the team must provide for instruction in Braille unless, after careful consideration, it is determined that the use of Braille is not appropriate. Fourth, the team must consider the communication needs of the child, especially if the child is deaf or hard of hearing. In that case, the team must consider opportunities for direct communication with other children and LEA personnel in the child's language and communication mode. For example, if a high school student is the only deaf child in the school and communicates primarily by American sign language, the team must consider opportunities for the child to communicate with peers and other school staff in American sign language. Last, the team must determine if the child requires assistive technology devices and services. For example, if a child is quadriplegic, the team might recommend a special computer with a mouthstick and an adapted computer table for the child.

IEP Components

There are ten components of an IEP. Each must be documented by a statement(s) on the IEP form to meet legal requirements. Each component is detailed below.

The Child's Current Level of Performance

This is a statement in narrative on the IEP reflecting the child's performance in areas of special need as determined in the evaluation and discussed in the eligibility conference. A direct relationship should exist between this statement and other components of the IEP. The statement is a reflection of the areas of special need, the child's eligibility for special education, or how the disability affects the child's involvement in the regular curriculum. It tells the reader the level of accomplishment prior to beginning instruction. For example, if a fifth grader was learning disabled, the eligibility conference participants might have indicated that his inability to recognize words by sight and phonics interfered with his learning in the regular classroom. This would have been an area of special need that interfered with learning and needed to be addressed in the IEP. In making a statement of present levels of performance on the IEP, the team might write, "John is unable to sound out three-letter words and is unable to identify half of the 220 Dolch sight words. This prevents him from success in the regular curriculum, as the curriculum focuses on reading 20-page stories on a fifth grade level. John is able to use context clues to assist in decoding words."

Annual Goals and Benchmarks or Short-Term Objectives

Goals and objectives must be related to meeting the child's needs that result from his/her disability to enable him/her to be involved in the regular curriculum and to progress. They must also meet each of the child's other educational needs resulting from his/her disability. There should be a direct connection between statements made in present levels of performance and goals and objectives. Using the example above, an appropriate goal and objective for John might be the following:

Goal: In 30 weeks, when given a passage selected randomly from level 4 or level 5 of the regular education reading curriculum, John will read aloud at a rate of 100 words correct per minute.

Objective: In 15 weeks, when given a passage selected randomly from level 4 or level 5 of the regular education reading curriculum, John will read aloud at a rate of 40 words correct per minute.

The goal is measurable and tells us where we are going in relation to where we began prior to special instruction, i.e., present level of performance. The objective or benchmark is an intermediate step in reaching the goal. It is also specific and measurable. In the example of John, one goal and three objectives might be appropriate. In the case of a child with a severe disability, several areas would be addressed in present levels of performance and several goals and objectives would correspond. The number of areas addressed in present levels of performance and the number of goals and objectives would depend upon how many areas of special need were determined to interfere with learning in the regular curriculum.

Special Education and Related Services, Supplementary Aids and Services, and Program Modifications or Supports for School Personnel

Services provided to the child must assist the child in advancing toward annual goals and in moving toward involvement and progress in the general curriculum and nonacademic activities. Services must also educate the child with other children (with and without disabilities). For example, consider the case from the beginning of this chapter stating that the special education teacher was told to change children's IEPs to accommodate the lunch schedule. In addition, the change would affect the services required by these children, i.e., the students were to be integrated with nondisabled children at lunch time. It would not be proper or legal to change these children's services detailed on the IEPs just to accommodate a schedule. One assumes that the services detailed on the IEP, including eating lunch with nondisabled children, was to assist each child in making progress toward goals and objectives. To make this change because of a scheduling conflict would compromise meeting the children's needs.

The Extent, If Any, to Which the Child Will Not Participate with Nondisabled Children in the Regular Classroom

On the IEP there must be an explanation of the extent to which the child will not be educated with nondisabled children. The unstated assumption is that the child will be educated with nondisabled children and, if not, there must be a reasonable rationale. For example, it would not be appropriate to place a child in a self-contained special education class just because the child's "academic achievement in reading and spelling were two grade levels below average." A more appropriate rationale might include specifying the accommodations and supplementary services that have been attempted unsuccessfully despite the poor achievement in reading and spelling.

Modifications in the Administration of State or District-Wide Assessments of Student Achievement; and, If Not Participating, Why Not, and How the Child Will Be Assessed

Most states and LEAs administer assessments to children to measure their performance and many tie assessments to progress toward state and/or local standards or outcomes (*Education Week* 1998). Participation by students with disabilities in these state assessments varies from 10 percent in Colorado to more than 90 percent in Kentucky (Shriner 1993). The 1997 amendments of the IDEA stipulated that this decision should be determined at the IEP meeting, although some states (e.g., Illinois) have been making these decisions in IEP meetings prior to the federal mandate. If the IEP team determines that a child will not participate in the state or local assessment, it must state why the assessment is not appropriate and tell how the child will be assessed.

Inconsistent guidance has been available regarding the participation of students with disabilities in state and local assessments. An example of a form used to document this decision process appears in Figure 3.8.

The Projected Date for the Beginning of Services and Modifications and the Anticipated Frequency, Location, and Duration of Those Services and Modifications

The date that services and/or modifications will begin must be included on the IEP. In addition, how often services will be offered (e.g., how many sessions per week), where the services will be delivered (e.g., in the regular classroom or special class-

Student Name _____

Date of Birth _____

Year _____

Grade Placement for Assessment
Considerations

State Assessment Is Administered as Follows

Language Arts: Grades 3, 6, 8, 10

Mathematics: Grades 3, 6, 8, 10

Biological & Physical Sciences: Grades 4, 7, 11

Social Sciences: Grades 4, 7, 11

Fine Arts: State Determined

Physical Development/Health: State Determined

Accommodation Codes

1. Use of audiocassette for directions only.
2. Instructions provided in other modes (e.g., sign, Braille, native language).
3. Augmentative communication devices (e.g., braillewriter, computer, typewriter).
4. Use of tests in large print or Braille.
5. Use of calculators as allowable, according to IGAP instruction book.
6. Use of other assistive devices as used during routine instruction.
7. Modification of test site (e.g., lighting, space).
8. Modification of the time allowed.
9. Modifications as used during routine instruction or test taking.
10. Other (specify):

Rationale Codes

A Invalid due to lack of exposure to the curriculum
B Invalid due to inability to function in a similar test situation
C Invalid due to the nature of the student's disability
D Other (specify):

Participation in State Assessment

Write yes or no next to each learning area. If yes, note the accommodation code, *if needed*. If no, note the rationale code. (Use the additional space as needed.)

Learning Area	Code	Rationale	Other
Lang. Arts			
Math Code			
Biology/PS Code			
Social Sci. Code			
Fine Arts Code			
Phy. Dev. Code			

If the child will not participate in the state assessment, indicate how the child will be assessed:

_____

_____

FIGURE 3.8 *Example: State and Local Assessment Considerations*

room), and how long the services will be offered (e.g., the entire academic year or summer only) must be indicated. Sometimes teachers will not be specific enough in documenting this information. For example, an IEP might indicate the duration of services by writing "one year." If the service begins in October, the duration suggests that the service will be continued throughout the summer and be reviewed in October the following year. An LEA could be required to provide the service throughout the summer even though the intent was not to provide summer services.

How the Child's Progress Toward Annual Goals Will Be Measured

Specific assessments must be listed that will demonstrate how the child is progressing toward annual goals. In the case of John summarized above, his goal of improving reading fluency is general and the teacher must indicate how his progress will be measured. In this case, John's progress will be measured as detailed in the objective. It is projected that John will read, with fewer than 6 errors, at a rate of 100 words per minute from level 4 and 5 reading curriculum materials.

How the Parents Will Be Regularly Informed of the Child's Progress Toward Goals (at Least as Often as Nondisabled Children's Parents Are Informed)

Parents must be regularly informed of their child's progress toward annual goals and the extent to which progress is sufficient to allow the child to achieve goals by the end of the year. "Regularly informed" means as often as parents of children in regular classes are informed of progress. Often, parents of children in regular education classes are informed quarterly by means of a report card of progress. Sometimes, parents of older children receive mid-quarter progress reports. In any case, the frequency must match regular education and specifically address progress toward annual goals.

Detailed Transition Services

Transition services should be an integral part of IEP program planning and instruction. Transition is defined as

> a coordinated set of activities for a student with a disability that (A) are designed within an outcome-oriented process, which promotes movement from school to post-school activities, including post-secondary education, vocational training, integrated employment (including supported employment), continuing and adult education, adult services, independent living, or community participation; (B) are based upon the individual student's needs, taking into account the student's preferences and interests; and (C) include instruction, related services, community experiences, the development of employment and other post-school adult living objectives, and, when appropriate, acquisition of daily living skills and functional vocational evaluation (20 U.S.C. § 1401 (a)(19)).

For students age 14 or younger, if appropriate, a transition statement on the IEP must indicate needed services that focus on the student's courses of study. For example, if it is appropriate for a student to participate in vocational education, this must be indicated on the IEP. By age 16 or younger, if appropriate, a transition statement of needed services must be included. This statement may include interagency responsibilities or linkages as needed. More specifically, the IEP team must address goals in each of the service areas of instruction, community experiences, development of employment and other post-school adult living objectives, and as appropriate, acquisition of daily living skills and functional vocational evaluation. If the IEP team determines that no services are needed within a particular area, then a statement to that effect and rationale for the statement must be included in the IEP.

As an example, consider the case of Tim, a 16-year-old high school student labeled BD/LD. After gaining input from Tim, the IEP team wrote the following transition goal:

Tim will work in the field of building trades and live in an apartment with his
    friend.

Services needed by Tim to reach the transition goal included the following:

Tim will receive 60 minutes per week (two sessions) of social skills instruction from
    the BD/LD teacher in a special education classroom. Instruction will begin
    September 5 and end May 31.
Tim will receive five-week job trials from staff at the Area Vocational Center
    beginning September 5 and ending January 15. Job trials will occur off
    campus for two hours daily five days per week.

Transfer of Rights, at Least One Year Before Reaching the Age of Majority Under State Law

At least one year before the student reaches the age of majority in the state, each state has the option of including a statement in the IEP that the student has been informed of his/her rights under the IDEA and that those rights will transfer to the student upon reaching the age of majority.

Summary

In general, administrators must remember that the IEP is the centerpiece of federal law and the means for documenting free appropriate public education (FAPE). A review of special education litigation from 1978 to 1995 indicated that free appropriate public education was one of the most litigated areas (Maloney and Shenker 1995).

Each IEP must be individualized and based on a student's needs, not current configuration of services available within the LEA. For example, a second grade student was identified as having a severe learning disability. The LEA didn't have a self-contained classroom for students with learning disabilities at the primary level. Even though the child might have needed maximum services in a special education self-contained setting, the LEA decided to place the child in a resource setting. In this case, the placement was based on services available, not those needed by the student.

It is also important that areas of special need designated by the evaluation team and eligibility conference should tie directly to the IEP via present levels of performance, goals, objectives, and needed services. Goals and objectives should focus on reducing problems that have resulted from the child's disability and are interfering with the child's ability to learn in the regular classroom environment.

If administrators clearly communicate policy and procedures to all appropriate staff within the LEA, it is likely that children will receive free appropriate public education and the LEA can defend its position if there is conflict regarding placement.

PLACEMENT ISSUE: INCLUSION

Inclusion can best be viewed as an issue of individual placement. If a child is to receive all or some special services within the regular classroom, this placement configuration must be reflected in the IEP. It is the IEP team that determines specific special services a child needs to receive a free appropriate public education. Research "suggests that the most effective interventions for students with disabilities have the following characteristics: a case-by-case approach to decision making about student instruction and placement; intensive and reasonably individualized instruction combined with very close cooperation between general and special education teachers; and careful, frequent monitoring of student progress" (Hocutt, 97).

In inclusive schooling, "students attend their home school with their age and grade peers. It requires that the proportion of students labeled for special services is relatively uniform for all of the schools within a particular school district, and that this ratio reflects the proportion of people with disabilities in society at large. Included students are not isolated into special classes or wings within the school. To the maximum extent possible, included students receive their in-school educational services in the general education classroom with appropriate in-class support" (National Association of State Boards of Education 1992).

Requests for Inclusion

When a request for inclusion is made by a parent, it is far more useful for an administrator to be proactive rather than reactive. Any request for inclusion should result in an IEP meeting where the request will be carefully considered. In the IEP meeting, the following questions must be addressed:

1. Can education in the regular classroom with supplementary aids and services be achieved satisfactorily? Discussion on this matter might include expectations in the regular classroom and the student's ability to meet those expectations with or without assistance. If the answer is no, then:
2. Has the district included the student to the maximum extent appropriate?
3. Have steps been taken to accommodate the student in the regular class? Have supplementary aids and services in the regular class setting been considered? If no steps have been attempted, that is a matter of concern. In addition, steps should be more than token steps.
4. Is there benefit to the student with a disability in the regular class? The discussion might focus on the nature and the severity of the disability and the curriculum of the regular class. The team should look beyond academic benefit and consider nonacademic, social, language, and behavior benefits.
5. What might be the effect of the student with a disability on other students in the classroom? Considerations would include whether the student is likely to

monopolize the teacher's or aide's time to disrupt other students (Weishaar 1997, 262).

To address these questions in a systematic manner, the IEP team could use a specific planning process. This planning process serves two purposes: (1) to assure a free and appropriate public education and (2) to assure that an LEA can defend itself if its actions are questioned. The planning process includes the following sequence:

> At the IEP meeting to consider a request for inclusion, the regular education teacher could complete a simple chart that specifies teacher expectations for a particular class. Participants would then discuss the skills required to meet each teacher expectation and whether the student had the skills required. Where a mismatch between teacher expectation and student skill occurs, the team would determine what, if any, adaptations and/or special services are necessary. This information is then used to make a decision about the benefit of inclusion for the student and is reflected in the IEP. It is important to note that the IDEA presumes that all children will be placed in the regular classroom unless an IEP team determines that the child must be removed for special education services. It is also important to understand that this planning process does not presume that the child must have the prerequisite skills to be placed in the regular classroom. Rather, the planning process is a vehicle to communicate about the classroom, the child's needs, and the goals for the child without focusing on the emotionally charged term of inclusion. An example of a completed chart is detailed in Figure 3.9. By following this planning process, true consideration of a regular education placement with supplemental aids and services could be documented.

Inclusion is an issue that every administrator will have to address in his/her career. Rather than take a personal position on the issue or concept of inclusion for all children, it makes sense for an administrator to consider a request for inclusion as an individual issue of placement. If, after careful consideration by an IEP team, a child can be included in the regular classroom, then the IEP should reflect that placement. If not, the IEP should reflect any other placement that will afford the child an appropriate education. Inclusion is not an answer to all special education placement questions, but it should refer to several questions, such as, "Why not regular education?"

Summary

Understanding the identification and placement process in special education is essential for all administrators. If administrators are well versed in this process, children are more likely to receive appropriate services. Because this process is heavily regulated by the IDEA, it is easy for administrators to make a mistake. To assist administrators in increasing problem-solving skills in the identification and placement process, practical case studies for this chapter follow. These cases allow students to read, discuss, and answer questions about real-life situations.

Physical Aspects: SCIENCE
Class Size 24 Age Range 11–12 Boy/Girl no. 12/12
Arrangement of Desks Lab tables; 2 per table
Independent Study Centers
Distractions Lots of movement: work in small groups
Noise Students talk quietly during labs
Other Overhead projector used
Analysis of Student Skills

STUDENT INFORMATION
Name Mike
Eligibility Mentally Handicapped—Mild
Age 11 DOB ____ Sex M F
Skill Codes (optional):
 I Independent
 A Assistance Needed
 U Unable to Perform Task

Area	Expectation	Student Skills (I, A, U)	Adaptations
ACADEMICS:			
1. Reading	Text—5th grade level, 15–20 pages per chapter, 3 pages per lesson	Reads well orally. Good oral comprehension	Preread chapter in special education room. Mike will follow along during reading in regular class.
2. Written Work	Complete labs, study questions. Take quizzes/tests, written notes.	Cannot form sentences on his own	Peer tutor—special ed class & study hall. Reduce no. of questions on test & change expectations for passing grade. Notes: write one or two words
3. Math Skills	Use a calculator. Use measurements.	No experience with calculator or measurements	Special ed teacher will assist in classroom.
4. Following Directions	Teacher writes directions & gives directions orally.	Cannot understand lengthy directions	Teacher will simplify directions & repeat.
5. Motor Output			
6. Oral Language	Students talk quietly during labs.	Mike talks loudly.	Remind Mike to talk quietly.
7. Cognition	5th grade terminology	Understands beginning 3rd grade terminology	Reduce no. of new terms
BEHAVIORIAL:			
1. On Task	Students sit quietly.	Does not often sit still without something in his hands	Verbally encourage & compliment appropriate behavior—use chart if needed.
2. Disruptions	Use assertive discipline—name on board, check after name.	Usually follows classroom rules	

FIGURE 3.9   *Example: Planning Process for Inclusion (continued)*

3. Follows Rules	Classroom rules posted	May not be able to read	Review classroom rules & consequences in Special Education classroom.
4. Social Interactions	Work in lab groups of 2–3 students.	May not contribute to discussion	Place with good role models. Assign jobs with which he would be successful.
5. Follows Directions	Most directions oral, some written	Difficulty with some written directions	Give all directions orally.
6. Participation in Group	Perform specific jobs in lab group setting.	May not contribute to discussion	Assign Mike to record data.
7. Attention			
ORGANIZATION			
1. Preparation for Class	Bring book, folder, paper, pencil, assignment notebook.	Able to bring needed materials	None
2. Time to Complete Tasks	Take incomplete tasks home.	Able to take work home	Parents will check backpack daily.
3. Seating			
4. Participation Rules			
5. Class Routine			
6. Packs up for Leaving			
7. Homework	Read and complete study questions.	Reading level too difficult	Preread in special ed classroom. Write homework on assignment notebook (teacher or peer will do). Tutor will assist during study hall.
TEACHING TECHNIQUES:			
1. Lecture			
2. Class Discussion (explanation)			
3. Self-Directed Study			
4. AV Presentation	Copy notes from overhead.	Difficulty copying from board	Copy key words (will be underlined). Teacher will provide copy of overhead.

FIGURE 3.9 *Example: Planning Process for Inclusion (continued)*

5. Experiments	Make observations, measure, calculate, record data in groups.	Record data for group	Write 3–4 words or record numbers.
6. Group Work	Lab groups of 2–4 students	Works well with other students	Write 3 sentences. Read 1 orally.
7. Oral Reports	Individual & in small groups	Difficulty writing sentences	
8. Quizzes/Tests	Multiple choice, short answer, matching, essay	Cannot answer essay or short answer	Rewrite test to simplify (Sp. Ed teacher). Print/type tests.
9. Grades	Letter grade given on study questions, labs, quizzes, tests, reports	Cannot perform at 6th grade level	Teacher writes positive comments & grades where appropriate—grades based on efforts & ability. Confer with special ed teacher about final grade.
STIMULUS MATERIAL:			
1. Note Taking			
2. Use of Textbooks	Read orally & silently.	Cannot orally read or silently read text	Follow along during oral reading. Preread material in special ed class.
3. Worksheets			
4. Chalkboard			
5. Graphs	Make bar & line graphs.	Limited motor coordination to make graphs	Make partial graph.
6. Manipulatives	Use microscopes, measuring tools, calculators.	Limited manipulation skills	Use peers to assist.
7. Games			
8. Computer			
9. Lab Work			

FIGURE 3.9 *Example: Planning Process for Inclusion (continued)*

CASE 3.1: "BASKETBALL PLAYER OR SPECIAL EDUCATION STUDENT?"

Ms. McClure, special education administrator, looked up from her desk to see Mr. Wells, a school board member walk into her office.

Mr. Wells began by saying, "You may be able to help me. I attended the basketball game last night at the high school and Coach Fisher pulled me aside before the game began. He pointed out one of his players, Corey Black, who is on the junior varsity team this year. Apparently, Corey is a very talented basketball player. Coach Fisher thinks that with proper training and support he could play college basketball and maybe even professional basketball. He says he's never seen a player as talented as Corey in all of his years as coach. However, Coach Fisher is very concerned that Corey is labeled "learning disabled." He said the label may hurt his chances at playing college basketball. He was wondering if there was anything we could do to get him out of special education, maybe retest him. I told him I was going to be in the area today and I'd stop by to see you."

Ms. McClure was somewhat surprised as she said, "I'm somewhat familiar with Corey Black, and as I recall, Corey has difficulty with reading. How could he possibly succeed in regular education classes without help?"

Mr. Wells answered, "Coach Fisher has a plan to help Corey, both academically and socially. It might be a good idea for you to talk with him to see specifically what he has planned. He did mention that he has frequent communication with Corey's mother and she doesn't want him in special education. You know, Ms. McClure, how important basketball is in this school district."

Ms. McClure said, "I'll certainly look into the case, Mr. Wells. I'll try to contact Coach Fisher today."

Later that day, Ms. McClure reviewed Corey's file. As the only child of a single mother, Corey had received special education services since fourth grade, first in a self-contained class, then a resource class. Corey made good academic progress, although his last reevaluation indicated that he still functioned in the below average range in reading. This year, as a sophomore, Corey was placed in one special education class and received tutoring during his daily study hall. Other classes were in the regular program. Corey passed all classes in high school with C's and D's.

Ms. McClure contacted Coach Fisher the next day by stopping by his office at the high school. Coach Fisher indicated that having a special education label might hurt Corey's chances in college basketball. Ms. McClure assured him that Corey would not be discriminated against in college athletics.

Coach Fisher disagreed and stated that if Corey was taken out of special education he would be provided with daily tutoring, weekly monitoring of progress, and placement in low-track classes with teachers who would provide special accommodations for him. In addition, Corey was already working with a mentor after school hours so that he had a positive male role model in his life. He also said that Corey's mother agreed with him.

Ms. McClure suggested that a current reevaluation be conducted and Coach Fisher agreed.

Later that week, Ms. McClure contacted Corey's mother about the reevaluation. She confirmed that she fully agreed with Coach Fisher that Corey should be taken out of special education and agreed with the reevaluation. She indicated that she wanted Corey to graduate and attend college, something that no one in the family had ever accomplished.

The reevaluation was completed six weeks later and a date for an eligibility/IEP conference was established.

The meeting was scheduled after school in the conference room. Nine persons sat around the round table. They included Ms. McClure, special education director, Mr. James, special education teacher, Mr. Fisher, basketball coach, Mrs. Stringer, assistant principal, Mrs. Merrill, regular education English teacher, Mr. Charles, psychologist, Mrs. Cole, social worker, Mrs. Black, parent, and Corey.

Ms. McClure began the meeting by introducing the participants and saying, "We are here today to discuss the outcome of Corey's reevaluation and to determine if changes will be made in Corey's IEP. As you know, the reevaluation was initiated by Coach Fisher, but Corey was also scheduled for his triennial reevaluation. We will discuss the results of the reevaluation first. Mr. James, will you first summarize Corey's progress in his classes?"

Mr. James answered, "Yes. Corey has been my student in special English for the past two years. In addition, I have worked with him during his study hall for

(Continue)

CASE 3.1 (CONTINUED)

tutoring. Corey has passed all classes during the past two years and is making progress toward graduation. Most of Corey's grades have been C's with a B in industrial arts. Corey has indicated to me that he would like to work in automotive repair when he graduates from high school. We have discussed the possibility of taking classes at the vocational school next year. Corey still has difficulty reading, however. He works with me once or twice a week to get help with his regular classes. Often, we preread the material for class or study for tests. Corey really has benefited from this extra help. Behaviorally, Corey has not experienced any problems. He generally complies with teacher direction."

The social worker, Mrs. Cole, then updated the social history. She discussed Corey's home life and Corey's relationship with his mother and his mentor. She also stated that Corey had no problems at home nor did he have any health concerns. She ended by asking, "Mrs. Black, is there anything you wanted to add?"

Mrs. Black said, "No, I just want Corey to graduate from high school."

Mr. Charles, the school psychologist, then reviewed his evaluation. He said that he administered the Weschler Intelligence Scale for Children–Third Edition (WISC-III) and the Weschler Individual Achievement Test (WIAT) to Corey. On the WISC-III, Corey's scores indicated average potential, both on verbal and performance scales. On the WIAT, Corey performed within the low average range in reading, with below average scores in basic reading and low average scores in reading comprehension. In math, Corey performed in the low average range both in calculation skills and reasoning. In written language, Corey performed on the borderline between low average and below average. In oral language, Corey performed within the average range. Mr. Charles said that the test results did not represent any change from previous evaluations.

Ms. McClure then asked, "Coach Fisher, you have been working with the family and have proposed some changes in Corey's program. Would you tell us what you propose?"

Coach Fisher answered, "Corey is an exceptional basketball player and I think he may have a future in basketball. As you know, I have arranged for a mentor to work with Corey outside of school and this has had a positive effect on Corey. If Corey was taken out of special education, I could arrange for special tutoring on a daily basis

for him by a peer tutor. One of my assistant coaches would check his progress weekly, and we could place him in a regular practical English class for next year, along with other regular classes. Corey would not enter the vocational school, but continue to take academic classes, with the goal to enter college after graduation. If he still wanted to work in car repair, he could get training later. I really think Corey could succeed without special education."

Ms. McClure said, "It seems that Corey still has the same special needs in reading and spelling that qualify him as having a learning disability. The question is, does he need special education assistance to meet those needs? Corey seems to be progressing well in special education. Mr. James, you have worked with Corey for two years. What do you think?"

Mr. James said, "Corey needs help with reading and keeping up in regular classes. He also needs to be scheduled with teachers who are understanding of him. He could certainly continue in special education with those services. On the other hand, Coach Fisher is offering similar assistance within the regular education program. The only difference in his schedule would be placement in regular English class. Corey would also delay any training in car repair."

Ms. McClure asked, "Mrs. Merrill, you would be Corey's regular education English teacher next year. What do you think?"

Mrs. Merrill said, "I have taught practical English for 20 years and I have seen students succeed with less support than you plan for Corey. I think Corey would work well in my class provided he had extra assistance when needed."

Ms. McClure asked, "Corey, what do you think?"

Corey looked at the floor shyly as he said, "I want out of special education. I don't mind not going to the vocational school. If Coach Fisher thinks I could go to college, I'd like to go."

Ms. McClure said, "Mrs. Black, do you agree?"

Mrs. Black stated, "Yes, I do."

Ms. McClure stated, "It appears that the consensus of the team is that Corey still has a disability, but that with supplementary aids and supports coordinated by Coach Fisher, he may no longer need special education. Does everyone agree with this?"

No one said anything. Ms. McClure said, "Corey will no longer be eligible for special education services

(Continue)

CASE 3.1 (CONTINUED)

for next year. Mr. James, I would like for you to coordinate your program with Coach Fisher to assist him in arranging a program for Corey next year."

Ms. McClure said, "If Corey has difficulty next year with this plan, he could be referred for another evaluation and we could decide upon any changes at that time. Hopefully, that won't happen. Does anyone have questions? O.K., this meeting is concluded. Mrs. Black, I will give you a copy of the conference report that summarized the evaluation. Thank you for your time in attending this meeting."

During the next school year, Corey was placed in regular classes. Coach Fisher arranged for tutoring and regularly checked Corey's progress. Corey passed all classes with C's and one D. Corey was very successful in basketball, helping the team to win the state championship.

Note to readers: You will now be asked questions about this case. Before you read the Questions and Reflections section at the end of the book (Appendix A), you

should fill out a case study analysis (Appendix C), then answer the questions and share your ideas with the class.

Questions

1. What were the important issues concerning Corey's eligibility for special education services?
2. Was the outcome, i.e., discontinuing eligibility for special education services, in the best interest of the child? Why or why not?
3. What was the motive of Coach Fisher? Did his motive have an adverse or positive effect on the outcome?
4. Did the special education administrator proceed appropriately when faced with the request from the school board member? How do you know?
5. Describe a different outcome for this case.

CASE 3.2: "I KNOW WHAT'S BEST FOR MY CHILD!"

West Junior High School is typical of many junior high schools in suburban areas. It has about nine hundred students and has a diverse population. The special education program at West serves about 100 students, slightly more than 10 percent of the population. The program serving these students is departmentalized, meaning that each special education teacher teaches six sections of a required class, e.g., English, math, science. Seven special education teachers and five instructional assistants serve the learning disabled, behavior disordered, and mentally impaired students. A department chairperson is appointed annually by the board of education to coordinate the special education program. The duties of the chairperson include scheduling students in classes, changing schedules, changing IEPs, coordinating annual reviews, and advising the administration on discipline matters concerning students in special education. The chairperson also works as a liaison between the director of special education and the junior high school principal.

Mrs. Dust had been special education department chairperson for the past ten years. She enjoyed the administrative responsibilities and the special and regular education teachers viewed her as an asset to the school. In May, Mrs. Dust participated in IEP meetings for all incoming seventh graders to assist in planning schedules and IEPs. She traveled to the feeder schools to participate in the meetings.

One class, the behavior disorders class at Whiteside Elementary School, had three incoming students. The first two meetings went smoothly. The third meeting centered around a student, Will Brown. The BD teacher conducted the IEP meeting and Will's mother, Belinda Brown, was present. Will was self-contained in the BD class during his sixth grade year. His mother insisted that Will be placed in some regular education classes during seventh grade.

She said, "Will has made many improvements this year. He hasn't been in trouble during the past 6 weeks. I really think he deserves a chance in regular education. I know he can succeed academically."

(Continue)

CASE 3.2 (CONTINUED)

The BD teacher, Mrs. Ochoa, said, "Yes, Will has progressed nicely the past 6 weeks. However, I am concerned at how Will will adapt to changing from a small, structured classroom with one teacher to a large school with many teachers. It might be overwhelming. When Will becomes overwhelmed, he often acts out. It might be best to start out with all special education classes."

Mrs. Dust said, "I agree. The junior high is very different from elementary school. Most students adjust well when they have more special education classes initially. If they do well, we can always schedule more regular classes."

Mrs. Brown said, "I disagree. Will is more mature and wants the challenge of regular education classes. He will be more motivated to succeed if he is placed in classes that he wants. He doesn't want special education classes."

Mrs. Dust reluctantly said, "Well, I guess we could try some regular education classes, maybe math, PE, and industrial arts. Will seems strong in math and physical activities. If he has difficulty, we could always change the classes to special education classes."

Mrs. Brown said, "That would at least be a start. But I think we should think about more regular classes in the future."

Mrs. Ochoa said, "Will has strong academic skills, especially in math. His progress should be monitored frequently, though. I am concerned about his low tolerance of frustration."

Mrs. Dust said, "I will monitor his progress every other week. If I see a problem, I will contact Mrs. Brown."

Mrs. Brown was happy when she said, "Thank you. This is what Will wants and I know he will succeed."

Will's IEP reflected his placement in special education English, social studies, and science. Regular education classes were math, physical education, and industrial arts. Goals and objectives involved compliance with rules, respect for authority figures, and development of appropriate peer relationships.

In September, school began. Will seemed to adjust adequately. His only discipline problem involved two tardies to first hour class. In October, Mrs. Dust received a telephone call from Mrs. Brown.

Mrs. Brown said, "I am so pleased with Will's progress. He loves junior high and his classes. Because

he is doing so well, I thought we might place him in one more regular education class, maybe science. Will really likes science and I think he will do well with the regular education science teacher, Mr. Dobbs."

Mrs. Dust said, "Overall, Will has done a nice job in school. I suppose we could try him in Mr. Dobb's science class."

Mrs. Brown said, "Great. When can he begin?"

Mrs. Dust said, "The end of the first quarter is next week. I could probably change his schedule for the following week. Please ask Will to see me next week and I'll work out the schedule change. We can try this change on a trial basis and see how Will does."

The next week, Will's schedule was changed to include regular education science class. During the next few months, Mrs. Dust monitored Will's progress. He seemed to be passing all classes with C's and D's. He was, however, having difficulty socially in unstructured situations. In the cafeteria, for example, Will pulled a chair out from under another student because he wanted the student's place at the table. In another situation, Will was cursing loudly in the hallway. When a teacher confronted Will, he denied cursing and argued with the teacher. Will was sent to the office on both occasions and was given after school detentions.

In December, Mrs. Brown contacted Mrs. Dust by telephone and again requested a schedule change for Will.

She said, "Will is really bored in the special education English class. He reads well and likes to write. It's time to try him in a regular education English class. Don't you agree?"

Mrs. Dust replied by saying, "Yes, Will reads well, but I am concerned about his behavior difficulties in unstructured situations. I know you are aware of the two recent incidences resulting in after school detentions."

Mrs. Brown didn't seem too concerned as she said, "Yes, I am. I don't see these incidences as a big problem. Anyway, this doesn't have anything to do with his boredom in English class. His behavior may improve if he is challenged in his classes."

Reluctantly, Mrs. Dust agreed to the change. She knew Will was able to succeed academically, but as more changes were made, Will's behavior seemed to deteriorate.

(Continue)

CASE 3.2 (CONTINUED)

In early February, Mrs. Brown again contacted Mrs. Dust to request a schedule change.

She said, "I think Will needs all classes in regular education. He does not want to be associated with students in special education. He and I talked about placing him in regular education social studies and he agreed to work extra hard to pass the class. He also agreed not to get into any more trouble at school."

Mrs. Dust said, "Mrs. Brown, I am reluctant to make this change. Will seems to be having more behavior difficulty. He has a low tolerance of frustration. I'm concerned that he won't be receiving the support he needs if we make this change."

Mrs. Brown said, "He will still be in special education. Let's try the change for two weeks and see how Will does in the class."

Mrs. Dust again discouraged Mrs. Brown, but Mrs. Brown was very insistent and forceful. It seemed easier to placate Mrs. Brown by making the change.

Mrs. Dust said, "Mrs. Brown, I do not agree with this change, and if it doesn't work, I will not accept responsibility. I will agree to make the change for a two-week trial. If Will has one behavior incident in those two weeks, we will have to reconsider his placement."

Mrs. Brown said, "I understand, Mrs. Dust. I know what's best for Will and placement in regular education is what is best for him."

One week later in PE class, Will was cursing loudly. The teacher reprimanded him and Will cursed at the teacher. The teacher put his hand on Will's shoulder to lead him to the office. Will hit the teacher across the face.

When contacted by the principal, Mrs. Brown said, "I told Mrs. Dust that Will was in the wrong placement. She should have been monitoring Will's progress more. In addition, the PE teacher shouldn't have touched Will. If Will is touched, he will strike out."

Note to readers: You will now be asked questions about this case. Before you read the Questions and Reflections section at the end of the book (Appendix A), you should fill out a case study analysis (Appendix C), then answer the questions and share your ideas with the class.

Questions

1. Was it proper to change Will's placement three times to placate Mrs. Brown? Why or why not?
2. What is the systemic issue that needs to be addressed to avoid future problems? How should this issue be addressed by the special education administrator?
3. How should the IEP be changed procedurally? Describe what should have happened.
4. Was the parent correct when she said the child's program wasn't appropriate? Why or why not?
5. Was Mrs. Dust correct in saying that she would not accept responsibility if Will did not do well in the regular social studies class? Why or why not?

CASE 3.3: "I WILL NOT INCLUDE THIS CHILD IN MY SCHOOL!"

Mr. Brolin, Principal of Drake Elementary School, walked into the superintendent's office and immediately felt uneasy. Dr. Overton's secretary said to go into the office and that Dr. Overton and Dr. Harris, special education administrator, were waiting for him. Mr. Brolin had been a principal for twenty years and he knew that there was an important concern as he was not usually summoned to the superintendent's office.

Dr. Overton began the conversation by saying, "Mr. Brolin, we have a special problem we'd like to discuss with you. We have a family who just moved into our district, the Stevens, who have a twelve-year-old son, Jake. Jake is placed in a private day treatment facility for students with behavior disorders. Mr. and Mrs. Stevens and personnel from the private day treatment facility contacted me and requested that Jake be returned to the

(Continue)

CASE 3.3 (CONTINUED)

regular school setting, and your school would be his home school."

Dr. Harris added, "This is an unusual case and we need your input to decide how we will proceed, Mr. Brolin. As a twelve-year-old, Jake is a rather large boy for his age, about 150 pounds. Jake had gifted potential until the age of 5, when he contracted a case of encephalitis. He suffered a long-term fever and had several grand mal seizures, which damaged his brain. At this point, he is labeled 'traumatic brain injury.' His level of intellectual functioning at the present time is mild retardation, with an IQ of about 68. For the past year, he has been placed in the private day treatment facility. His parents also had difficulty with him at home and they have been attending family counseling at the day treatment facility. Prior to this placement, Jake was moved from one special education program to another. I talked to the special education administrator where Jake resided previously and he was totally frustrated with Jake and his family. Jake was in a program for mild mentally disabled children, but his behavior was too severe for this placement to be successful. He was then transferred to a self-contained behavior disorders program in the public school and even this placement was unsuccessful. Prior to the day treatment placement, he verbally threatened to attack his teachers and threatened to kill other students. During the year at the day treatment facility, Jake was physically restrained many times, especially during the first semester. When Jake was confronted by authority figures, he responded by cursing, throwing furniture, and verbally threatening others. On two occasions during Jake's first semester at the day treatment facility, Jake's actions resulted in minor injuries to three staff members. During Jake's second semester at the day treatment facility, Jake's behavior dramatically improved. He had only one act of violence directed toward a peer and only had to be physically restrained one time. The day treatment facility recommended that Jake be returned to the public school this year because he has improved. They also recommend trial placement in the regular classroom because they think Jake will respond to positive peer role models. As Dr. Overton said, we just received the request for an IEP meeting to return Jake to the regular school setting, possibly a regular sixth grade classroom with support services."

Mr. Brolin said slowly as the color drained from his face, "You mean the parents want us to place this child in *my* school?"

Dr. Overton said, "Yes, I'm afraid so. The day treatment staff are supportive because they think a normal learning environment will help Jake behaviorally. They think a personal assistant would be necessary. My feeling is that we should at least attempt this placement."

Mr. Brolin stood up as he said, "I will not under any circumstances take this child into my building. I am responsible for the education and well-being of 400 students and many staff members. I refuse to take this child!"

Dr. Overton also stood up and said, "Listen, Mr. Brolin, this may be temporary, but I think we owe it to the child and his family to try to make this placement work. In fact, I insist that we meet with the parents."

Mr. Brolin stated emphatically, "After twenty years, you are going to insist that I take a child into my building who has the potential to hurt people. I simply won't do it!"

Mr. Brolin walked out of the superintendent's office and went back to his building. He was worried about his behavior with the superintendent. He had never refused to do anything in the past. He always tried to do the best he could even though he didn't agree with all requests. However, he thought, this was different. He would feel terrible if he agreed to this placement and someone got hurt.

Back in the superintendent's office, Dr. Harris and Dr. Overton talked.

Dr. Harris said, "Wow, I didn't expect this type of reaction from Mr. Brolin. However, with time, he'll come around and support us."

Dr. Overton said, "He'd better or he may not be principal of that building or any building in the district. Dr. Harris, go ahead and arrange for the IEP meeting. Schedule it at Mr. Brolin's building and invite the regular education teacher for sixth grade and any special education teachers you feel might be involved."

Jake was ultimately placed in Mr. Brolin's building and assigned to the regular education sixth grade teacher. A one-to-one assistant was assigned to Jake. A nonaversive behavior management program was implemented using direct treatment strategies, positive programming, and reactive procedures. A highly struc-

(Continue)

CASE 3.3 (CONTINUED)

tured program was designed to take into account Jake's cognitive abilities, instructional needs, and behavior. Jake's program included several school jobs and was implemented in a variety of school settings throughout the day. The majority of his time was spent away from his regular sixth grade peers.

The initial implementation of the program was difficult. The first one-to-one assistant resigned within three months. Two one-to-one assistants, one in the morning and one in the afternoon, were hired. Jake also received the direct services of a behavior specialist, inclusion facilitator, social worker, speech therapist, and physical therapist. Because Jake could not eat breakfast prior to leaving home in the morning due to medication issues, Jake's first hour of school was spent preparing and eating breakfast.

Under the current conditions, Jake's behavior improved. He had not engaged in any physical altercations in the past six weeks. However, his program was con-

stantly updated and reviewed to address behavior and academic challenges.

Note to readers: You will now be asked questions about this case. Before you read the Questions and Reflections section at the end of the book (Appendix A), you should fill out a case study analysis (Appendix C), then answer the questions and share your ideas with the class.

Questions

1. If a similar student transferred to your building tomorrow, how would you, as building administrator, prepare for the student?
2. Was Mr. Brolin's behavior acceptable in the superintendent's office? Why or why not?
3. Did the program, as implemented, provide a free and appropriate public education? Was the program in the least restrictive environment? How do you know?

CHAPTER 4

CONFLICT RESOLUTION IN SPECIAL EDUCATION

This chapter provides an examination of conflict in special education. First we discuss the basic foundations of conflict. Next we review methods of resolving conflict that frequently involve the special education administrator. These methods include principled negotiation, mediation, and due process hearings. After reading this chapter, analyzing the cases, and engaging in the practice exercises, you should be able to:

- Describe the origins of conflict and typical responses to conflict.
- Use effective communication skills in a simulated conflict situation and identify those skills in case studies.
- Implement the strategy of principled negotiation in a simulated conflict situation.
- Develop an understanding that conflict resolution strategies occur along a continuum from less to more formal.
- Discuss legal and procedural aspects of mediation and due process.

See semantic map detailing Chapter 4 on page 65.

FOUNDATIONS OF CONFLICT

Understanding Conflict

Consider the following potential conflict situations that have frequently occurred in special education administration. Think about how you, as an administrator, would address the situation.

1. Mrs. Teller, the speech therapist, calls you on the phone, and tells you that she will not be able to start therapy with her students until mid-September. You just left the building principal's meeting where one topic of conversation was the date that speech therapists would begin therapy. The principals were unhappy that therapists usually begin serving children one and one-half weeks after school begins, when regular education teachers work with students the first day of school. You told the administrators in the meeting that therapy would begin on September 1, which was earlier than last year.

2. You are attending the evaluation and individualized education plan (IEP) conference of a third grade boy. Paul was just made eligible for learning

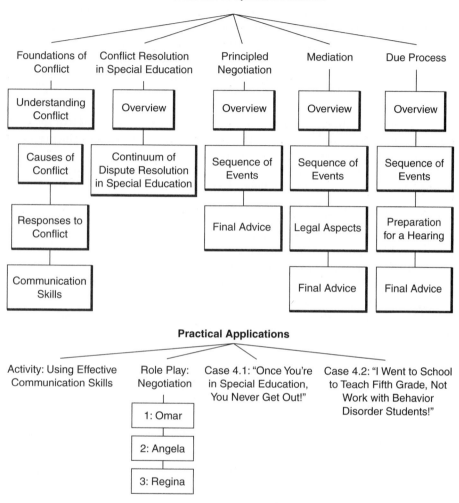

Conflict Issues in Special Education

Practical Applications

disabilities and physically handicapped services, with the related service of occupational therapy. His parents turn to you and state that they want a particular occupational therapist to be employed by the school district because of her expertise in a particular area needed by Paul. You already have a competent occupational therapist on staff.

3. You answer a telephone call from an elementary building principal. She tells you that she wants to suspend a behavior disorders (BD) student from the bus for the "rest of the year" because of continuing misbehavior on the bus, and she doesn't care what the special education law says.

Each of these three scenarios is a situation involving *potential* conflict with an-other person or persons. How should you respond to these conflict situations? Should you respond aggressively? In scenario 1, for example, would you tell the therapist that she has to begin working September 1 no matter what the reason for her delay? In responding in this manner, are you the winner and is she the loser? Would it be better to appeal to a higher authority?

In scenario 2, is it best to confront the parents aggressively by stating that you already have a competent occupational therapist on staff and that you have no intention of employing another one? Or perhaps you think it might be best to delay answering and try to ignore the request, hoping that once Paul begins occupational therapy, his parent's request won't have to be addressed.

In scenario 3, should you get angry and tell the building principal that she can't legally do what she is proposing? Another response might be to tell the principal to do what she thinks is correct and take the consequences of her actions later.

Think about a recent conflict that you have experienced, either professionally or personally. Try to answer the following questions to determine how you handle conflict: Who was involved? How did you feel? How do you think the other person felt? What did you want? What did the other person want? Was the conflict resolved? If so, how? If not, what happened? Asking yourself these questions about a recent situation will help you analyze how you resolve conflict.

All administrators meet with conflict daily. In the field of special education, conflict is inevitable, and special education administrators must learn to expand their repertoire of conflict resolution approaches to become a successful administrator. When you are asked, "What is the first phrase that comes to mind when the word conflict is mentioned, do you have some of these thoughts?"

> "Oh, no, here it (or he or she) comes again!"
> "I am so tired of dealing with this!"
> "I have to draw a line somewhere and this is it!"
> "I don't care what they think, we should take this issue as far as necessary to prove that we are right!"
> "Don't those parents (or teachers or other administrators) understand that we don't do that here?"

If you focus on these (or other) negative thoughts about conflict, it is unlikely that you will be a successful administrator. You may also become disengaged, bitter, and generally unhappy with your chosen field.

The most important concept to understand is that *conflict is a normal, everyday occurrence that can be a positive force, encouraging creativity and growth in people.* Administrators can choose to view conflict in a *positive* light and see it as an *opportunity* to develop personally and to enact change, or they can view conflict in a negative light, which could result in hurt feelings, anger, and unhappiness.

Causes of Conflict

To adequately resolve conflict, it is important to understand the cause of conflict in any given situation. Much of the work on causes of conflict originates with the control theory of William Glasser (Glasser 1984). This theory attempts to determine why and how people behave. To summarize Glasser's theory, everything we do is behavior and all behavior is purposeful. The purpose of all behavior is to satisfy basic innate needs. All behavior is an attempt to control ourselves and our world as we continually try to satisfy these needs. If we understand what need(s) we are striving toward, it is possible to define the problem and build conflict resolution strategies on common needs of both parties.

Most conflict situations involve both parties striving to meet one or more basic psychological needs. These needs include the following:

1. Need for belonging, e.g., loving, sharing, cooperation.
2. Need for power, e.g., achieving, accomplishing, being respected.
3. Need for freedom, e.g., making choices.
4. Need for fun, e.g., laughing, playing (Bodine, Crawford, and Schrumpf 1994).

Limited resources and differing values may also contribute to conflict. Limited resources include lack of money, time, or property. When conflict originates with limited resources, it is often easier to resolve than other types of conflict. For example, if a parent is unable to work with her child on daily homework assignments due to evening job commitments, (i.e., lack of time), the conflict could be resolved by providing peer tutoring at the end of each day to complete homework. Differing values involves people having different beliefs. Conflicts originating with differing values often are difficult to resolve. For example, a parent requests a particular placement in a certain location for his child. The special education administrator feels that the principle of granting this request is wrong, i.e., no parent should be allowed to choose a particular placement in a specific location. The special education administrator may be right, but clinging to this principle or value, may, in the long term, escalate conflict.

Resolution of conflict is almost impossible when one party feels its psychological needs are being threatened by the other party (Schrumpf, Crawford, and Usadel 1991). To illustrate the importance of understanding basic psychological needs as a foundation of resolving conflict, consider the example that follows.

Many conflicts in special education originate in differences of opinion between parents and professionals about a child's special education program. The arena for voicing these differences and planning services for a child may be the IEP meeting. Parents often enter these meetings with the following needs:

- The desire to work with school staff (need to belong).
- The desire for options from which to choose for their child (need for freedom or to make choices).
- The desire for school staff to listen to and value their input (need for power and belonging).
- The desire for special education meetings to be comfortable, not painful.

If one or more of these basic psychological needs are threatened in the IEP meeting, it is possible for conflict to result. For example, if parents are *told* what will happen to their child in terms of programming, some parents might disagree and be upset that other options aren't being considered. This results in conflict.

Another example is seen in the third scenario on page 65, where the principal wants to suspend a BD student from the bus for the "rest of the year." It is essential for the special education administrator to understand the psychological needs of the principal to resolve conflict. The principal probably wants to protect her sense of freedom in regard to making decisions in her own building. She may also want to demonstrate to other students and staff that a student will be disciplined if he or she engages in serious misbehavior on the bus. Understanding these needs will help the special education administrator define the nature of the problem and formulate options to deal with conflict.

Responses to Conflict

There are three basic responses to conflict: aggression, avoidance, and principled negotiation (Fisher, Ury, and Patton 1991). An aggressive response is characterized by threats, aggression, and/or anger, where the ultimate goal is to win. The thoughts of the aggressor might include, "I am not going to give in" or "I'll try to be fair, but I will stick to my position on what's acceptable because I know I'm right." This is a reactive approach to conflict, often resulting in an increase in anger and frustration, an increase in perceived threat to psychological needs, more people getting involved in the conflict, and escalation of the conflict (Bodine et al. 1994; Schrumpf et al. 1991).

An example of this type of response would be if a special education administrator decides that children with severe disabilities should be fully included in the regular classroom, and the administrator tells teachers that this model will be implemented and provides inservice so that teachers will know how to implement the model. Parent meetings are held to convince parents that full inclusion is appropriate for children with severe disabilities. Teachers feel that they have no choice to individually implement the most appropriate program and that they must go along with the program even if they don't completely agree with it. Although this example is extreme, it illustrates a win-lose response, where the administrator wins and other parties lose. This is not a response to conflict that would likely result in long-term resolution.

An avoidance response to conflict includes withdrawal from the situation or ignoring the problem. One party might hope that the conflict will go away if it is ignored. Basic psychological needs are not met. For example, the person avoiding conflict is not in control of his/her life and sometimes views him/herself as a victim. In this type of response, all parties are losers, because they aren't able or willing to stand behind their convictions and often give in to avoid conflict. In the situation where one party is angry, an avoidance response may have merit in the short term to allow that party to cool off. An example of an avoidance response would be if the special education administrator gives in to parental demands for special education services, no matter what the child's needs or cost to the district. The goal in this situation is for the administrator to avoid conflict with the parent. The avoidance response is not recommended as a method of resolving conflict, and the administrator's response in this case is illegal because the child's right to a free and appropriate public education is disregarded.

A preferred method of resolving conflict is called a principled response (Bodine et al. 1994), a communication response (Schrumpf et al. 1991), a problem-solving response (Kreidler 1984), and principled negotiation (Fisher et al. 1991). In this type of response, one party employs conflict resolution strategies, i.e., negotiation, mediation, and addresses the needs and interests of both parties, who cooperate to create a solution acceptable to all. This conflict resolution method can be characterized as a win-win method, where both parties listen with empathy, clarify each other's positions, and search for solutions that meet the psychological needs of both parties. An example is where a parent demands that his second grade child who is mildly mentally impaired be fully included in the regular classroom. Instead of responding by trying to convince the parent that this placement is not appropriate for the child, the special education administrator approaches the situation with an open mind and convenes an IEP meeting to discuss the issues. The parent is able to freely state his position and the administrator listens with empathy, perhaps asking clarifying questions. The administrator is also able to state her position, as are other participants in the meeting. By listening with empathy, both parties' needs for power are addressed. Ultimately, the administrator is aware and clarifies the parent's underlying interests, which include the parent's desire for his child to experience a normal classroom (need for belonging). Several solutions are generated to meet this need for belonging. By generating several solutions, the parent's need for freedom (of choice) is addressed. Some solutions recommend a full day in the regular classroom and others involve partial inclusion in the regular classroom. After discussing the demands of the regular classroom and the academic and social strengths and weaknesses of the child, all parties agree to a solution of including the child for the afternoon program in the regular classroom. The classroom teacher requests and receives assistance from an aide during that time period.

This is a powerful method of resolving conflict. Many conflicts would not escalate if the special education administrator employed this problem-solving response. Principled negotiation is so important to the resolution of conflict that it will be considered in more detail later in this chapter. Some conflicts, however, may have to move to another level of resolution, e.g., due process.

Communication Skills

The foundation of conflict resolution is effective communication skills. Without good communication skills, it is unlikely that resolution of conflict will occur in a lasting manner, and it is possible that conflict could escalate. All administrators should be knowledgeable about and practice effective communication skills. The goal of good communication is for both parties to understand each other and to be understood. Sometimes, statements by the special education administrator are ineffective because the administrator uses communication "roadblocks" or "pitfalls" (Schrumpf et al. 1991). These roadblocks stop one party from understanding and from being understood. Examples of the roadblocks are:

- A teacher walks into the special education administrator's office to discuss Maria. Before the teacher has an opportunity to talk, the administrator interrupts her. As the teacher again tries to discuss the child, the administrator again interrupts the teacher. The teacher leaves, feeling frustrated. In this case, interrupting the teacher blocks communication.
- An IEP meeting is conducted on a tenth grade student and the student's transition plan is discussed. As the parent is talking about what the student will do when he leaves high school, the special education administrator states that he would encourage the student to enter trade school because the student has poor academic skills. The parent states that she would like the student to go to college. The administrator again states his advice and the parent doesn't offer another opinion, but feels frustrated. In this case, offering personal advice blocks communication.

- In an IEP meeting of a first grade student with learning disabilities, the teacher states that the child should be retained in first grade because of poor academic progress. She states that she has retained other similar children and that retention has been successful. The teacher then begins to tell a detailed story about retaining a child three years ago and how the child did well academically as a result. The parent is in tears. In this case, the teacher bringing up her own experience with another child's retention did little to further communication.
- A teacher and a special education administrator are sitting in the teacher's lounge discussing a student in special education. They are very critical of the student's parent and his ability to help his child at home with homework. The teacher states, "He obviously doesn't care." Another teacher at a nearby table knows the parent and understands that he is single and works two jobs to make ends meet and often is not home until 7:00 P.M. This teacher is offended that the administrator and teacher are so critical and judgmental of the parent without understanding his personal situation. In this case criticism and making judgments blocks communication.
- In an IEP meeting, the parent of a child with severe autism demands that the school pay for a special alternative therapy for her child. The special education administrator laughs as he says, "Are you serious? The district can't possibly afford this treatment for one child." The parent walks out, stating, "I'll have my attorney contact you." In this case, laughing or ridiculing the parent and her request block communication.

Effective communication typically focuses on four basic skills: active listening, empathic listening, using "I" messages, and using clarifying responses.

Active listening involves using nonverbal behaviors to demonstrate that you are listening and understand what the other person is saying. Active listening skills include maintaining eye contact, facing the person speaking, smiling, nodding, and leaning forward.

Empathic listening involves recognizing the feelings of the person speaking, reflecting those feelings, and restating what you think the other person is saying. For example, if a parent says in an angry tone of voice, "I don't think it's fair that third graders are assigned so much homework!", she is probably feeling frustrated with the amount of homework for her child. The other person, reflecting feelings, might say, "It sounds like you're feeling frustrated about the amount of homework Kaitlyn has to complete each night." The parent then can agree or disagree with this reflection, furthering communication and understanding. The other person could also restate what she hears the parent stating by saying, "I hear you saying that your experience is that third graders shouldn't have as much homework as they do on a daily basis." Again, the parent can then agree or clarify what she actually intended to say, furthering communication and understanding.

Using "I–messages" is a way of using communication to focus on the situation, not on the child's or parent's or other person's personality and character (Ginott 1965). When we begin communication with the word "you," communication often hits a roadblock, because the message focuses on the personality and character of the other person. For example, a special education teacher in an IEP meeting suggests placing Keesha in the regular classroom for reading and the regular classroom teacher responds by saying, "You can't do that. I have too many groups." This "you–message"

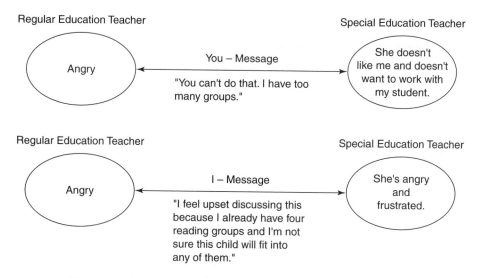

FIGURE 4.1   *I–Message vs. You–Message*

blocks communication and escalates a potential conflict situation (Figure 4.1). As another example, a parent requests that the school district provide speech therapy for her 3-year-old child five times per week and the speech therapist recommends therapy two times per week. The special education administrator states to the parent, "You don't understand, Mrs. White. The speech therapist knows what is best for your child. Therefore, we need to implement her recommendation." Again, the "you-message," in an unspoken manner, attacks the character and personality of the parent.

As an alternative, it is suggested that messages begin with "I" so that communication can be enhanced. In the speech therapy example above, it would be much better for the administrator to say, "I feel that the child's needs might best be met with speech therapy twice a week because Jim has made many positive gains with this model during the past year." Although the parent might not agree, the statement is a reflection of the administrator's thoughts and feelings about the situation and not an indirect attack on the parent's personality and character. In another example of placing Keesha in the regular classroom for reading, the regular education teacher might have used more effective communication by saying, "I am a little upset discussing this because I already have four reading groups and I'm not sure Keesha will fit into any of them" (Figure 4.1). At the very least, communication is not blocked when "I–messages" are used.

When a communicator uses clarifying responses, he or she is trying to understand the other person and gain more information by asking open-ended questions such as the following:

- What is your understanding of the problem?
- What happened next?
- How did you feel about that?
- Can you help me understand what happened?

These questions are nonthreatening and serve to enhance communication and understanding.

CONFLICT RESOLUTION IN SPECIAL EDUCATION

Overview

As a way to ensure parental participation in the identification, evaluation, program, and placement of children in special education and to protect children's rights, Individuals with Disabilities Education Act (IDEA) requires states to provide administrative hearings, i.e., due process hearings, with an impartial hearing officer to parents and local education agencies (LEAs) who are in conflict. If the parties are not satisfied with the outcome of the due process hearing, one or both parties can appeal the decision to the judicial court system.

Since the federal law was enacted in the 1970s, there has been general dissatisfaction with this formal process to resolve conflict because of the cost, adversarial nature, and frequent inability to provide mutually satisfying solutions to conflict (Schrag 1996). In addition to this dissatisfaction in special education conflict resolution, the 1960s and 1970s were a time of change when religious and peace activists began to understand the importance of teaching conflict resolution skills to children. In 1965, a Presidential Commission on Law Enforcement and the Administration of Justice encouraged experimentation with alternative dispute resolution strategies (Schrag 1996). At the same time that educators were developing conflict resolution programs in the schools, neighborhood justice centers were growing in the United States, with the primary purpose of providing mediation services for interpersonal and community disputes (Miller 1994). During the early 1980s, two important organizations emerged with the purpose of developing alternative ways of resolving conflict. They included the National Institute for Dispute Resolution and the National Association for Mediation in Education.

As a result of the general dissatisfaction with the formal processes for resolving conflict in special education and the general movement to implement alternative dispute resolution strategies in communities and schools, several less formal alternative strategies for resolving conflict in special education have emerged.

Continuum of Dispute Resolution in Special Education

Conflict resolution in special education can best be viewed along a continuum (Figure 4.2). At one end of the continuum are less formal strategies and at the other end are more formal strategies. Less formal strategies include principled negotiation (Fisher et al. 1991) and mediation. More formal strategies include due process hearing and litigation. Characteristics of these strategies are included in Figure 4.2.

In the remainder of this chapter, the most frequently used conflict resolution strategies are discussed. They include principled negotiation, mediation, and due process. It is very important that special education administrators approach conflict using a less formal strategy, preferably principled negotiation and/or mediation. It is recognized that there are some situations and issues that are best addressed at a more formal stage of resolution, i.e., due process. However, the authors are convinced through experience that many issues would never have to reach the more formal stages of conflict resolution if less formal strategies were employed as early as possible when conflict occurs. Goldberg and Huefner (1995) state, that "many disputes

Less Formal   More Formal

$\longleftarrow$ $\longrightarrow$

Principled Negotiation	Mediation	Due Process	Litigation

- Emphasis on relationships between parties
- Focus on future; avoid blame
- Responsibility to define issues and determine solution rests with disputants
- Flexible
- Negotiator/mediator is neutral and confidential
- Provides private resolution
- Less costly
- Less time consuming
- Attorneys often not involved
- Voluntary

- Emphasis on issues, facts, positions
- Focus on past; assigns blame
- Tends toward win–lose solution
- Parties define issues and positions; third party makes decision
- Governed by rules and procedures
- Full protection of due process
- Can be useful to establish precedent for similar cases
- Issues can be public
- More costly
- More time consuming
- Attorneys often involved
- Mandatory upon request

Adapted from: "Designing Dispute Resolution Systems in the Health Care Industry" by Slaiku, K. A., *Negotiation Journal, In Practice Dispute Systems Design: A Special Section*, pp. 395–400.

FIGURE 4.2   *Resolution of Conflict in Special Education Continuum*

have gone to due process hearings because the parties lacked the skills to defuse volatile situations. Relationships have been destroyed because both parties thought they needed to prove that they were *right*" (p. 541).

PRINCIPLED NEGOTIATION

Overview

Principled negotiation was developed by Fisher and Ury of the Harvard Negotiation Project (Fisher et al. 1991). Its use, initially, was in the areas of diplomacy and commercial conflicts. The work has been adapted to give teachers, administrators, and students essential conflict resolution strategies in the school setting (Bodine et al. 1994; Kreidler 1990). Negotiation can be defined as a problem-solving, conflict resolution process where the parties voluntarily discuss their differences in an attempt to reach an agreement. In negotiation, a third party is not involved, whereas in mediation there is a neutral third party. Negotiation is a powerful resolution strategy and has been largely underutilized in resolving special education conflicts (Goldberg and Huefner, 1995).

Fisher, Ury, and Patton (1991) discuss four aspects of principled negotiation:

1. Separate people from the problem.
2. Focus on interests, not positions.
3. Invent options for mutual gain.
4. Insist on using objective criteria.

It is important when negotiating to separate people from the problem. In conflict, emotion often runs high and it is easy to direct anger, disappointment, etc. toward the other party. This process does little to resolve conflict and, in fact, may escalate the conflict. Effective communication often helps separate the person from the problem. For example, using "I–messages" addresses the situation, while using "you–messages" addresses the other party's personality and character.

The second aspect of principled negotiation—focus on interests, not on positions—is often overlooked when resolving conflict. The objective of conflict resolution and negotiation is to satisfy the underlying interests of both parties. This will be next to impossible as long as both parties insist on focusing on their particular positions. Underlying interests relate to why each party wants what it wants. Behind each party's underlying interests are the basic psychological needs each party is striving to obtain. The negotiator is searching for common or compatible underlying interests. For every common interest, there are usually several possible solutions. Shared or compatible interests can be viewed as the building blocks to a mutual agreement (Figure 4.3). In the situation described in Figure 4.3, the negotiator, (possibly the special education administrator) would strive to identify interests common to both parties and meet the basic psychological needs identified. By doing this, the focus shifts from each party's position to the following:

- A focus on finding mutually satisfying options and then solutions that will assist the child in making academic and social gains in school.
- A focus on working together to find a solution.
- A focus on mutual respect and good communication skills.

The common interests and meeting basic psychological needs form the basis for generating options for a mutually satisfying agreement.

The third aspect of principled negotiation involves generating options for a mutually satisfying solution. If both parties understand and identify common interests, the next step is to generate at least three possible options that address common interests and meet basic psychological needs of both parties. In generating options, it is important not to judge any of the options, as this may stifle creativity.

The fourth aspect involves using objective criteria for determining if a solution is working. This process involves specifying how the parties will know that the proposed solution is working. This evaluation must be agreed upon by both parties and should be part of the final agreement.

Sequence of Events in Principled Negotiation

The work in principled negotiation has been adapted and expanded to the school setting to train students and adults in basic negotiating skills to resolve conflicts. Bodine, Crawford, and Schrumpf (1994) provide an excellent model from which to work in resolving conflicts as a negotiator. The steps are described below and are applicable to resolving conflict in special education.

1. Begin the negotiation process.
   - State and agree upon ground rules: take turns talking and listening (without interruption), cooperate to resolve conflict, discussion will be confidential.

Situation: In an IEP meeting, the parents want 9-year-old Alphonso, who has Down syndrome, fully included in the regular education fourth grade class. The school staff, including the special education teacher, the regular education teacher, the special education administrator, and the building principal, are opposed to the placement.

The charts below illustrate that underlying common interests are essential to a mutually satisfying agreement. Focusing on positions probably won't culminate in a mutually satisfying agreement.

> Mutually Satisfying
> Agreement Built on
> Common Interests and
> Meeting Basic Psychological Needs

Parent Interests (Basic Psychological Needs)	School Staff Interests (Basic Psychological Needs)
• Parents want to work with school staff (need for belonging). • Parents want to be respected for who they are and what they do (need for power). • Parents want options for their child (need for freedom). • Parents want staff to listen to their input (need for power and belonging). • Parents want their child to achieve academically and socially in school (need for belonging).	• Staff wants to work with parents (need for belonging). • Staff wants to be respected for who they are and what they do (need for power). • Staff wants options for the child (need for freedom). • Staff wants parents to listen to their input (need for power and belonging). • Staff wants child to achieve academically and socially in school (need for belonging).

> No Agreement

Parent's Position	School Staff's Position
We want our child fully included in the regular classroom.	We do not want this child fully included in the regular classroom.

FIGURE 4.3   *Focus on Interests: Building Blocks for a Mutual Agreement*

2. Define the problem.
   • First person tells his/her view of the problem: I was . . . , I think . . . , I feel . . .
   • Second person actively listens and summarizes first person's view of the problem.
   • Both parties reverse roles and repeat.
   • Each party can clarify the information by making statements or asking open-ended questions.

3. Focus on interests.
   - Each person states his/her wants and the reasons for wanting to resolve the conflict. "I want . . . I want to solve this problem because . . . If we don't resolve this conflict, I . . . "
   - Each party summarizes what the other person wants and why, i.e., uses empathic listening skills.

   Note: To resolve a conflict, this stage is critical. It is essential that both parties move from their positions and focus on common interests.

4. Create options for mutual gain.
   - Both parties create at least three options that address both party's interests.
   - Both parties try to be creative and don't judge any of the options.

5. Evaluate each option and choose a solution.
   - Parties elaborate on options, combine options.
   - Parties evaluate each option by asking, "Is it fair? Can we do it? Do we think it will work? How will we know it is working?"

6. Create an agreement.
   - Agreement could be written.
   - Plan of action is formed (i.e., who, what , where, when, how).
   - Each person tells what he or she will do to implement the agreement.

In using this negotiation process to resolve conflicts in special education, one might wonder if both parties must understand the process to use it successfully. For example, if a parent confronts the special education administrator with a problem, is it necessary for both the parent and administrator to be knowledgeable of the conflict resolution process? The answer is, no. Ideally, it would be nice if everyone were trained in negotiation strategies. In fact, it has been suggested that LEAs conduct widespread training of teachers, administrators, and parents in the skills of negotiation (Goldberg and Huefner 1995). The reality is that this training probably will not occur. However, if one party (i.e., the special education administrator), is trained in the skills of negotiation, it can be very successful in resolving conflicts. When the special education administrator refuses to react to the other party's position and instead uses good communication skills to address underlying psychological needs and interests, it is possible that resolution can occur.

Final Advice

This negotiation process takes practice and commitment on the part of the special education administrator to be successful. Therefore, at the end of this chapter role-play situations are presented to provide a vehicle for practice. In addition, several exercises address basic communication skills. It is recommended that the special education administrator take a copy of the negotiation steps outlined above into any situation where there may be conflict and refer to each step, attempting to move through each step. This "real-life practice" is the most valuable practice of all and may resolve many conflicts that might have ended in a more formal, and costly, resolution process.

MEDIATION

Overview

Mediation, like principled negotiation, can be categorized as an alternative dispute resolution strategy. Along the continuum shown in Figure 4.2, it is somewhat more structured than principled negotiation, but still considered a less formal strategy.

Mediation has been used since the late 1970s as an alternative dispute resolution strategy in civil litigation cases involving contested divorces, and child custody, visitation, and support issues (Schrag 1996). It has been used in many different disciplines, including business disputes, consumer disputes, small claims courts, environmental issues, public policy conflicts, consumer disputes, and international conflict (Baruch Bush 1992). It has also been adapted to resolving educational conflict, and programs for peer mediation are gaining widespread acceptance in the schools (Dobbs, Primm, and Primm 1991; Savoury, Beals, and Parks 1995). Because of its appeal as a cost-saving and successful alternative to resolving special education disputes, mediation was available in 39 states by the mid-1990s (Symington 1995). In 1997, states and LEAs were mandated by IDEA to make mediation available on a voluntary basis to resolve disputes in special education.

Mediation has been relatively successful in resolving disputes in special education. Agreement rates in states have been documented at 80 percent and mediation is cost-effective when compared with due process (Schrag 1996). It has also been suggested that mediation is dependent upon skilled and well-trained mediators (Schrag 1996).

Mediation can be defined as a conflict resolution process where a neutral third party assists the disputing parties in reaching a mutually satisfying agreement. It is an informal process, but provides structure, i.e., a beginning, middle, and end. The focus is on creative problem solving and communication. Mediation has been referred to as principled negotiation facilitated by a neutral third party (Goldberg and Huefner 1995). The mediator is a trained and skilled facilitator, but he or she doesn't have the power to impose a decision or to enforce a decision or agreement.

To fully understand mediation, it is useful to compare it with the more formal conflict resolution strategy of due process (Figure 4.4). Mediation is a voluntary process, meaning either party can decide that it does not want to use mediation. Mediation does not delay due process, but can occur concurrently with a request for due process. Many times, a request for due process will be made and an agreement using mediation will occur in the "eleventh hour" prior to the due process hearing. Mediation provides a structure for disputing parties to fully discuss the issues and to negotiate a mutually satisfying agreement. Good communication is emphasized by the mediator in an attempt to find mutual interests to form the basis of an agreement. Mediation is also future-oriented and not focused on assigning blame.

Sequence of Events of Mediation

Although models of mediation vary, there are several common steps across all models (Schrag 1996). They include the following steps:

1. Introduction and opening statement.
   The mediator usually makes an opening statement about the nature of mediation, the mediator's role, a review of ground rules, and information about how the parties may reach agreement and what the agreement means.

Mediation	Due Process
Nonadversarial	Adversarial
Informal: conference style	Formal: litigation style
Focus on future	Focus on past
Win-win	Win-lose
Enhances communication	Diminishes communication
Disputants determine outcome: mutual problem solving	Third party determines outcome: hearing office orders decision
Flexible structure	Strict procedural rules
Focus to identify mutual interest	Focus on polarized positions
Open communication by participants	Communication by participants stifled (representatives speak for both parties)
Emotional commitment	Emotional detachment
Low cost	High cost
Confidential	Can be confidential or public
Often concluded in less than one day	Hearing can last several days
Voluntary	Mandatory upon request
Minimal number of documents and participants	High number of documents and participants

Adapted from: Whelan, R. J. (1996). *Mediation in Special Education,* Lawrence, KS.

FIGURE 4.4   *Comparison: Mediation and Due Process*

2. Uncovering common interests.
   Each party has the opportunity to make an uninterrupted statement about what he or she wants and why. After each person talks, the mediator can ask questions, summarize, or seek information to clarify that person's understanding of the conflict.
3. Collaboration.
   Using good communication skills, the mediator helps both parties discuss feelings and concerns and review proposed solutions.
4. Caucusing.
   Meeting with each party individually (caucusing) may occur, at the discretion of the mediator. In the caucus, the mediator will further clarify what the party wants and what alternatives he or she is willing to consider. Caucusing is usually confidential, unless the party agrees to share caucus information.
5. Resolution and agreement.
   If agreement is reached, the mediator writes the agreement and it is signed by all parties. If no agreement is reached, the mediator advises both parties of the next step in resolving the conflict, i.e., due process.

Legal Aspects

Until the 1997 reauthorization of IDEA, mediation was available only in some states. In 1997, Congress mandated that all states make mediation available on a voluntary basis. Mediation procedures in IDEA include the following (IDEA Regulations, 34 C.F.R. § 300.506; Council for Exceptional Children, 1998).

1. Mediation is voluntary and cannot be used to delay or deny parents' right to due process.
2. Each state must maintain a list of mediators. If a mediator is not chosen randomly, both the parents and the school must be involved in the selection process and agree upon the mediator.
3. The LEA or state education agency (SEA) may establish procedures to require parents who don't choose mediation to meet with a neutral party who would explain the benefits of and encourage mediation.
4. The SEA will pay the cost of mediation.
5. Mediation will be scheduled in a timely manner at a convenient location.
6. Any agreement reached in mediation must be in writing.
7. Procedural safeguards notices must be given to parents engaged in mediation.
8. The discussions that occur during mediation must be confidential and may not be used as evidence in future due process hearings or litigation. However, the final written agreement may be used in future proceedings. Parties in the mediation may be required to sign a confidentiality pledge.
9. Attorneys' fees may not be awarded for mediation at the discretion of the state for a mediation conducted prior to filing a complaint.

Final Advice

If other less formal conflict resolution strategies are not successful, mediation is an excellent option to resolve the conflict. Sometimes having a neutral third party who is a skilled negotiator is necessary to move both parties beyond their respective positions to a mutually agreeable resolution. Even if mediation is unsuccessful and the parties engage in a due process hearing, the mediation can serve to clarify important issues in the conflict.

DUE PROCESS

Overview

The right to a due process hearing has been required in the federal statutory law (IDEA and its predecessor, Education for All Handicapped Children Act) since 1975. The statutory law was passed by Congress in an effort to provide procedural protections to children with disabilities. Due process is a formal, adversarial procedure or event used by parents and LEAs to resolve conflict relating to a child's special identification, evaluation, program, and/or placement. On the continuum in Figure 4.2, it represents one of the most formal procedures used to resolve conflict in special education.

Due process hearings are conducted litigation style, where an impartial third party, the hearing officer, listens to evidence presented, including the examination and cross-examination of witnesses. Based on the evidence presented, the hearing officer renders a decision to resolve the conflict. The decision is binding unless it is appealed to the federal or state judicial system. Due process hearings can be requested by parents or LEAs. In a due process hearing, there is a "winner" and a "loser." During a due process hearing, the focus is often on the past and on polarized positions. There are often attorneys representing both parties. The parties rarely engage in any meaningful dialogue. Due process hearings can be confidential or public and they often include many witnesses. Hearings

- SEA is required to develop a model form to assist parents in filing a complaint.
- In filing a request for a hearing to the LEA, the parent must provide a written notice that includes: the name and address of the child and the name of the school the child attends, a description of the nature of the problem relating to the proposed initiation or change, including facts related to the problem, and a proposed solution to the problem.
- Both parties must disclose evidence to be used at the hearing 5 business days prior to the hearing.
- At least 5 business days prior to a hearing, each party shall disclose all evaluations completed by that date and recommendations based on those evaluations that are intended to be used at the hearing.
- Both parties have the right to be accompanied and advised by counsel and individuals knowledgeable of children with disabilities.
- Both parties have the right to present evidence and confront, cross-examine, and compel the attendance of witnesses.
- Both parties have the right to a written verbatim record of the hearing or at the option of the parents, an electronic verbatim.
- Both parties have the right to written or, at the option of the parents, an electronic verbatim of the findings of fact and decisions.
- Findings of fact decisions must be public, provided confidentiality is maintained.
- The decisions and findings may be appealed to state or district court of the United States, or first to the SEA if required in that state.
- Except in cases involving alternative educational settings, unless the LEA and parents otherwise agree, the child shall remain in the then-current placement.
- If applying for initial admission to school, with the consent of the parents, the child shall be placed in a public school program until proceedings end.
- Parents may have the child who is the subject of the hearing present.
- Parents may open the hearing to the public.
- Unless the hearing officer grants an extension the final decision in a hearing must be reached within 45 days of the hearing request.

Source: Individuals with Disabilities Education Act Regulations, 34 C.F.R. 300, 507–514 (1999).

FIGURE 4.5   *Due Process Legal Procedures*

may last several days at a high financial and emotional cost to participants. Often, relationships are damaged after a due process hearing. Due process hearings are governed by many legal procedures. These procedures are summarized in Figure 4.5.

In a survey of due process hearings in all states from 1994 to 1996, there was a steady increase between 1991 and 1995 in both number of hearings requested and percent of requests resulting in convened hearings (Ahearn 1997). On average, 34.8 percent of hearings requested actually resulted in a hearing being held (Ahearn 1997).

Sequence of Events of Due Process

When a request is made for a due process hearing by a parent, the request will often be given to the special education administrator or superintendent. It is important at this stage to assist the parent in completing a written request for the hearing and to forward the request to the state education agency (SEA) immediately. At this point, depending upon SEA regulations, it is important to consider mediation. Mediation will not delay the timelines in due process and may provide a way to resolve the conflict prior to the hearing. It is assumed that, if possible, the special education administrator has already attempted principled negotiation to resolve the conflict.

If a parent wants to initiate a due process hearing, she or her attorney must provide notice to the school district that includes the name of her child, her address, the name of the school her child attends, a description of the problem, and a proposed resolution of the problem. After a due process hearing has been requested, it is likely that the LEA will engage the services of an attorney well versed in special education law to represent the LEA. If this is the case, records for the child will be forwarded to the attorney and the special education administrator, superintendent, and attorney will confer to discuss strengths and weaknesses of the case, potential witnesses, and documents needed. The attorney will prepare questions for prospective witnesses and will discuss the questions and strategy with all witnesses at a pre-hearing conference. In addition, the attorney will often discuss what to expect in terms of examination and cross-examination (e.g., hostility, attacks on credibility, their status as experts, and how to answer questions).

At the actual hearing, which may last for several days, the sequence of events generally follows these steps:

1. Opening statement by the hearing officer.
2. Opening statement by the school district representative.
3. Opening statement by the parent's representative.
4. Direct examination of school district witnesses by the school district representative.
5. Cross-examination of school district witnesses by the parent's representative.
6. Direct examination of parent's witnesses by the parent's representative.
7. Cross-examination of parent's witnesses by the school district representative.
8. Closing statement by the school district representative.
9. Closing statement by the parent's representative.
10. Closing statement by the hearing officer.

A written report outlining findings of fact and decisions by the hearing officer is received by both parties. In the written order, timelines are detailed for implementing the order or appeal to the judicial system, or if the SEA requires, appeal to the SEA for review.

Preparation for a Hearing

Although the LEA attorney will prepare the case for the school district and become the spokesperson, the special education administrator will be essential in providing background information on the case and preparing teachers for their pivotal testimony. To assist the attorney in preparing the case, the following points are useful for the special education administrator:

1. Be as fully informed as possible as to the exact issues in the case and assist the attorney in understanding the issues.
2. Gather all records concerning the child and share them with the attorney. Often records exist in several locations and it is the administrator's job to ensure that a complete set of records is available.
3. Organize the records in a logical order for the attorney, e.g., chronological, topical.

4. Parent contact records should be gathered and a chronology of events leading to the request for due process hearing should be constructed.
5. Be honest with the attorney. If something occurred that was not procedurally correct, inform the attorney. If this information isn't shared, it will in all likelihood come out in the hearing.
6. Identify all professionals serving the student as well as the evaluators involved in the last evaluation, and share this list with the attorney.
7. Inform the attorney of any known weaknesses in the potential witness list, e.g., friend of parent, "weak" teacher.

Teachers often provide very important information as witnesses during due process hearings. They can be on a witness stand for many hours undergoing intensive, detailed questions about teaching techniques, behavior management techniques, materials used, the IEP process, etc. For example, the following dialogue could take place in a hearing where the special education teacher is cross-examined by the parent's attorney.

Parent Attorney:	Ms. Li, were you Hakim's special education teacher during the past school year?
Teacher:	Yes, I was.
Parent Attorney:	I assume then that you participated in writing Hakim's IEP.
Teacher:	Yes.
Parent Attorney:	Please look at the goal written for Hakim on page 6. Would you read it to me?
Teacher:	It says, "Hakim will read a list of 25 survival words at 100 percent accuracy."
Parent Attorney:	I don't see where this goal was evaluated. Did you evaluate the extent to which this goal was met?
Teacher:	Yes, the IEP team conducted an annual review and . . .
Parent Attorney:	(interrupts) I understand that you say you conducted an annual review, but where on this IEP is it documented that you evaluated Hakim's progress on this goal?
Teacher:	We always evaluate goals on IEPs.
Parent Attorney:	It is not documented on the IEP, so how am I to believe that Hakim's goal was properly evaluated?
Teacher:	We discussed Hakim's progress in the meeting.
Parent Attorney:	I propose that you didn't evaluate Hakim's progress. If you had done so, there would be some type of documentation on the IEP. Conducting an IEP meeting and doing what you are supposed to do at an IEP meeting are two different things, aren't they?
Teacher:	(looking upset) I guess so.

One can see from this dialogue that intense questioning can undermine even the most confident teacher. The special education administrator, along with the school district attorney, can help prepare witnesses for a due process hearing. The following are useful ideas to prepare teachers as witnesses.

1. Review the child's records and be prepared to discuss the child's progress over time.

2. It is essential to be well prepared. Being overprepared is better than not being prepared. Try to anticipate prospective questions and prepare accordingly.
3. Be honest in answering questions.
4. If not sure what to say when asked a question, ask for clarification or look at your attorney and ask for clarification. This strategy will buy time for you to think.
5. Don't answer "what if" questions. Stay with your actual experience with the child.
6. Remain unemotional and calm when answering questions as much as possible, even though you may be nervous on the inside. Answer questions in a "matter-of-fact" manner.
7. Don't be afraid to put forth the best possible case. The other side will also do this.
8. Demonstrate the significant concern the school district has shown over the years for the child.
9. Focus on the amount of talent which has been made available to the child.
10. If possible, focus on the suggestions, revisions, etc. which were proposed by the school district to enhance the student's performance and to resolve concerns of the parents.

Attorney's Fees

If the parents win in the due process hearing, a court may award reasonable attorneys' fees as part of the costs to the parents. The thinking is that parents would not have had to spend money on an attorney if the school district had proceeded correctly in the first place. At times, prior to a hearing, the school district may offer the parents a plan to settle the dispute. If the parents don't accept the plan and ultimately the hearing officer rules that the plan offered prior to the hearing was appropriate, attorneys' fees might not be awarded. Circumstances where attorneys' fees might be given to the parent include the following:

- If the offer is made within ten days before the hearing begins, or
- If the offer is not accepted within ten days, and the court or hearing officer finds the relief finally obtained by the parents is not more favorable to the parents than the offer of settlement (IDEA Regulations, 34 C.F.R. § 300.513).

Attorneys' fees can't be given to parents if the parent's attorney attends an IEP meeting unless the meeting is convened as a result of the due process hearing or judicial action or, at the discretion of the state, as a result of mediation conducted before filing a request for the hearing (IDEA Regulations, 34 C.F.R. § 300.513). A court can reduce the amount of attorneys' fees when the court finds that the following conditions have occurred.

1. The parent unreasonably protracted the final resolution of the controversy.
2. The amount of fees awarded unreasonably exceeds the hourly prevailing rate in the community.
3. Considering the nature of the action, the time spent and legal services furnished were excessive.
4. The attorney representing the parent did not provide to the LEA the appropriate information in the complaint (IDEA Regulations, 34 C.F.R. § 300.513).

In addition, attorneys' fees may not be reduced if the court finds that the LEA unreasonably delayed the final resolution of the action or there was a violation of procedural safeguards.

Final Advice

Although some due process hearings are impossible to avoid, the special education administrator should attempt to resolve conflicts in a less formal, less costly manner. Even if a hearing request has been made, it is often worthwhile to consider mediation, for example. If conflicts are resolved in a less formal manner, relationships will be preserved, costs will be contained, and both parties have an opportunity to win.

Administrators often are not well versed in less formal methods of resolving conflict, yet it is advantageous to all parties to use these methods. Less formal methods are not regulated or mandated. To practice the essential skills in resolving conflict, two activities follow. The first is an activity where partners practice using effective communication skills, which form the foundation of conflict resolution. Second are three role-play situations where students are presented with a conflict situation, assigned roles, and practice negotiation skills as outlined in the text.

After these practice activities, students will read, discuss, and answer questions about two practical cases dealing with conflict resolution in special education.

A C T I V I T Y

Using Effective Communication Skills

For this exercise, work with a partner. The first person talks for one minute uninterrupted about a recent conflict. The partner uses the following effective communication skills: active listening, empathic listening, "I-messages," and clarifying responses. The partners then switch roles.

At the end of the exercise, discuss the following:

1. How easy or difficult was it to allow a person to talk uninterrupted for a minute? How easy or difficult was it to use effective communication skills?

2. As the person talking about a conflict, did you feel heard and understood? Why or why not?

3. Can you think of a school-related conflict where using effective communication skills might have helped to resolve the conflict? If so, discuss the situation.

R O L E   P L A Y :   O M A R

Instructions

For this role play, work with a partner. One person will assume the role of the special education administrator and the other person will assume the role of Omar's parent. Read the background information and each person's position. If you play the part of the special education administrator, use the outline for negotiation provided earlier in this chapter and try to negotiate a resolution to the conflict with the parent.

Situation

Omar is a fifth grader at Martin Luther King, Jr. Elementary School. He does not like going to school. Omar's report card indicated that he was doing poorly in all subjects and that he was not completing his assignments. His parent is upset because Omar is imaginative and creative, loves to read, converses like an adult, and is capable of doing superior work. Omar's teacher called the parent last week to discuss referring Omar for testing for possible placement in a special education program for children with behavior disorders. The parent refused to sign the consent for the evaluation. The parent called the special education administrator to complain about the teacher and the quality of education Omar is receiving. The special education administrator invited the parent to a meeting. The parent believes Omar is having problems because his teacher does not challenge him and he is bored.

Background

Omar has been in the school for four months. The family moved to this community in the summer. Omar was tested in the second grade and placed in a class for the gifted at his former school. Omar's current teacher has taught fifth grade for 25 years and is well respected in the district.

Special Education Administrator's Position

You want to support the teacher. You have consulted with the building principal and the other fifth grades are full. You don't want to move Omar to another class. You think Omar could have emotional problems.

Parent's Position

You want Omar served by the gifted program and changed to a different fifth grade classroom where the teacher has a good reputation for challenging students like Omar.

ROLE PLAY: ANGELA

Instructions

For this role play, three people will assume the following roles: special education administrator, principal, and parent. Read the background information and each person's position. If you play the role of the special education administrator, use the outline for negotiation provided earlier in this chapter, and try to negotiate a resolution to the conflict.

Situation

Angela is a third grade student with behavior disorders who is in a self-contained special class at Lincoln Elementary School. She is a bright, manipulative, and very disruptive student. Lately, she has been extremely disruptive on the school bus, e.g., hitting, kicking, spitting at other students and the bus driver. The principal has removed her from the bus on two other occasions, each time for two days. This means Angela's mother has to take off time from work to take Angela to and from school. Yesterday, Angela threw a book on the bus and hit another student in the head. The principal called the parent and said that Angela would be removed from the bus for five days.

The parent is furious and calls the special education administrator. The parent says that her boss will not allow her to be late to work and leave early. She is angry that the principal refused to consider alternative discipline for Angela. The parent is well versed in parents' rights for children with disabilities.

An IEP conference is arranged for the next day.

Background:

The building principal has been a good administrator, but tends to react impulsively, especially if a student has been hit or hurt. The parent is well educated and knowledgeable. This situation could become a due process case in the future. Up to this point, the parent has worked well with the principal and special education administrator.

Special Education Administrator's Position

You think the principal has gone beyond reasonable discipline and yet you understand the seriousness of the discipline and safety issue. You want to support the principal and also explore other modes of discipline. You also have legal concerns about the child's removal from school without alternative transportation.

Parent's Position

You do not want Angela suspended from the bus for behavior relating to her disability. You want the principal to agree to alternative discipline, maybe after-school detention.

Principal's Position

You want the right to discipline as you see fit in your building. You have given Angela many warnings prior to suspension and you don't feel she deserves any more chances. You're not too concerned about the parent's anger. She will just have to understand that Angela's behavior won't be tolerated, and that the punishment fits the behavior.

ROLE PLAY: REGINA

Instructions

For this role play, three people will play the following roles: special education supervisor, parent, and first grade teacher. Read the background information and each person's position. If you play the role of the special education supervisor, use the outline for negotiation provided earlier in this chapter, and try to negotiate a resolution to the conflict with the parent.

Situation

The special education supervisor is attending an evaluation and IEP conference today for a first grader in Mrs. Wilson's class. When the meeting convenes, it is apparent that Regina, a first grader, will be eligible for learning disabilities assistance for reading. It is March and Regina can only read three-letter words. Mrs. Wilson, Regina's teacher, told the special education supervisor before the conference that Regina's mother was very opposed to placement in special education.

Special Education Supervisor's Position

You feel that all children who are eligible for special education assistance should receive the help to which they are entitled. You want to work to develop a positive relationship with parents, but it is the child who should receive an appropriate education, and you will not compromise on this point. If that means challenging the parent, you are not afraid to do so.

Parent's Position

Your husband was in special education and you know that he never got out of special education. Your spouse is not much help to you as he works all day and drinks every night. You don't want Regina to end up like this. You are angry, upset, and very much opposed to placement in special education.

First Grade Teacher's Position

You have been teaching first grade for 25 years and are considered an excellent teacher. You know Regina will not be successful academically without special education assistance. You have threatened to retain Regina if she does not receive help from special education.

CASE 4.1: "ONCE YOU'RE IN SPECIAL EDUCATION, YOU NEVER GET OUT!"

Mrs. Kalimah had been a first grade teacher for 25 years and was highly regarded in the field of education. She was a traditional teacher who worked hard to ensure that all her students learned to read by the end of the year. Her class this year was small with only 20 students. Still, she was concerned about David Smith's progress. It was January and David wasn't comfortable with simple sight words and had great difficulty sounding out words like "cat" and "hat." Today, David's mother agreed to meet with her after school to discuss David's progress. Mrs. Kalimah felt that the only way for David to learn to read was if he received special education assistance. To qualify for help, David would have to be evaluated, and this was the subject of today's conference with Mrs. Smith.

At 3:15 P.M., Mrs. Kalimah met with Mrs. Smith in her classroom. Mrs. Kalimah began the meeting by saying, "Mrs. Smith, I asked you to meet with me today because I am concerned about David. He is such a sweet boy and he tries hard in school. I know you work with him as much as you can at home. However, I am very

concerned about his reading progress. David is having difficulty reading at a preprimer level. He struggles over sounding out simple words like 'bat' and 'mat.' Sometimes I'm not sure he really understands that symbols stand for sounds or that words can be sounded out. He also struggles with common sight words like 'and' and 'the.' He seems to remember them one day, but forgets them the next day. I've worked with many children over my 25 years as a teacher, and I really think David could have a learning disability."

Mrs. Smith looked up and said, "My husband had a learning disability and the school didn't help him at all! Once he got placed in special education, he never got out. He can't even find a steady job now. He's really not much help at home. I don't want that to happen to David. I want David to graduate from school. I don't want him in special education."

Mrs. Kalimah continued, "Special education can help David learn to read, Mrs. Smith. I'm also concerned about promoting David to second grade if he doesn't receive some special help."

(Continue)

CASE 4.1 (CONTINUED)

Mrs. Smith reluctantly said, "Well, I guess it wouldn't hurt to let David be tested, but I'm not going to allow him to go into special education."

Relieved, Mrs. Kalimah reviewed the evaluation consent form with Mrs. Smith and Mrs. Smith signed the form.

Six weeks later, Mrs. Smith received a notice that a meeting would be held to discuss David's evaluation. The evaluation conference was held after school in the principal's conference room. Around a large table, six participants waited for Mrs. Smith to arrive. They included Mr. Turner, special education supervisor; Mrs. Kalimah, David's teacher; Mrs. Ramirez, principal; Mr. Boyle, psychologist; Mrs. Diehl, learning disabilities teacher; and Ms. Welston, social worker. Mrs. Smith arrived about five minutes late and took the last empty seat.

After introductions, Mr. Turner began by saying, "We are here today to discuss the evaluation of David Smith and his possible eligibility for special education services. Mrs. Kalimah, would you begin by telling us about David's progress in first grade and why you referred him for the evaluation?"

Mrs. Kalimah stated, "David has been in my classroom since the beginning of the year. I have been concerned about his reading progress almost since then, but I decided to wait until after Christmas to see if maturity might make a difference. It didn't. David has great difficulty reading. I am really concerned about David's success next year in second grade. I really don't think he will succeed without special help. He's really a sweet, compliant child and I hate to see him fail."

The social worker, Ms. Welston, gave her report next. She reported that David's development had been unremarkable. Ms. Welston said that it was difficult for the family to make ends meet due to Mr. Smith's lack of a job. Ms. Welston then asked Mrs. Smith is she had anything to add.

Mrs. Smith said, "I can tell you one thing. David isn't going into any special education class. My husband was in special education and it didn't help him at all!"

Mr. Turner replied, "We'll discuss special education after we review the evaluation, Mrs. Smith."

The psychologist reviewed his findings. He stated that David had average overall intelligence on the Weschler Intelligence Scale for Children–Third Edition. However, David exhibited weaknesses in his verbal abil-ity and this was reflected with a verbal IQ of 80. His performance IQ was 115 or high average. In reading, Mr. Boyle confirmed Mrs. Kalimah's observations. David was far behind his peer group in basic reading skills and was performing on a preprimer level. Spelling skills were also delayed, but math skills appeared to be average. Compared to his overall ability, David had significant weaknesses in reading and his short-term memory was weak, suggesting a learning disability.

Mrs. Diehl reported in her observation of David in class that David was attentive during instruction, but obviously could not complete the reading tasks assigned to him. He was not able to succeed in an existing reading group and had to be taught by himself in reading.

Mr. Turner concluded by saying, "I understand the team to indicate that David has a learning disability in the areas of reading and short-term memory. Does everyone agree with this conclusion?"

Everyone nodded in agreement, except Mrs. Smith. She said, "Does this mean David will go into special education?"

Mr. Turner said, "It appears that David needs special education assistance to learn to read, Mrs. Smith."

Mrs. Smith angrily stated, "Then I disagree. I said earlier that I will not allow David to go into special education and I won't."

Mrs. Kalimah said, "Now, Mrs. Smith, you know David needs special education help. He won't be successful in reading without special help. In fact, I don't know how I can promote David to second grade unless he is in special education."

Mrs. Smith stood up and said, "You are going have to figure out some other way to help David because he is not going into special education. Once my husband went into special education, he never got out!"

Mr. Turner stood up and said, "David may need special education help all the way through school, but there is nothing wrong with receiving help."

Mrs. Smith walked out of the room and everyone looked surprised. Mr. Turner said, "I knew Mrs. Smith didn't want David in special education, but I thought that once she heard how much he needed help, she would give her consent. I think we have two options. One, we could go ahead and make David eligible for special education and request a due process hearing. Second, we could reconvene this meeting and try to talk

(Continue)

CASE 4.1 (CONTINUED)

to Mrs. Smith with the idea that she needs time to think and that we need to address the issue using a different approach. I suggest we try the second approach first."

The participants agreed and another meeting was arranged with Mrs. Smith. The second meeting was scheduled a week later in Mrs. Kalimah's classroom with the same participants.

After everyone was seated, Mr. Turner began the meeting by saying, "Mrs. Smith, it seems that we differ on how we can help your son in school. Today I'd like for us to agree to cooperate with each other so that we can resolve our differences. In doing so, I ask that we take turns listening to each other and talking. I really think that we can resolve our differences about David's education."

Mrs. Smith said tentatively, "OK, I'll listen, but I'm not changing my mind."

Mr. Turner continued, "Thank you. Mrs. Smith, what is your understanding of David's progress in school?"

Mrs. Smith thought for a few seconds, then said, "I knew David might have trouble learning to read. In kindergarten, he struggled to learn the alphabet and I knew that reading would be hard for him. I work with him at home as often as I can. You know, I work two jobs and sometimes I'm not home until eight at night. I just want him to learn to read. I know, from seeing my husband struggle, how important it is to read."

Mr. Turner responded, "It sounds like you know that he is frustrated with school and that you want him to succeed in school."

Mrs. Smith nodded and said, "Yes. I want so much for him to learn to read and I can see that it is really hard for him." Tears welled up in Mrs. Smith's eyes as she talked.

Mrs. Kalimah said, "Mrs. Smith, I've been teaching first grade for many years and David isn't the only child who has difficulty learning to read. Many times, maturity plays a role. Some children are ready to read earlier than other children. David seems like he's not quite ready, but that doesn't mean he'll never be a successful reader. In fact, it's quite possible that, with help, he will learn to read."

Mrs. Smith said, "Do you really think so?"

Mrs. Kalimah replied, "Yes, I do. I would never give up on David. He needs special attention with his read-

ing now. That doesn't mean he won't be a successful reader or student or adult."

Mr. Turner said, "It seems like the evaluation confirmed what you already know about David's reading, Mrs. Smith."

Mrs. Smith answered, "Yes, I guess it did. It's just that it was hard for me to hear that."

Mr. Boyle, the psychologist, said, " The testing indicates that David is a bright child and that something is blocking his ability to learn to read now. David may need help removing that block."

Mr. Turner said, "Mrs. Smith, what do you want to happen to David?"

Mrs. Smith said, "I want him to learn to read, maybe with more individual help, and to graduate from high school. I don't want him to quit school."

Mr. Turner continued, "I agree with you. I think your goals are exactly the same as everyone at this table. What are some ways that we could achieve the goals of learning to read and graduating from high school?"

Mrs. Kalimah said, "I have been working closely with David on reading this year, but maybe I could work with him after school three days a week for 15 minutes. Maybe the extra help for the remainder of the year would make a difference. But I am concerned about second grade."

Mr. Turner asked, "Mrs. Smith what are your concerns about second grade?"

Mrs. Smith said, "I am really worried about second grade. I know that David can't keep up, especially in reading."

Mrs. Diehl, the learning disabilities teacher said, "Mrs. Smith, I will be working with a small group of second graders in reading next year. What I plan to do is see them in a group for about 30 minutes a day and I will go into the second grade class during reading and work with those students on an individual basis. I will also be developing extra practice work in basic reading skills for those students. I think David would benefit from the extra attention."

Mrs. Smith said, "Isn't that special education?"

Mrs. Diehl said, "Yes. But children don't see me as the special ed teacher. They see me as the reading teacher and another teacher in the regular classroom. Also, I would suggest that David spend the majority of his day in second grade."

(Continue)

CASE 4.1 (CONTINUED)

After further discussion, Mrs. Smith agreed to placing David in the learning disabilities program for the following year. She was appreciative of the extra assistance that David would receive for the remainder of this year with his first grade teacher, Mrs. Kalimah. Mrs. Smith signed the consent for placement and the team wrote David's IEP.

Note to the reader: You will now be asked questions about this case. Before you read the Questions and Reflections section at the end of the book (Appendix A), you should fill out a case study analysis (Appendix C), then answer the questions and share your ideas with the class.

Questions

1. What was Mrs. Smith's position initially? Likewise, what was the school district's position initially?
2. If the two parties, Mrs. Smith and school district personnel, had stayed with their positions, what might have occurred?
3. What happened during the second meeting that resulted in conflict resolution? What steps of the negotiation process can be identified?
4. How was the communication different during each of the two conferences?

CASE 4.2: "I WENT TO SCHOOL TO TEACH FIFTH GRADE, NOT TO WORK WITH STUDENTS WITH BEHAVIOR DISORDERS !"

Anna Kowalski was the special education director of a large suburban unit school district of 6,000 students. She worked with a special education supervisor, four school psychologists, two social workers, and approximately 70 special education teachers and paraprofessionals. The district served approximately 650 students with disabilities. Most students with mild and moderate disabilities were served within the district. Approximately 50 students with severe disabilities were served by working with other local special education cooperatives and area private schools.

In the district, three elementary behavior disorders (BD) classes were located in King Elementary School. One class served kindergarten through second grade, one served third and fourth grades and one served fifth and sixth grades. Each class had approximately 12 students and was staffed with a special education teacher and a paraprofessional. The building also had three learning disabilities (LD) classes. Overall, the building served 350 students in kindergarten through sixth grade, and each grade had two sections. The building principal, Ms. Black, was a former special education administrator and had been principal at King Elementary for three years.

One day, a third grade teacher was walking with her students to the cafeteria. In the hallway, the BD teacher from fifth and sixth grades was physically dragging a screaming and kicking student from her class down the hall toward the office. The BD teacher said, "I told you that if you threw your books one more time today at another student, you would go to the principal's office to call your mother and that is what we are going to do!" The student's face was red and he was flinging his arms and trying to kick the teacher. He was also yelling profanities. The third grade teacher stopped her class until the BD teacher had taken her student past the group.

Later that day, there was a discussion in the teacher's lounge about the incident among a group of four regular education teachers and one LD teacher. The discussion focused on why teachers in this building had to "put up" with those severe behaviors from BD students.

One teacher stated, "I was on playground duty yesterday and I had to break up a fight between two students from the BD class and I'm tired of dealing with these students. I went to school to teach fifth grade, not work with BD students! If I wanted to work with BD students, I would have gone into special education."

Another teacher added, "King Elementary is the only school in this district to house three classes for BD students and that's not fair."

A third teacher said, "I know that I will get phone calls from parents after the violence my students witnessed in the hallway! What am I going to say?"

(Continue)

CASE 4.2 (CONTINUED)

The LD teacher suggested writing a letter to the board of education detailing the behaviors of the students in the BD class and requesting action. As the LD teacher was making her suggestion, Ms. Black, principal, walked into the lounge. The teachers told Ms. Black what they were planning and Ms. Black told the group that they certainly had the right to complain and write the letter.

Two days later, all teachers in the building, with the exception of the BD teachers, signed the letter and sent it to the board of education.

No one in the building talked with Ms. Kowalski, special education director, or with Mr. Brown, the district superintendent, about the letter. A teacher from King Elementary called Ms. Kowalski later that day and told her that a letter had been sent to the school board. Anna Kowalski immediately contacted the superintendent and informed him about the letter. The superintendent called Ms. Black, building principal, to inquire about the letter and was told she was "vaguely aware" of the concerns, but not of the letter.

The superintendent, in his weekly communication packet with the school board, informed board members of the letter they were to receive and that he and the special education administrator were working with the King Elementary staff to resolve the issues.

The superintendent and Anna Kowalski then arranged an after-school meeting with the staff at King Elementary. The superintendent conducted the meeting and asked staff to express concerns about the BD programs in the building.

One teacher stated, "I really don't understand why we have to locate all elementary BD students in this building! When I am out on the playground, I constantly have to discipline these students. They are not good role models for other students."

Mr. Brown responded by saying, "It seems that you are upset about the presence of these children in one building. We want to work with you to resolve the issues, but we can't do this unless we are informed of your concerns. It appears that these are long-standing concerns and this is the first time that Ms. Kowalski and I have been made aware of the concerns."

The meeting was lengthy and the tone was positive. At the conclusion of the meeting, Anna Kowalski offered to meet with teachers the following week regarding specific concerns. The teachers expressed appreciation that Mr. Brown and Ms. Kowalski had taken the time to listen to their concerns. They also apologized about not informing the superintendent and special education administrator first instead of sending a letter directly to the board of education.

The next day, the superintendent had a heated meeting with Ms. Black, the principal. He told her that he was very upset that she had not informed him about the letter and that she originally told him she was "vaguely aware" of the letter. Ms. Black was told in no uncertain terms that either he or the special education administrator were to be informed of any concerns regarding special education in the future.

At the next school board meeting, there was a lengthy discussion of issues raised in the letter concerning BD students at the school. The superintendent was able to inform board members about the meeting and that the issues were being addressed. He promised to keep the board members informed about the resolution of the conflict. He also informed board members of the possible role that Ms. Black, principal, played in possibly "stirring up" the problem issues. In other words, he stated that the issues could possibly have been resolved at the administrative level.

Note to the reader: You will now be asked questions about this case. Before you read the Questions and Reflections section at the end of the book (Appendix A) you should fill out a Case Study Analysis (Appendix C), then answer the questions and share your ideas with the class.

Questions

1. How should Ms. Kowalski, special education director, address conflict with the following: King Elementary staff? King Elementary principal? District superintendent? Board of education? Parents?

2. What issues of programming for elementary BD students are related to this conflict? How might these issues be addressed?

3. How should the special education administrator approach the BD teacher(s) about how the student in the case was managed (i.e., force the student down the hall, kicking and screaming)?

4. What issues about line of authority are a concern?

PROGRAM EVALUATION IN SPECIAL EDUCATION

In this chapter, issues dealing with program evaluation in special education will be reviewed. After reading the chapter and analyzing the cases, you should be able to:

- Discuss the forces that have shaped special education program evaluation.
- Describe program evaluation issues.
- Understand the impact that standards-based reform, alternative assessment, and high school completion have had on special education.
- Discuss success of special education.

See semantic map detailing Chapter 5 on page 93.

OVERVIEW

Special education faces a number of hurdles in the application and implementation of law and in meeting public expectations. One of the most difficult areas of application and implementation deals with program evaluation and individual student assessment of students with disabilities. Program evaluation and student achievement, for the student with a disability, are dependent upon each other, but are difficult to coordinate and more difficult to attain. Why? It may be that to this point the regular education initiative has not grasped the importance of assimilating special education into the whole of education or has not decided upon an evaluation format that will meet the dictates of legislation and district needs.

If special education is ever to be integrated into general education principles the entire school/school district must become responsible for the curriculum and also be accountable for student achievement.

PROGRAM EVALUATION DEFINED

What is program evaluation? Popham (1993) proposed that the concept of program evaluation became a specialty as an outcome of the Elementary and Secondary Education Act (ESEA) of 1965. The act included a specification that programs be evaluated yearly as part of the funding process. From the inception of ESEA to the present,

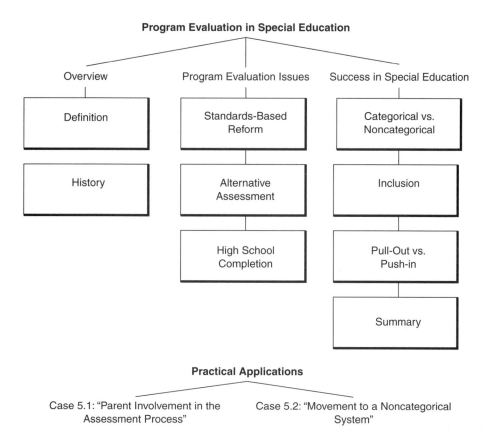

program evaluation has become the standard for regular education as opposed to an infrequently applied approach demanded by a federal program. The operative words in program evaluation have been "regular education."

In the preface to their text, *Testing Students with Disabilities,* Thurlow, Elliott, and Ysselldyke (1998, 3) state, "Today, the topic of testing students with disabilities is near the top of the list of district and state priorities. If it is not, it probably should be. Why? Because districts and states are being pushed to be accountable for the results of education, for how well students are performing. And states and districts are realizing that to have good educational accountability systems, it is important to be sure that all students are included, and this means students with disabilities."

Thurlow, Elliott, and Ysseldyke (1998) go on to give six reasons why students with disabilities should be in an accountability system. The reasons are:

1. For an accurate picture of education.
2. For students with disabilities to benefit from reform.
3. To make accurate comparisons.
4. To avoid unintended consequences of exclusion.
5. To meet legal requirements.
6. To promote high expectations.

As reported in *Research to Practice: A "Blueprint" for Closing the Gap in Local Schools* (Abbott et al. 1999), there are several key questions that should be addressed in establishing a research model.

- Are local school partnerships established using a model?
- Have interactions between teachers and researchers been established?
- Have research-based practices increased?
- What is the effect on formative measures of student outcome?
- What is the extent of teacher satisfaction?
- Does participation increase rather than decrease from year to year?

This blueprint and other attempts at integrating practice and research may assist educators in translating program results into reliable reportable information.

This chapter will review the issues dealing with program evaluation and the evaluation of specific programs within special education.

Scenarios

1. "You don't have any options. Reading between the lines I believe that the law says that you must offer the same assessment to the students in special education as the students in your regular education program, and you must report the findings in your newspaper. I have been reporting on school issues for a long time and cannot understand your hesitancy in showing the improvement or lack of improvement in your special education students," stated Hart Berkowski, editor of the local newspaper.
   - How would you answer Hart Berkowski?
2. Dr. Sellenriek was in her fourth year as assistant superintendent of the Frontenac School District. She was meeting with her administrative council. The council was made up of principals, department chair representatives, and teachers from elementary, middle school, and the high school. "Let's move on to the second agenda item. The school board has decided that the district's schools will move from a pull-out to a push-in program for our special education students. We have until September to develop the program. Here is what I need from you. I need a list of the issues that we should discuss in order for the special education push-in program to be successful. As you noticed on the agenda I have allowed for forty-five minutes for you to get together by level to develop the list. We will have a day-long meeting this summer to develop my usual approach of implementing a *First Day, First Week, First Month, and First Year Manual* for everyone to follow. Let's take a break and when we come back get into your groups. Thanks ahead of time for all your help."
   - What would you list as important issues to consider as the district moves toward a push-in program?

PROGRAM EVALUATION IN SPECIAL EDUCATION

What is the state of program evaluation in special education? How does the state of program evaluation affect public confidence in educational programming for general and special education? Does special education work?

Through the late eighties formal program evaluation in special education focused on process indicators rather than the outcomes of the individual student or student groups (Johnson 1998). Goertz (1996) indicated that special education has had a limited influence in standards-based reform. Malouf and Schiller (1995) believed that the long-standing gap between research and practice in special and regular education should be considered a national concern.

As educators and parents began to review federal law (Goals 2000: Educate America Act, 1993; Improving America's Schools Act, 1994; IDEA—amended, 1997) in light of programs for special education students, the concept of evaluation began to change. Questions dealing with student outcomes, achievement in comparison to age-appropriate peers, and post-school success began to take the forefront (Sage and Burrello 1994).

With the implementation of IDEA amendments of 1997, which requires the reporting of students with disability assessment, the importance of assessment grew. Even with the emphasis on assessment the actual number of states that report information on statewide assessment of students with disabilities is less than twenty percent (*Twentieth Annual Report to Congress on the Implementation of the Individuals with Disabilities Education Act,* 1998).

There are two basic reasons why there is a discrepancy between the importance of assessment and the actual numbers being involved in district assessment. The first reason deals with the focus that is put upon district and school assessment results. It is felt that by including the assessment of students with disabilities a school district's overall assessment may be compromised. The second reason deals with the feeling by parents and educators that it is important to protect students from stress. Roach, Dailey, and Goertz (1997) followed 12 state systems and found the following issues when dealing with the inclusion of special education students with disabilities in general education accountability:

- General accountability systems that rely heavily on student achievement are inadequate for monitoring the progress of students with disabilities if they are not included in the assessment.
- Accountability systems may mask pockets of poor achievement by school or populations within schools, if data are not collected and reported in sufficient detail.
- State compliance staff feels pulled by federal compliance requirements when a state significantly collapses special education monitoring items into a more general, performance-oriented state format.
- Parents, teachers, and students are concerned about the potential implication of new graduation and diploma requirements on students with disabilities. Alternatively, some educators and policymakers are concerned that current diploma and graduation requirements may give students with disabilities an unfair advantage in the system.

By July of 2000 IDEA required that all students with a disability be given an option of an alternate assessment. This will change the way districts report overall assessment data in their school district report card.

PROGRAM EVALUATION ISSUES

Standards-based reform, alternative assessment, and high school completion will be the focus of attention for special and regular educators alike through the early 2000s as a means of determining success. The concept of measurable results through improved accountability and improved collection of data will assist educators and the public in determining program success. The reform movement towards standards carries with it the additional variables of assessment, accountability, and consequences.

To implement standards-based reforms across the continuum it is necessary to determine how to assess every child's movement toward the standards. This creates problems for districts as they face the difficult task of formulating alternate assessments that accommodate one segment of the continuum—students with disabilities.

When is an alternate assessment used? Ysseldyke (1997) suggested that alternative assessments are used when a student does not fit into the regular program of assessment.

School districts have a host of reasons why certain students should not be part of a district's assessment plan. Some of these reasons are:

- The issue of relevance.
- The use of alternate curriculum.
- IEP mandates.
- The negative effect of the students with disabilities test scores on overall district results.

One of the variables used to determine the success of a school district is the level of high school completion. The graduation rate of 29 percent, diploma or certificate of completion, for students with disabilities remained basically the same for years 1992 through 1996 (*Twentieth Annual Report to Congress on the Implementation of the Individuals with Disabilities Education Act,* 1998). With additional emphasis by IDEA upon high school graduation, pressure will continue on school districts to adjust graduation requirements to include students with disabilities.

What is the graduation rate for students with disabilities in your district, your state? What is your district doing to promote a greater graduation participation rate for students with disabilities?

HOW SUCCESSFUL ARE SPECIAL EDUCATION PROGRAMS?

There continues to be a great debate as to the evaluated merit of special education programs. An overview of selected findings from the literature will show how difficult it is to point to a program or concept, which should be used successfully with a large segment of the special education concept. One of the initial problems deal with the significant number of students excluded from assessment systems (Olson and Goldstein 1997). Without a substantial database relevant conclusions could not be drawn. Even after the publication of IDEA (1997) only thirteen states had publicized performance data on students with disabilities (Ysseldyke et al. 1998).

Selected Research

- Tucker (1989) indicated that little conclusive research has been published which indicates success or failure in either achievement or realization of the concept of LRE (least restrictive environment).
- Despite statements that students with disabilities achieve more in general settings than in segregated settings, research by Hiebert, Wang, and Hunter (1982) does not substantiate the claims.
- In a study on the use of instructional time in an inclusive setting, Hollowood, Salisbury, Rainforth, and Palomboro (1994) reported that time allocation fell within the upper ranges as reported in other studies.
- Ammer (1984) identified poor communications between the classroom teacher and the specialist, disagreements about instructional techniques, curriculum, and standards as problems associated with pull-out programs.

Through the late eighties and early nineties accessibility to programming had been a major source of data used to indicate success or failure of a program. With new direction from IDEA (1997) accessibility will no longer stand alone as the impetus for defining success.

What are the trends in programming? What is being said about these trends?

Categorical vs. Noncategorical Programming

Until the early nineties it was easier to define what constituted a special education program. A student was identified and put into a category of disability. Today not only is there a "categorical drift" (Ysseldyke, Algozzine, and Thurlow 2000) but there is also a programming drift.

Special education teachers are being asked to teach students with different disabilities within the same classroom whether they are trained to teach the various categories or not. Wang, Reynolds, and Walberg (1994) indicated that between 1988 and 1990 there was a 131 percent increase in the number of teachers employed in cross-categorical settings. Has your district or a district close to you moved into the cross-categorical programming mode? Review the literature for a more in-depth understanding of the issues revolving around the categorical/noncategorical debate.

The Inclusive Setting—How Successful Is It?

Educators and the parents of children with disabilities will agree that inclusion is one of the most controversial issues facing special education. Many parents believe that inclusion truly meets the spirit of LRE. What does the literature say concerning the success of inclusion?

The National Center for Educational Restructuring and Inclusion (1995) reported that students placed in inclusion programs showed academic gains, improved standardized test scores, and reached IEP goals. Students also had fewer incomplete assignments, reacted more positively with peers, and positively increased attitudes toward schooling.

Baker and Zigmond (1995) reported that in a study of five elementary schools special education students were receiving a good general education in the inclusive setting but received very little special education.

Solend and Duhaney (1999) reviewed the literature dealing with the impact of inclusion on academic and social performance of students with disabilities. The authors concluded that the impact varied. They went on to say, "The inclusion movement has the potential to have a positive impact on students with and without disabilities and their teachers. However, these positive outcomes are not being realized for some students placed in inclusive settings, which can result in a concomitant negative reaction to inclusion on the part of their teachers."

Pull-Out and Pull-In Programs

An answer to the instruction of students with disabilities and students requiring remedial help, but not diagnosed as needing special education resources, has been the pull-out program. Although there have been attempts to offer alternatives to the pull-out it remains the most often used scheduling device. The pull-out program can be organized following different formats but in each instance the student leaves the regular education classroom to attend a self-contained program. The amount of time for the pull-out is determined by the IEP and is often influenced by the scheduling for the school and grade level.

Will (1986) proposed a regular education initiative, which would offer alternative programming for students in segregated settings. A form of the regular education initiative is the "push-in" program. In the push-in program the special education service is provided in the regular education classroom—both the regular education teacher and the special education teacher work together to benefit all children.

An example is in order. Students from a fourth grade class and students from a self-contained learning disabilities class come together for social studies instruction. The fourth grade teacher and the learning disabilities teacher develop the lessons and team teach the combined class.

Meyers, Gelzheiser, and Yelich (1991) reported that in a study of push-in programs teachers believed that their collaboration was more focused on instructional planning. Teachers also viewed the interaction as having improved their instructional skills. The study further indicated that students in the push-in program and the non–special education students were positively impacted by the process.

McLeskey, Henry, and Axelrod (1999) studied reports to Congress and determined that students with learning disabilities were being educated in larger numbers in less restrictive settings. They suggest that because of this trend teachers would take on greater responsibility for the education of students with learning disabilities in the regular education classroom.

Vaughn and Klingner (1998) examined the perceptions of students with learning disabilities toward their educational settings. Among other findings a majority of the students preferred to receive specialized instruction outside the regular education classroom for part of the day.

Special education has seen a number of changes of the type of delivery service that is provided for the student with special needs—from segregated settings to categorical self-contained classes, from pull-out to resource, from inclusive to push-in, an ever-evolving process. When we look back at this evolving special education process we will begin to see that what mattered was heightened teacher/preservice teacher and administrator training, parent involvement and training, a continuum of placement opportunities, and proper use of program evaluation techniques.

In the first scenario, portrayed at the beginning of the chapter, Hart Berkowski challenged the local school district's efforts at reporting the assessment of the special education program. He essentially was demanding that the same assessment protocol be used in both regular and special education classes. An essential part of your answer should be "yes" we must assess; "no" we are not obligated to use the same assessment tools. We are bound by IDEA (1997) to provide an assessment of established standards for our special education students. In many instances we will provide alternative assessments for our students. If a student's IEP indicates that she or he can be assessed with the same assessment tools as regular education students then she/he will be part of the district's general report card.

In the second scenario, the assistant superintendent is asking the council to assist the district in moving towards a push-in program. The council should consider:

- The change process.
- The issues that will confront the general education faculty.
- The issues that will confront the special education faculty.
- The issues that will confront the students and parents.
- Seeking information from other districts that have initiated a pull-in program.

SUMMARY

With the reauthorization of IDEA and public pressure to offer quality programs to all children, public schools are faced with an inevitable fact; they will evaluate the achievement of all students with disabilities. The details of what the evaluation programs will look like have yet to be worked out.

CASE 5.1: "PARENT INVOLVEMENT IN THE ASSESSMENT PROCESS"

Dr. James Dillingsworth, superintendent of schools, talking to his administrative council states, "I am not sure that we can meet the mandates that the state department of education has issued concerning the assessment of our special education students. We have a very good process for evaluating our programs through district assessment plan for the regular population of students, but we don't really evaluate our special education programs—or am I wrong? Look at this section of IDEA (1997)":

(A) IN GENERAL. Children with disabilities are included in general and district-wide assessment programs, with appropriate accommodations,

where necessary. As appropriate, the state or local education agency—

(i) develops guidelines for the participation of children with disabilities in alternate assessments for those children who cannot participate in State and district-wide assessment programs; and

(ii) develops and, beginning no later than July 1, 2000, conducts those alternate assessments.

(B) REPORTS. The State educational agency makes available to the public, and reports to the public with the same frequency and in the same detail as it reports on the assessment of nondisabled children, the following:

(Continue)

CASE 5.1 (CONTINUED)

(i) the number of children with disabilities participating in regular assessments.

(ii) the number of those children participating in alternate assessments.

(iii) (1) The performance of those children on regular assessments (beginning no later than July 1, 1998) and on alternate assessment (no later than July 1, 2000), if doing so would be statistically sound and would not result in the disclosure of performance identifiable to individual children.

(II) Data relating to the performance of children described under sub clause (I) shall be disaggregated—(aa) for assessments conducted after July 1, 1998; and (bb) for assessments conducted before July 1, 1998, if the State is required to disaggregate such data prior to July 1, 1998.

"I am particularly concerned about the beginning part that states, 'Children with disabilities are included in general and district-wide assessment programs, with appropriate accommodations, where necessary,' and how this relates to parent involvement. I believe that most parents think of testing as what happens to their child as part of the special education referral and induction process. We all know that there has been a great deal of energy in this state to put accountability of

schools before the general public. The field has been broadened to now include special education. Folks, it isn't going to go away and it shouldn't."

"What I would like to discuss today and get some consensus on is how do we assist the parents of students with disabilities understand their rights and responsibilities in the assessment and accountability process. How do we get them involved in the process? How do we get the parents to understand that a large number of students with disabilities—80+ percent—can participate in our general district education assessment program? Let's brainstorm ways to deal with the issue."

Note to the reader: You will now be asked questions about this case. Before you read the Questions and Reflections section at the end of the book (Appendix A), you should fill out a case study analysis (Appendix C), then answer the questions and share your ideas with the class.

Questions

1. How would you involve parents in the assessment process?
2. What can we do to inform the general public about assessment issues?
3. How can we involve the media?

CASE 5.2: "MOVEMENT TO A NONCATEGORICAL SYSTEM"

Chad Palmer had been a strong supporter of special education while serving three terms on the Stanford School District Board of Education. During his tenure he led the board in hiring more special education staff, changing the title of the director of special education to assistant superintendent, adding additional funds to the special education budget, and purchasing computers and software to assist students in the program.

After leaving the board Chad became involved in Stanford Chamber of Commerce and helped to develop partnerships between local corporations and the school district. It was during his presidency of the State Chamber of Commerce that Chad had the opportunity to visit other cities and states. During his visits he would always ask about special education.

From his visits and discussions he began to believe that special education students would be best served in a noncategorical setting.

Yesterday he called John Reed (superintendent of schools), Tasha Reynolds (school board president), Bernie Smith (assistant superintendent for special education) and asked to meet with them.

"Tasha, John, Bernie, thanks for meeting with me." He shook their hands, sat down, and continued speaking, "As you know, from my tenure on the board I have tremendous empathy for our special education students. I have spent the last few years away from district operations but never have moved too far from my desire to help make this district's special education the best in the nation."

(Continue)

CASE 5.2 (CONTINUED)

John Reed sat back in his chair and remembered how Chad had prodded him to find "creative ways to move money into special education." They had a very good relationship because both of them wanted the best for all the students in the district. John also knew that Tasha had not been around Chad's high energy, singleness of purpose, hard-charging personality. He watched Tasha as Chad spoke.

Chad looked at Tasha and Bernie and said, "I know that you will agree with me that the closer we can get our special education students to regular education the better it will be for them and for the regular education students. What I would like for us to discuss is moving our special education program into a noncategorical setting for all of our students. As we speak it would seem impossible to evaluate our special education program because there are so many ways that we deal with them. That is why I believe that we should treat them all equally, all the same way. Do I need to review the concept?"

Tasha looked perplexed. "Chad I can appreciate all that you have done for the district and the community. You won't remember this but we met a number of years ago at a board meeting when the agenda dealt with the Family Life Program. I felt at the time that your liberal leanings might get the district in trouble with various groups that did not agree with you. But you certainly were organized and made a splendid statement at the end of the curriculum committee's presentation. You managed to bring the various groups together. What I have a problem with is moving into a program that will totally change the way we do things in the district. I do know a little about our special education program. I know that we get very few complaints. I know that for the most part parents feel that their children are receiving excellent help by the special education teachers. Now how do you think that changing to a noncategorical inclusive setting would help our students?"

Chad thought for a moment, then said, "In visiting school districts all over the United States I believe that this is the direction we should take. I think that you should at least look at moving the district's program in the noncategorical direction, then we can truly evaluate our program. John, Tasha, and Bernie, I thank you for meeting with me today. I know that you will think about this change because it is good for our students." Chad then left the superintendent's office.

John looked at Bernie and asked, "What do you think about his idea of moving into a noncategorical program?"

Note to the reader: You will now be asked questions about this case. Before you read the Questions and Reflections section at the end of the book (Appendix A), you should fill out a case study analysis (Appendix C), then answer the questions and share your ideas with the class.

Questions

1. You are the assistant superintendent of schools responsible for special education. What would you say about moving into a noncategorical program?
2. What do you believe would be the best of all settings for the students in the special education programs?
3. How should the president of the board of education deal with the request from the former board of education president?

CHAPTER 6

FISCAL ISSUES IN SPECIAL EDUCATION

This chapter provides a review of how special education is funded. Mechanisms for funding at the federal and state levels are described, as well as unintentional consequences of each type of funding. Medicaid as a funding source for special education funding is discussed. After reading this chapter and analyzing the cases, you should be able to:

- Describe the general funding sources for special education.
- Describe funding formulas used to distribute federal and state monies for special education.
- Discuss possible consequences of funding formulas.
- Discuss trends impacting the future of funding of special education.

See semantic map detailing Chapter 6 on page 103.

OVERVIEW—HOW IS SPECIAL EDUCATION FUNDED?

It is essential for special education administrators to become familiar with state and federal funding mechanisms in special education. Special education administrators have the responsibility of planning programs and services to provide a free and appropriate public education (FAPE) to all eligible children within the local education agency (LEA) and they must be able to justify costs to superintendents and school boards. In addition, special education administrators must become knowledgeable of funding sources to access available funds. The costs of special education services is a continuing controversy, both in the community and with school boards (Shapiro, Loeb, and Bowermaster 1993; *Wall Street Journal* Oct. 20, 1993).

The method of funding appears to influence placement decisions made about individual children (Dempsey and Fuchs 1993; Hasazi et al. 1994). Following are two illustrations of problematic situations that arise within an LEA where fiscal issues are central to the situation.

1. Budding School District agreed to move two seventh grade, multiply impaired students back to their home school, North Junior High, for the next school year.

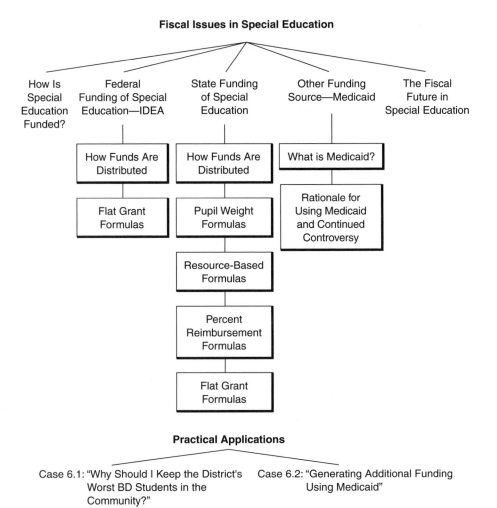

Fiscal Issues in Special Education

How Is Special Education Funded?

Federal Funding of Special Education—IDEA

State Funding of Special Education

Other Funding Source—Medicaid

The Fiscal Future in Special Education

How Funds Are Distributed

Flat Grant Formulas

How Funds Are Distributed

Pupil Weight Formulas

Resource-Based Formulas

Percent Reimbursement Formulas

Flat Grant Formulas

What is Medicaid?

Rationale for Using Medicaid and Continued Controversy

Practical Applications

Case 6.1: "Why Should I Keep the District's Worst BD Students in the Community?"

Case 6.2: "Generating Additional Funding Using Medicaid"

The students had been transported to a neighboring school district 20 miles away for special education services. In making the building accessible, a wheelchair ramp would need to be built in the cafeteria. Budding School administrators would save significant costs in transportation for these two students. When they made a request to the state board of education to use the cost savings for transportation to make the building accessible, they were told that transportation funds could not be used for any purpose except transporting students. The cost of the ramp would have to come from local funds.

2. John, a fourteen-year-old student with behavior disorders, was placed in a resource room at the local high school. During the first month of school, John was involved in three fights with peers and was insubordinate with teachers. It

was obvious that John needed more structured special education services, but a self-contained BD program was not available within the LEA. In the past, the LEA opted not to implement a self-contained BD program within the school district because it was less costly to place the student in a private day treatment program. Instead of creating a local program within the school district, all eligible students in need of self-contained programming were placed in a local, private day treatment program for behavior disorders. Consequently, John was placed in the private day treatment facility. It was actually cost-effective for the school district to make this placement as the state reimbursed the school district for about 90 percent of the private school tuition.

In the first situation, although the LEA saved considerable money by serving the two multiply impaired students within their home district, the savings could not be used to offset the additional cost of building a ramp. Dwindling local funds had to be used for the ramp. If transportation funds were more flexible, the cost savings could have followed the students by making the building accessible without significant additional cost to the LEA. In the second situation, the student needed a self-contained placement for students with behavior disorders, which was not available in the LEA. Instead, the student was placed in a private day treatment facility, which was more restrictive. There was a cost incentive to place the student in the private setting because most of the tuition was reimbursed by the state. If special education funds were more flexible, the funds could have been used to initiate a self-contained program within the LEA.

LEAs receive funds for special education services through three sources: federal government (IDEA), state government, and local school taxes. In 1987–88, the federal portion of special education funding was approximately 8 percent, the state portion of funding averaged about 56 percent, and the local portion of funding averaged about 36 percent (Parrish and Chambers 1996). Figure 6.1 illustrates the sources of

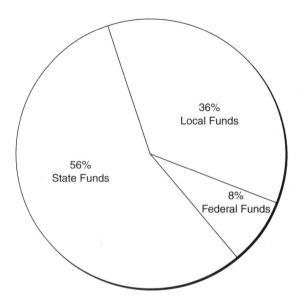

FIGURE 6.1   *Sources of Funding for Special Education*

funding based on these averages. These averages varied greatly from state to state. For example, federal funding of special education ranged from 65 percent of total expenditures in Kentucky to 3 percent in Minnesota, and state funding of special education ranged from 90 percent of total expenditures in Hawaii to 17 percent or less in New Hampshire and Oregon (Parrish and Chambers 1996). Federal and state funds are funneled into the LEA through various funding distribution formulas. Individual states and the federal government have different policies and procedures for distributing funds for special education.

FEDERAL FUNDING OF SPECIAL EDUCATION—IDEA

The federal government, through the Individuals with Disabilities Education Act (IDEA), provides supplemental funding for special education services to individual states. Each state must submit a state plan to receive these funds. In the state plan, there must be an assurance that the state adheres to the statutes and regulations of IDEA. Once approved, each state receives funding (averaging 8% of total special education costs across the country). Other federal laws (i.e., Section 504 of the Rehabilitation Act and the Americans with Disabilities Act) do not provide funding for special education.

How Funds Are Distributed

A summary of federal funding methods can be seen in Figure 6.2. Historically, federal IDEA funds have been distributed to states based on the state's number of students receiving special education services, called a flat grant. The total federal Part B allocation of funding under IDEA was divided by the number of students identified for special education across the country. The result was a single dollar amount per student. The more special education students identified in the state, the more federal funding the state received. This funding formula is still used, but the 1997 amendments to the IDEA added an element of census-based funding and greater flexibility in the use of funds.

Flat Grant (based on the number of students with disabilities)
- Definition: Total monies allocated by Congress are divided by the total number of students in special education in each state.
- Result: Amount of money a state receives increases with an increased number of children with disabilities; higher-cost and lower-cost students receive the same amount of funding.
- Concerns: Overidentification of students with disabilities.

Flat Grant (based on census)
- Definition: Monies allocated by Congress are distributed to each state based on the total number of students in both special education and regular education. Often a percentage of funds are allocated based on the number of students in each state who are economically disadvantaged.
- Result: States with more students identified as disabled do not receive more funds.
- Concerns: Accountability or assuring that funds are spent on children in special education; some students with special needs might not be identified.

FIGURE 6.2   *How Are Federal Funds Distributed?*

Census-based funding is another type of flat grant formula that distributes funds based on the total number of students, regular and special education, not just the number of students in special education. Because it is believed that poverty results in conditions that could lead to disability (Parrish 1996), the total number of students who are economically disadvantaged often becomes an element in the formula. In the 1997 amendments to IDEA, a new funding process went into effect when appropriations reached $4.9 billion. In this new process, LEAs receive funds, based on their previous year's allocation for special education (i.e., "hold harmless clause" or an assurance that the LEA will not receive less funds under the new formula than the old), and then additional funding using the following formulas:

1. 85 percent from the total population enrolled (including regular and special education students).
2. 15 percent from the total number of students who are economically disadvantaged.

The 1997 amendments also added that during a fiscal year in which monies appropriated for IDEA exceed $4.1 billion, the LEA may treat as local funds up to 20 percent of the amount of money it receives under IDEA that exceeds the amount received the previous year. This means the LEA would have greater flexibility in the use of up to 20 percent of the excess federal funding it receives.

The federal funding formula in 1975 originally indicated that states were to receive up to 40 percent of the national average per pupil expenditure (APPE) for each child with a disability. However, allocations never were funded at that level. The federal allocation never exceeded 12.5 percent of the national APPE (Parrish and Chambers 1996).

The federal funding formula, like all funding formulas, has weaknesses and has been criticized. Because funds are primarily distributed as a flat grant (i.e., a fixed amount of funds are dispersed per child), the amount of funding a state receives increases with an increased number of children with disabilities. Therefore, there may be a built-in incentive to overidentify students with disabilities and serve them in lower cost placements. Thomas (1973) suggested that this type of funding formula encourages overidentification of children with mild disabilities as these children are less expensive to serve.

One may assume that the intent of the 1997 amendments to IDEA was to move toward a neutral funding formula, one that didn't reward states for identifying more students with disabilities because overidentification had become a major issue. In addition, by providing more flexibility with federal dollars, costly assessment could be avoided and some students might be better served outside of special education. However, even census-based funding may be criticized. For example, concerns about accountability have been raised—that is, how to assure that the funds are used to support programs for students with disabilities. It is also feared that students with legitimate needs may not be identified or served if special education is deemphasized.

STATE FUNDING OF SPECIAL EDUCATION

All states have formulas to provide for a portion of the cost of special education. States vary on the portion of funding for special education and the formula used to allocate funds. As stated earlier, the average states' portion of special education funding was 56 percent in 1987–88—with a variance of 90 percent in, for example, Hawaii and Idaho to 17 percent or less in, for example, Kentucky and Virginia (Parrish and Chambers 1996). In a review of data from a study of states' special education finance systems (Parrish 1996), it was evident that 18 states used pupil weights as a method of disbursing funds, 10 states used resource-based formulas, 11 states used percent reimbursement, and 11 states used flat grants to disburse funds for special education.

Two-thirds of all states are engaged in special education finance reform (Parrish 1996). Reform is related to higher costs associated with special education and has been driven by several demographic, political, and social factors.

1. Enrollments in the general school population and the resulting costs continued to increase. After an initial decline in overall school enrollments from the mid 1970s to the mid 1980s, enrollments began to increase. Student enrollment increased from 39 million in 1986 to 44 million students in 1994 and will continue to rise to about 49 million by 2002 (Parrish and Chambers 1996). Therefore, costs for educating all students will continue to increase.
2. In addition to general increases in school populations, special education populations continued to increase by 15.56 percent between 1987 to 1988 and 1992 to 1993 (Parrish and Chambers 1996). The following factors influenced this increase:
    a. New amendments to IDEA resulted in adding new preschool children and infants with disabilities. Adding two new categories of disabilities under IDEA—traumatic brain injury and autism—also resulted in more students with disabilities.
    b. Population and family structure changes resulted in more students living in high-risk conditions (i.e., poverty, substance abuse, HIV), which are associated with a higher rate of disability.
3. Educational reform and the demand for higher standards resulted in more students unable to meet the increased standards, thereby increasing the population of students with disabilities.
4. There are concerns over fiscal incentives for more restrictive, higher cost placements in special education. There is a wide variance in how states serve special education students, with nine states serving more than 60 percent of special education students in regular education and six states serving less than 15 percent of special education students in regular education (O'Reilly 1995).

How Funds Are Distributed

Although each state has an individual formula to distribute funds for special education, funding formulas can be categorized into four categories: pupil weight, resource-based, percent reimbursement, and flat grant (Parrish 1996). The manner in which each funding formula is used in each state will vary and some states will use more than one formula. For example, a flat grant in one state may be based on a certain amount of reimbursement for each special education teacher, and in another state may be based on a certain amount of reimbursement for each special education student. Flexibility is also an issue, in view of the fact that some states allow special education funds to be used only on special education students and other states allow the funds to be used on other students in need of services. Following is a description of each funding method, an example, and the incentives built into each method. Each method is summarized in Figure 6.3.

Pupil Weight Formulas

In this funding method, each student identified as disabled is assigned a weight that is a multiple of the cost to educate a student in regular education. Different types of students in different types of placements might have different weights. For example, students with behavior disorders in self-contained placements might cost 2.5 times as much to educate as students in regular education. The LEA is then reimbursed 2.5 times the reimbursement for regular education students. As with all funding systems, there appear to be fiscal incentives to place students in a particular manner. Because pupil weights are tied to a particular type of disability and/or placement, there may be an incentive to overidentify students in that particular category or placement which generates more funding.

Resource-Based Formulas

In resource-based funding formulas, funding is based on a particular resource supplied (e.g., teacher or classroom unit, rather than students). If classroom units are used, each unit is defined in terms of the resources and costs needed to operate them. The number of classroom units are determined by applying class size standards and the total funding is established by multiplying the cost per unit by the number of units. The amount of funding received by a particular LEA will vary depending upon the settings in which students receive services. For example, if State A reimbursed five times more for self-contained settings for students with learning disabilities, the LEA will receive five times more for each classroom unit of, say, 15 students. The overall result might be that only 7 percent of students with learning disabilities in State A are educated within the regular classroom and 93 percent of students with learning disabilities are educated in self-contained settings.

Because classroom units or teachers are counted in a resource-based funding formula, class sizes might be maximized to qualify for more funding for additional classroom units and children's needs might be defined by existing placement types (Hartman 1992; Dempsey and Fuchs 1993). There might be little incentive for classifying children as disabled because the state might limit overall funding or enforce an enrollment cap.

Percent Reimbursement Formulas

In this type of funding formula, the LEA receives a percentage of actual or eligible costs of special education services. The percentage could vary depending on type of expenditure item and amount of reimbursement (e.g., 100%, 50%). This approach could be combined with other approaches, like a percentage of student program costs or personnel costs. For example, State A might reimburse LEAs 25 percent of the salaries of certified special education teachers in the state. In this case, since the local costs are

Pupil Weight Formulas
- Definition: Each student with a disability is assigned a weight that is a multiple of the cost to educate a student in regular education. School districts receive funds based on these multiples.
- Results: Amount of money a school district receives increases if the district has more programs with higher weights.
- Concerns: Districts may overidentify students in categories of disabilities that are weighted.

Resource-Based Formulas
- Definition: Funding to school districts is based on a particular resource supplied (e.g., teacher, classroom unit). Each unit is defined in terms of the resources or costs needed to operate them. Total funding to school districts is determined by multiplying the cost per unit by the number of units. Often, a limit on overall funding is enforced.
- Result: Amount of money a school district receives varies depending upon the settings in which students receive services. If self-contained programs generate more funding per unit, the school district with many self-contained programs will receive more money.
- Concerns: Childrens' needs might be defined by existing placement types; little incentive for classifying children as disabled because of possible enrollment caps.

Percent Reimbursement Formulas
- Definition: The school district receives a percentage of actual or eligible costs of special education services.
- Result: If the state reimburses a small percent of special education costs, districts might have fewer special education programs.
- Concerns: If the state reimburses a small percent of special education costs, there might be an incentive to identify fewer students as disabled, fill special classes to capacity, and encourage transfer of higher-cost to lower-cost programs.

Flat Grant Formulas (based on number of students with disabilities)
- Definition: Funds are distributed to school districts based on the total number of students in special education in each school district.
- Result: Amount of money a school district receives increases with an increased number of children with disabilities.
- Concerns: Overidentification of students with disabilities; higher-cost and lower-cost students receive the same amount of funding.

Flat Grant Formulas (based on census)
- Definition: Monies allocated by the state are distributed to each school district based on the total number of students in both special education and regular education. Often, a percentage of funds are allocated based on the number of students in each school district who are economically disadvantaged.
- Result: School districts with more students identified as disabled do not receive more funds.
- Concerns: Accountability or assuring that funds are spent on children in special education; some students with special needs might not be identified.

FIGURE 6.3 *How Are State Funds Distributed?*

relatively high (i.e., 75%), there might be an incentive to identify fewer special education students, fill special education classes to capacity, and encourage transfer from higher cost to lower cost special education placements (Hartman 1992). If the state reimbursed a higher percentage of personnel costs, the reverse would hold true.

Flat Grant Formulas

Flat grant formulas are the simplest to understand and explain. Typically, funds are distributed by reimbursing the LEA a particular amount for each child identified as disabled. Funds could also be distributed by total student population, disabled and nondisabled, or by any other type of unit. Flat grants do not recognize the varying costs of resources throughout the state or the varying costs of an individual's placement. If a child is placed in a high cost classroom for children with autism (e.g., five students, one teacher, two aides, various related services personnel), the amount of reimbursement would be the same as for a child receiving speech and language services for thirty minutes a week.

One incentive in this type of funding would be to overidentify students as mildly disabled. For example, if State B distributed $5,000 per child identified as disabled, the LEA would receive more funding in direct proportion to the number of students identified as disabled. Another incentive would be to identify and place in special education more students with mild disabilities. The reasoning behind this incentive is that all types of children with disabilities (higher cost and lower cost placements) would receive the same amount of funding, and students with mild disabilities would be less costly to serve (Thomas 1973).

If the flat grant formula disperses funds based on the number of students in the general school population, there is little or no incentive to make a particular type of placement because the amount of funding will not change.

OTHER FUNDING SOURCES—MEDICAID

In addition to federal, state, and local sources of funding, Medicaid is often used by LEAs to supplement the cost of special education and related services for eligible children with disabilities. For example, if the related service of speech therapy is included on a child's IEP, the IEP team has determined that this service is necessary to provide a free and appropriate public education (FAPE). If the speech therapy service also meets the state's Medicaid definition of medical necessity, it is included as a service in the state's Medicaid plan. If the child is Medicaid-eligible, the service is reimbursable by Medicaid. This reimbursement provides additional income to support the education of children with disabilities.

What is Medicaid?

Medicaid is a program that provides medical coverage and health care assistance to the medically and categorically needy population. Categorically needy clients are eligible based on a state formula linked to the federally established poverty level. Medically needy clients are those persons who require coverage whose income, while low, is above the poverty level. For medically needy clients and categorically needy clients, each state establishes the standard for qualification.

Medicaid is administered by both the state and federal governments. Specifically, each state establishes and operates its own program within federal guidelines and benefits are paid by a match of state and federal monies.

Benefits provided by Medicaid vary from state to state. The federal law mandates that states provide a core group of services including physician services, laboratory and X-ray services, in-patient hospital care, and early and periodic screening, diagnosis, and treatment (EPSDT). Other services, such as physical therapy, case management, speech therapy, and audiology, are optional services that states may choose to provide, but are not required to provide. Each state submits a state plan that defines mandated and optional services that the state Medicaid program will provide.

Medicaid is an open-ended entitlement program. Therefore, all persons who meet the state's eligibility requirements outlined in the state plan must be provided the services, regardless of cost. Because each state must pay for a percentage of the program's cost, costs are controlled by states limiting eligibility and services as outlined in the state plan.

Although some states allow reimbursement for some optional services (e.g., speech therapy, occupational therapy), all states must reimburse for early and periodic screening, diagnosis, and treatment (EPSDT). Enacted in 1967, EPSDT was designed to discover, as early as possible, disabling conditions in children and to provide continued follow-up and treatment. All children from birth through age twenty-one who are eligible for Medicaid are also eligible for EPSDT services. If a service, e.g., occupational therapy, is not available under the state's Medicaid program, the same service may be provided through the state's EPSDT program as it is a mandated service. Under EPSDT, each state must establish periodic examination schedules to meet standards of practice for medical, vision, dental, and hearing services. If a Medicaid-eligible child needs services as detected in a EPSDT screening, the child is entitled to services, including but not limited to, diagnostic services, occupational therapy, physical therapy, speech and language therapy, and hearing services. These services can be billed by and reimbursed to the LEA if the LEA is registered as a provider of services for Medicaid. In addition, the LEA can utilize the EPSDT option as part of the child-find and diagnosis components for early childhood. It can also provide reimbursement for Medicaid-eligible children who benefit from schoolwide screenings in vision, hearing, and speech and language therapy.

Rationale for Using Medicaid and Continued Controversy

When LEAs began using Medicaid funds for reimbursement of special education services, some administrators, board members, and community members were reluctant to participate. Some school board members felt that using Medicaid funds for educational services was "double dipping." In other words, local community members paid local taxes to support the schools and, via Medicaid, paid federal taxes for the same service. LEAs, then, would have received funds twice, once from local tax dollars and once from Medicaid dollars, for the same service.

Another concern of some community members was that LEAs would contribute to the depletion of Medicaid funds. For example, one local school board member voted against requesting Medicaid reimbursement for children with disabilities within the LEA because of a personal situation. The board member indicated that her mother was eligible for and used Medicaid. Recently, the mother had to be placed in a nursing home and was told that Medicaid would not cover the cost of the nursing home. The board member expressed the concern that if school districts did not use Medicaid funds, her mother might have had better coverage.

A third concern was that educational services were not medical services and Medicaid provided medical services to clients. By reimbursing an LEA for, say, physical therapy services for a child, the LEA was, in effect, providing and requesting reimbursement for a medical service, something LEAs were not allowed to do.

Although these reasons might be based on faulty logic or misinformation, they were very real and affected the manner in which Medicaid was initially accepted by some local school boards and community members. In the experience of the authors, these perceptions have largely been overcome, as many LEAs across the country are using Medicaid funds to supplement costs for providing services to children with disabilities. Overall, legislation, case law, and many policy interpretations of IDEA and its predecessor, PL 94–142, recognize that education agencies, state, local, and federal, are responsible fiscally for special education services, but that they are not the *only* agency fiscally responsible for these services (Kreb 1991).

THE FISCAL FUTURE OF SPECIAL EDUCATION

Parrish (1996) discussed several indicators of the future direction of special education financing. They include the following:

1. In all likelihood, the population of children eligible for special education services and the general population will continue to grow.
   - Social conditions that are indicators of conditions associated with disabilities (e.g., poverty, teenage pregnancy) continue to increase resulting in more children with disabilities.
   - Continued emphasis on education reform, including increased academic standards, will result in more students unable to meet the standards and eligible for special education services.
2. As a result of continued population growth, special education expenditures will continue to grow, causing a continued strain on special education budgets over the next ten years or so.
3. The general climate of fiscal conservatism will continue to force LEAs to restructure current services using existing funds.

Parrish (1996) also discussed how LEAs can make more efficient use of current funds.

1. A reduction in the current fiscal incentives to further identify special education students would limit the expected population growth in special education.
2. Increasing integration across categorical areas might result in unified systems to serve all students in need of special assistance.
3. Greater fiscal flexibility at the local level would allow LEAs to design programs that would result in better meeting the needs of local students in need of special assistance.

4. An increase in needs-based funding would result in placing funds where they are most needed as opposed to tying funds to certain types or intensity of services provided.

5. A change from fiscal accountability to outcome-based or results-based accountability would allow an LEA to use funds to design programs to meet the local needs of students. Results of student improvement would serve as fiscal accountability.

It is clear that the methods of funding special education services continue to change and evolve. It is important that special administrators have a good understanding of funding methods and sources of funds to appropriately serve the needs of all children, including those with disabilities. To assist you in developing these understandings, this chapter concludes with two practical case studies emphasizing the difficulties that administrators face in dealing with fiscal issues in special education.

CASE 6.1: "WHY SHOULD I KEEP THE DISTRICT'S WORST BD STUDENTS IN THE COMMUNITY?"

Phil Kuchta had been the director of Longman Special Education Cooperative for ten years. The cooperative consisted of nine rural school districts. Each district was within one and one-half hour from a large metropolitan area in the Midwest. Each district provided its own special education services to students with mild disabilities. The districts provided cooperative programs for some students with moderate disabilities.

Behavior disorders programming had always been a source of conflict. All districts operated resource and self-contained programs for students with behavior disorders. However, some students were unable to be served in the local programs due to the severity of the behavior disorder. In these cases, the student was enrolled in one of three private day treatment facilities close to the metropolitan area. The placement always involved transporting the student at least one hour each way on a bus. Because of the nature of the disability and the long bus ride, problems inevitably arose (e.g., fights) on the bus. The district then had to employ a bus aide to ensure safety on the bus. It was also apparent that once a student was placed in the private facility, the student rarely returned to the home school. If the student did return, it was often unsuccessful, resulting in the student returning to the private facility.

Superintendents on the governing board of Longman Cooperative had, on occasion, expressed unhappiness about the placement of students with severe behavior disorders. Not only was the tuition expensive, but the transportation costs were high. The superintendents complained about spending considerable funds on the few students who caused them the most trouble in their schools and in the community. In addition to the costs, sometimes a student would misbehave at the private facility and would have to be sent home in the middle of the day, resulting in running an additional bus to the facility. The superintendents were very aware that these students were not successful in the community, even if they did return.

Phil Kuchta recognized these problems for several years. He was also well aware of the funding mechanisms within the state that provided a fiscal incentive to place students in private facilities. The state required that the local school district pay the entire tuition cost. The state would then reimburse the district for all tuition costs exceeding two local per capita tuition costs (i.e., what it cost to educate each district student). This meant that if the private facility tuition cost was $15,000 per year, the school district would pay the entire tuition cost up front. A year later, the state would reimburse the district. If the per capita was $4,000, the district would not be reimbursed for $8,000, or two times what it cost to educate each district student (per capita tuition cost). This cost of $8,000 was less than would be necessary to provide a program for this student locally.

(Continue)

CASE 6.1 (CONTINUED)

After many discussions with the governing board superintendents, it was agreed that it might be advantageous to implement a program to serve students with severe behavior disorders within the cooperative. Phil Kuchta prepared a proposal to implement an alternative program for students with severe behavior disorders. Although the cost would be greater before and after reimbursement, he felt that the advantages outweighed the disadvantages. He prepared a packet of information to be forwarded to governing board members prior to the next monthly board meeting. The proposal would then be discussed at the meeting and, hopefully, voted on during the following meeting. Phil wanted to implement the program during the fall. By presenting information to the board in December, with action taken in March, there would be enough time to plan the program in detail. The planning would include the following: renovation of a building, employment of personnel, ordering materials, curriculum development, policies and procedures development, providing staff training, conducting IEP meetings on prospective students, and community public relations activities.

Phil reviewed the packet for the governing board one last time before he gave it to his secretary for distribution. The following information was included:

Proposal

Longman Special Education Cooperative Alternative Program

Governance The Longman Governing Board will establish an alternative school program for students with severe behavior disorders in Longman Special Education Cooperative. The program will be funded by local funds. The Longman member districts will be charged an assessment based on the start-up costs for setting up the program. Districts with students enrolled will pay tuition based on the costs to operate the program. Districts with students enrolled in the program will claim state pupil reimbursement. The local districts will be responsible for transporting students to and from the program.

Rationale The Longman member districts have placed an average of 13 students annually in private day treatment facilities for behavior disorders since 1991. The range of students placed was from 8

students in 1991 to 17 students during the past school year. The rationale for changing the programming of these students includes the following:

- Of 42 students placed in the private day treatment facilities since 1991, only 4 students have been successfully transitioned in the school or the community. It is anticipated that a local program would have greater success.
- Operating the program locally will allow for local control of the curriculum and provide for maximum opportunity for successful reintegration into the schools and community. In essence, the students will never leave the community. Education and therapy will focus on student strengths and will provide support to the family. Education and therapy will become a "wraparound" program, involving the student, family, community, and, as appropriate, local school.
- Although local districts would be responsible for transporting students to and from the program, transportation time would be less than half of the time necessary to transport students to private facilities. In addition, it is anticipated that behavior problems on the buses would be minimal due to minimal time spent on the bus. It is also likely that students would not be removed from school in the middle of the day for behavior problems, thereby eliminating making additional bus runs in the middle of the day.

Student Eligibility Students with severe behavior disorders in the public schools may be referred to the alternative program before considering placement in a private facility. Students in grades 7 to 12 who are currently in private day treatment facilities because of their severe behavior disorders will be considered for a less restrictive placement in the alternative program. Any student referred to the alternative program will have received a functional analysis of behavior while in the local school program.

Curriculum The education of any child in the alternative program might occur in the community, the classroom, or a combination of those settings. The goal would be to provide each student with a program that will allow the student the opportu-

(Continue)

CASE 6.1 (CONTINUED)

nity to return to the public school as soon as possible and to become a successful member of the community. The individualized curriculum could include job skill education, community employment, life skill education, counseling, etc.

Personnel The alternative program will include a full-time coordinator/teacher. This person will have extensive experience in teaching students with behavior disorders and supervising BD/LD teachers. The coordinator/teacher will act as head teacher and be in charge of the day-to-day operation of the program. The program will also include a full-time social worker, who will chair IEP team meetings, provide wraparound services, counseling, and act as case manager to coordinate activities and resources to assure a smooth transition for the student back to the public school and home community. The social worker will also seek assistance from other state and local agencies to assist in removing the barriers in the home, school, or community that are making it difficult for the student to succeed. A full-time program assistant/job coach will assist the coordinator/teacher in the classroom and travel into the community to assist the student in obtaining and maintaining employment. High school credit could be assigned by the IEP team for nontraditional activities such as counseling and/or working in a job as well as traditional coursework.

Student/Teacher Ratio Class size will be consistent with the state rules and regulations governing special education. Students with severe disabilities will be served at a ratio of 5:1. A full-time aide must be added when enrollment reaches 6 students. A full-time aide will allow 5 additional students to be added, for a total of 10 students. If the enrollment reaches 11 students, an additional teacher must be employed. At 16 students, an additional aide must be employed. The program will serve a maximum of 20 students with two full-time teachers (one of whom would be coordinator/teacher), two full-time aides, and a full-time social worker.

Staff Qualifications and Professional Development All professional personnel must be certified or eligi-

ble for certification in the area of specialization, e.g., behavior disorders, social work. Support personnel must have a high school diploma with at least 30 semester hours of college coursework. Professional development will be provided to all personnel through Longman Special Education Cooperative.

Location St. Mary's School in Reedville has a vacant school building that is available to rent. This building would be appropriate to meet the physical needs of the program with minimal renovation.

Fiscal Considerations

Cost Comparison Between Local Alternative Program and Private Day Treatment Facility

	Public alternative program Tuition Total	Private facility Tuition Total
Before state reimbursement	$15,135	$14,436
After state reimbursement	$11,309	$7,820

Start-Up Costs: $31,000 (to be divided equally among member districts)

State Private Facility Incentive

In this state there is an incentive to place students with disabilities in private facilities. Local school districts may pay similar costs up front for educating students, but more reimbursement is generated for students educated in a private facility.

For example, if the school district placed all severe BD students in a private day treatment facility at an annual tuition rate of $17,000 per year, they pay $17,000 up front. However, this state will reimburse the cost of private facility payments above two per capita tuition costs. If the district per capita is $4,000, the cost to the district after reimbursement is $8,000.

If the district implements its own public school day treatment program, employs the teachers, purchases equipment and materials, etc., and sets the annual tuition at the same rate of $17,000 per child, the most they can receive for pupil reimbursement is $2,000 per child annually.

(Continue)

CASE 6.1 (CONTINUED)

Therefore, it is more cost-effective to contract with a private facility to provide a program than it is for the district to implement a program. However, this is not always the most appropriate placement for the student.

The governing board meeting was held the following week. The superintendents were not pleased at the prospect of increased cost to educate students with severe behavior disorders. Phil Kuchta was prepared for this argument, as he stated, "I understand that spending more local funds on these students is not what you want to do. However, I think you are already spending these funds by providing transportation to distant facilities and making additional bus runs. I also know that these students eventually return to the community, often as dropouts. They are unable to hold jobs and sometimes get into legal difficulties in the community. If these students are helped within the community, the chances are much better that they will become contributing members who can work for a living. It is always better and more cost-effective to use taxpayer's money to support education rather than the probable welfare and cost of incarceration."

The superintendents decided, in principle, to support the proposal. They directed Phil and the board attorney to contact and negotiate with the owners of the school building to rent the facility. Phil indicated that he would forward renovation cost and rent cost to the superintendents prior to the next meeting.

The following month the superintendents voted unanimously to support the proposal, even though the cost was somewhat higher. Overall, they felt that they would have greater control over the students' quality of education and transportation costs would make up for some of the increase.

Note to the reader: You will now be asked questions about this case. Before you read Questions and Reflections section at the end of the book (Appendix A), you should fill out the case study analysis (Appendix C), then answer the questions and share your ideas with the class.

Questions

1. If you were a superintendent on this board, what questions might you ask the special education director?
2. What were the barriers that might have prevented the superintendents from supporting the proposal? What were the advantages of the local program?
3. What type of reimbursement would the districts receive for the local public school program and what placement incentive is inherent?
4. How were start-up costs going to be funded? Why do you think they were to be funded in this manner?
5. Describe a more neutral funding formula that would support placing students in local public school programs.

CASE 6.2: "GENERATING ADDITIONAL FUNDING USING MEDICAID"

Joan Zhou, director of special education at Parkville School District, dreaded the meeting at 1:00 P.M. today with district speech and language therapists. It wasn't that Joan disliked the therapists and it wasn't that Joan felt that the therapists didn't provide a valuable service. They did provide a valuable service to many children and were very professional. After pondering why she wasn't looking forward to the meeting, Joan decided that part of the reason was that every time she met with the therapists, they complained about being over-worked and having too many children on their caseloads. In part, they were correct. Most of the therapists had seventy students on their caseloads and traveled to at least two schools. In fact, Joan worked to support the employment of a sixth therapist last year and approved more funds for testing and teaching materials.

On the other hand, Joan felt that the therapists weren't open to new ideas in serving children. For example, one time Joan made arrangements for a speech and language therapist from another district to talk

(Continue)

CASE 6.2 (CONTINUED)

with the therapists about how she served students with language disorders within their special education classes and how the therapist and learning disabilities teacher worked together to serve these students. Joan didn't intend to imply that this was something she wanted every therapist to attempt. She was just trying to provide possible ways to serve students appropriately with growing caseloads. The therapist making the presentation did a great job, but the therapists in Joan's district complained about how her ideas would never work in this district.

Today, Joan was talking to the therapists about their future role in documenting services provided to children eligible for Medicaid services. Joan knew this would be a difficult meeting, but felt strongly about taking advantage of all sources of funds for special education. The superintendent and board of education had also approved of the billing for Medicaid services. The district would contract with BLC, Incorporated, to provide fee-for-service billing services.

Joan walked into the district conference room promptly at 1:00 P.M. She began the meeting by saying, "Thank you for taking time out of your schedules to come to this meeting today. We are going to talk about implementing a new program in this district—billing Medicaid for speech and language services rendered to eligible students."

She continued to explain by saying, "We currently have approximately 400 students in this district who receive speech and language services. At this time, about 60 students are eligible for Medicaid health services. Today I want to give you an overview of what Medicaid is and how we will begin to be reimbursed for speech and language services given to Medicaid-eligible children in this district."

Before she could continue, Sandy, who had been a therapist for 20 years, asked, "Are we going to be required to do more paperwork? We already have too much, and more paperwork would take us away from serving students."

Joan answered, "That's a good question, Sandy. Yes, there will be some documentation required and I will address that this afternoon."

Joan then continued by explaining Medicaid to the group. She said that Medicaid reimbursement was available for services provided by speech and language therapists to eligible children. Although Medicaid was a health service for needy children, the federal and state governments had agreed that certain IEP-related services could be reimbursed. Surrounding districts had been billing Medicaid for the past few years for speech, physical therapy, occupational therapy, psychological evaluations, and social work services and have received between $20,000 to $40,000 per quarter.

The meeting continued and Joan distributed written procedures for documenting services. The procedures on the handout included the following:

Procedures—Medicaid   Reimbursement—Speech and Language Therapy

The services provided by speech and language therapists are covered by the state's Medicaid plan and thus are eligible for reimbursement. These services are to be documented using codes listed. The two letter codes give both the type of service and the time spent providing the service. The recording of services must be by date and are applicable to those students with Medicaid coverage.

- Ongoing treatment services must be recorded on BLC's monthly service log. This log will be preprinted for your use provided your caseload is submitted to BLC.
- Please list your caseload by service site.
- BLC will complete a data match with the State Department of Public Aid to identify those students with Medicaid coverage.
- Service logs will be preprinted listing only those students with Medicaid coverage.
- New students can be added to the monthly service log and BLC will complete data matches.
- Please include appropriate diagnostic codes and category of service codes. The unit of service for speech therapy services is 15 minutes, with a maximum of 12 units.
- Please include your name and title and sign the form.
- You will also record screening services on a blank sheet of paper.

(Continue)

CASE 6.2 (CONTINUED)

- List students on paper with dates of the screening. Clearly mark"Speech/Language Screening."
- Send completed logs to BLC on a monthly basis.
- Make sure student names (first, last) are correct and include date of birth as well as the student's resident school district.
- Please include your name and title and sign the sheet.

As Joan verbally presented information on the handout, Nancy raised her hand and said, "It will be impossible for me to complete this paperwork and work with students. By the time I finish these forms, I won't have any time left to work with students."

The other therapists nodded in agreement as Pam said, "Do you have any plans to employ someone to complete clerical work for us?"

Lisa spoke up by saying, "I'm not sure a clerical person would help. I think we need another therapist."

Joan responded by saying, "I know you are already overwhelmed with your caseloads. However, this is a source of funding I don't think we can ignore. We are contracting with BLC, Inc. to assist us with the paperwork. After you initially submit your caseloads, you will receive a monthly list of only those Medicaid-eligible students. All you have to do is document service and add any new students."

John, who had been quiet to this point, asked, "Who will receive these Medicaid reimbursements that we generate? Will the therapists receive more funding as a result?"

Joan responded, "These funds have to be used to supplement services already in place or to add new services. They can't be used to fund another therapist, because we won't know from quarter to quarter how much reimbursement we will receive. As you know, the special education administration is moving into a new building. These funds could be used to renovate the building. It is possible the funds could be also used to purchase more tests and materials for the therapists."

John said, "So the money doesn't have to be used in the program that generated the reimbursement?"

Joan answered, "No, it doesn't. It will be used to supplement special education wherever it is needed."

Erica asked, "I morally disagree with using these funds. It seems like we are paying taxes to support the Medicaid program and then using the funds to pay the school district for services we already have local tax dollars for—it's almost like we're double-dipping into the taxpayers pockets."

Joan said, "That question has been raised and debated. It is clearly legal for the school district to become a provider for some services. The federal law, IDEA, indicates that it is acceptable to use other sources of funding to provide services for children. In this case, Medicaid will pay someone to provide speech therapy services. It may as well be the local school district."

The meeting lasted another hour. Joan promised to arrange another meeting in the next month to further discuss the procedures. She offered to have a representative of BLC review documentation procedures and to ask a speech therapist from a neighboring school district involved with Medicaid reimbursement to discuss general procedures.

Even though the meeting was difficult, Joan felt that she was making the right decision to pursue Medicaid reimbursement. She even thought that some of the funds generated should be used to support materials and tests for the therapists. Perhaps the therapists would be more supportive if they knew some funds would support their program.

Note to the reader: You will now be asked questions about this case. Before you read Questions and Reflections section at the end of the book (Appendix A), you should fill out the case study analysis (Appendix C), then answer the questions and share your ideas with the class.

Questions

1. How well did the special education director answer the speech and language therapists' questions?
2. Were there other supports the special education director could have implemented to gain the support of the speech therapists?
3. Should Medicaid reimbursement be used to employ another speech and language therapist? Why or why not?

CHAPTER 7

HUMAN RESOURCES ISSUES IN SPECIAL EDUCATION

Chapter 7 presents a concise review of issues facing the human resources function of school districts. After reading the chapter and analyzing the cases, you should be able to:

- Describe the human resources function of a school district.
- Identify the human resources issues that are associated with special education.
- Provide potential solutions to the human resource problems associated with special education.

See semantic map detailing Chapter 7 on page 120.

The following two scenarios depict aspects of a human resource department familiar to most school districts: orientation of general and special education staff to a new program, and retention of special education staff. In the first scenario, the school district is moving toward an inclusive system. The superintendent wants any division between special education and regular education blurred. She defined inclusive as, ". . . approaching teaching and administration as if there were no general education or special education. Each person involved in the educational process must understand the needs of every student and be willing to develop an instructional program that meets the student's needs." She has already presented the plan to the current staff. She is now interested in an orientation plan for new staff. In the second scenario the same district is trying to retain its special education staff in light of retirements and resignations.

1. Ralph St. George, director of special education services for the Lake Orzark School District, was asked by his superintendent to develop an orientation meeting to present her plans for an inclusive educational program. The superintendent was interested in an orientation program that would help the district's new faculty and new administrators better understand each other's roles. She wanted to keep some of the traditional aspects of an orientation program while adding areas that would strengthen the new staff's understanding of the special education program. The superintendent was trying to build an inclusive philosophy among her staff. She believed that faculty and administration needed to look at regular education and special education as one system. She felt what better way to begin, than by developing an understanding of the shared responsibility that regular education and

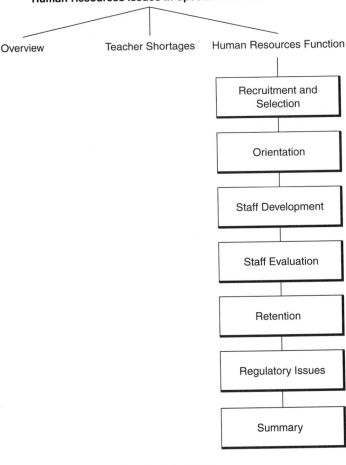

Human Resources Issues in Special Education

Overview   Teacher Shortages   Human Resources Function

Recruitment and Selection

Orientation

Staff Development

Staff Evaluation

Retention

Regulatory Issues

Summary

Practical Application

Case 7.1: "New Technology"   Case 7.2: "The OCR Complaint"

special education have toward the educational process during the orientation of new staff.

• What components should be included in the new orientation program?

2. The board of education of the Lake Orzark School District was concerned about the number of retirements and vacated positions among the district's special education staff. They wanted to know why faculty was leaving the special education program and what might be done about it. They asked Ralph St. George to determine why special education teachers would leave the program and what a district could do to retain its staff.

• What reasons for leaving special education should be included?

• What can the district do to retain staff?

In the first situation, Ralph St. George was asked by his superintendent to develop an orientation plan for new staff that would begin to lead them toward understanding the inclusive nature of education while retaining some of the traditional orientation program. Ralph might submit an orientation program that is composed of two parts: general orientation information and information that will reinforce the special education program. In the general portion of the program, all new faculty and staff should be introduced to the policies, procedures, the planning process, and the decision-making process, areas that represent the traditional information given during the initial meeting for new staff.

In the specific portion of the orientation program, a dialogue should be established that assists new teachers and administrators in understanding the relationship between special and general education. It is important for the incoming staff to understand the superintendent's inclusive philosophy. Examples of two activities that might be included in the orientation program are:

- Role-play a situation that calls for a classroom teacher, a special education teacher, and an administrator to break down the barriers associated with providing accommodations for a student with a disability.
- Bring current faculty, new faculty, current administrators, and new administrators together to discuss responsibilities that each have towards special education.

In the second scenario, the board of education asked that Dr. St. George research the reasons a large number of special education teachers leave or transfer from special education. They also asked him to detail what the district was doing to retain its special education staff.

Dr. St. George might report that nationally, special education teachers are leaving or transferring to other positions in education because of stress and burnout. He might also review the stressful issues leading to burnout: lack of involvement of special education teachers in district decisions, problems associated with IEP meetings, paperwork, and isolation from the regular education staff. He might recommend that to curtail these problems the district should offer opportunities for special education faculty to be involved in the district's decision-making process. He might also point out that problems associated with IEP meetings, the large amount of paperwork, and isolation of the special education faculty from the regular education faculty are the main causes of stress and burnout among special education faculty. To help alleviate these and other problems associated with burnout, Dr. St. George might recommend the initiation of a joint special education and regular education committee to review and develop solutions, which the board of education would consider for implementation.

OVERVIEW OF HUMAN RESOURCES

Although the term "personnel department" is still used in school districts, the more common term used to describe the personnel function is "human resources." A school district's human resources department is responsible for recruitment, selection, orientation, staff evaluation, contract negotiations, association/union issues, compensation, and development—which deal with all personnel. This chapter will focus on recruitment, selection, orientation, development, staff evaluation, the retention of certified personnel, and regulatory issues dealing with personnel.

Figure 7.1 depicts what a typical human resources department organizational chart might look like as well as responsibilities of the department. The board of

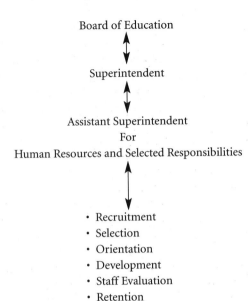

FIGURE 7.1   *Human Resources Organizational Chart and Selected Responsibilities*

education is at the top of the chart. The superintendent reports to the board. The assistant superintendent reports to the superintendent and is responsible for each aspect of the human resources department. It also shows the human resources programs reviewed in this chapter.

The board of education, by state constitution, is responsible for implementing and carrying out the educational program for the district through the superintendent. The board is also responsible for all federal and state rules, regulations, and laws. The board of education spends a majority of its time reviewing and approving actions dealing with budgets, planning, curriculum, human resources, and discipline.

The superintendent is the chief executive officer of the district and is responsible for every aspect of the district. In Figure 7.1, the aspects shown flow through the superintendent to the board of education. Although the assistant superintendent or director of a program may develop and present reports to the board of education, the accuracy of the material within the report or program is the responsibility of the superintendent.

Figure 7.1 lists six aspects of the human resources function that will be reviewed. One of the most important roles that the human resources department has is the recruitment and selection of faculty and staff. After faculty and staff have been hired, the next phase of the process, orientation, is put into place. To refine and develop skills, the human resources department prepares, presents, and documents the development of faculty and staff. The last two aspects of the flow chart deal with evaluation and retention of staff.

TEACHER SHORTAGES

In many school districts, there are more positions available than there are faculty to fill the positions that have been vacated or newly established. It is important to understand the magnitude of the issues facing school districts in terms of regular and special education faculty. The Secretary of Education, Richard W. Riley noted that "schools have been forced to put any warm body in front of the classroom" (*New York Times,* Jan. 9, 2000). The *Times* article goes on to project that there will be a vacancy rate of 250,000 teachers per year for ten years. This teacher shortage of 2,500,000 teachers has caused Congress and presidential hopefuls to develop proposals to bring more people into the profession.

The teacher shortage impact has been felt from the small Belle Glade, Florida, a tiny farm community, which was searching for two first grade teachers, to Texas, which has an estimated need for 20,000 teachers (*New York Times,* Aug. 15, 1999).

The *New York Times* (August 15, 1999) reported on teacher shortages in Los Angeles. The Los Angeles School District hired 1,600 teachers but had a vacancy of 2,500 teachers. Of those hired, 58 percent did not have teaching credentials.

In an article from the *Salt Lake Tribune* (Sept. 27, 1999), Mel Miles, director of human resources for Davis School District stated, "But if this trend continues, all districts in Utah are going to be in a frightening situation where we simply will not have enough qualified individuals to fill all the positions."

The need for special education teachers indicates the same trend. Boe et al. (1996) reviewed data from the Bureau of Labor Statistics, which projected a need for an additional 236,000 to 326,000 special education teachers by 2005. News reports similar to a lead article in the *St. Louis Post-Dispatch* (1999), "Finding, and Keeping Teachers Is a Challenge. Vacancies in Special Education Abound, continue to be a source of attention by major newspapers and other national media.

Singer (1993) estimated that attrition in special education would continue at a rate of 10 to 12 percent a year. The 1998 issue of *Occupational Outlook Quarterly* indicated that there would be a projected employment change of 59 percent in the area of special education before 2006. The *Cincinnati Enquirer* (Oct. 15, 1999) reported that 265 emergency teaching certificates were granted to people teaching students with learning and behavior disorders in Kentucky. An additional 123 teachers were given probationary certificates to teach special education students.

Why is there a shortage of special education teachers? The literature points to burnout as the focal point for the majority of special education teachers leaving the profession. What are factors that cause burnout? Dworkin (1985) indicated that burnout was caused by a sense of powerlessness and isolation. Sarason (1979) believes that colleges of education fail to prepare preservice teachers for the real world of teaching in which autonomy is not a characteristic of day-to-day operations.

Burnout is associated with a number of activities related to special education responsibilities. Greer and Wethered (1984) pointed to due process hearings, diagnostic testing requirements, and placement team meetings, as issues that contribute to stress. Parent complaints and interference, administrative pressures, time issues, new state and federal mandates, case law, parent advocates, state assessment, lack of staff development, isolation from colleagues, insufficient time to prepare for classes, and lack of resources may also be added to the list of those things that add stress to the life of a special education teacher. Olson and Matuskey (1982) indicated that paperwork, pupil-teacher relations, and student discipline are major contributors to the loss of special education teachers.

Berg (1994) recommended six strategies for dealing with burnout brought about by role conflict, problems in decision making, and reducing misunderstandings between regular and special education teachers. Included in the recommendations are:

1. Establishing clear lines of authority and responsibility;
2. Soliciting teacher input for decision making;
3. Facilitating social support groups;
4. Involving staff in the selection process;
5. Involving teachers in the evaluation process by providing opportunities for goal setting and self-evaluation; and
6. Encouraging mentoring relationships between veteran faculty and beginning teachers.

Weiskopf (1980) recommended that teachers reduce stress by:

1. Understanding the emotional demands of the job;
2. Understanding and setting realistic goals for themselves and their students;
3. Utilizing volunteers and aides to assist in the daily routines of a school day;
4. Trying to maintain communications with other faculty members;
5. When possible using team teaching and other techniques to break up direct contact with students;
6. Continuing to apply intellectual skills outside the job;
7. Developing/continuing physical exercise;
8. Maintaining hobbies and activities; and
9. Utilizing new techniques to offset routine.

The teacher shortage makes it difficult for school districts to maintain the numbers needed to adequately staff classrooms. In the next section, the recruitment and selection processes will be discussed in light of the shortage in the teaching profession.

HUMAN RESOURCES FUNCTION

Recruitment and Selection

Today's human resources departments are challenged with recruitment issues of a magnitude not faced by districts during the seventies, eighties, and early nineties. Special education has not been immune from these phenomena. As indicated above, the crisis is based on a lack of special educators to fill vacancies that exist.

Recruitment may be seen as all of the activities in the personnel process, which help to locate quality staff. It may entail internal transfers or the search for external personnel to fill the vacancies that reoccur in every organization. Typically, school districts advertise for vacancies by posting openings with universities, utilizing direct mailing to recent graduates, using the Internet, Web pages, and participating in job fairs.

The primary purpose of selection is to match vacancies to qualified applicants who will succeed in the job, remain in the position, will continue to develop professionally. The selection process has four phases.

Selection Process Phases

The first phase deals with the selection process as policy. Human resources policies dealing with selection may include employment standards, educational level, preparation for positions, expected skills, interpersonal skills, employment discrimination, merit, promotion and advancement, job descriptions, and union negotiated policies.

Authorization to hire personnel is the second phase. In this phase, the number of faculty and the necessary funds available are allocated and monitored.

The third phase deals with advertising for the position. Besides the usual method of advertising in professional journals and newspapers, posting openings with universities, and utilizing direct mailing to recent graduates, there now exists the use of Internet. School district Web pages offer a tailor-made advertisement opportunity for teachers and administrators looking for a position in a particular area of the country.

The fourth phase encompasses screening files for potential candidates. In this phase, the human resources department reduces the number of candidates to those that best fit the available positions. Unfortunately, this phase of the process has become complicated by the fact that there are fewer and fewer candidates in the labor pool.

The final phase in the selection process will vary from district to district. A district may utilize a committee composed of faculty and administration, administration alone, or the human resources personnel may select a candidate to fill a position.

Orientation

Directly associated with the selection of special education and regular education staff is the orientation process. It is important for the human resources department to develop a program, which assists in helping the newly hired faculty member to be successful. One way of doing this is to team the newly hired faculty member with a mentor teacher. The mentor assists the new faculty member in acquiring knowledge of policies, procedures, and school programs. This initial orientation can be of great assistance in the retention of staff.

Staff Development

The school district that has established a policy of continual staff development has positioned itself strategically to succeed. The heart of the process of education is the individual teacher. What should a district consider in preparing a staff development program for individuals?

Teachers grow through three types of activities (Joyce 1988): the formal system of staff development, the involvement with the school or school district (informal), and personal activities. Offering opportunities to grow in each of the realms is very important, especially in an area such as special education where the rate of turnover is exceptional.

The Office of Educational Research and Improvement (1986) suggests that individual staff development should begin at the point of orientation. He describes a process that tailors initial in-service instruction to specific needs. The implications for special education are important to note. New and valued special education teachers need to have programs that reflect issues dealing with: parent communications, paperwork, stress, linking coursework to classroom practice, support, pupil-teacher relations, student discipline, pressure for more inclusive classrooms, integrating special education and regular education, and dealing with regular education administration.

Staff Evaluation

Very few people escape having assessments completed on their on-the-job performance. The pace and magnitude of assessments in education have increased due to pressures from the media, federal and state agencies, and the educational profession itself.

Appraisal is a process that is designed to assist in the judgment of a person's performance against a standard established by the school district. The system of appraisal is formal in nature, has been approved by a board of education. The process has been taught to the appraisers, is systematically used throughout the district, and is essential in reaching the goals established by and for the program, unit, school, and district.

Anyone responsible for appraisal must be prepared and be certified to appraise. Directly related to a successful appraisal system is feedback. A complaint most heard about appraisal is the lack of feedback the teacher appraisal receives. Each person being appraised must be assured of the right to due process.

Special education presents a problem for many regular education administrators responsible for the evaluation of both regular education teachers and special education teachers. Administrators often feel that they do not know enough about special education to adequately evaluate special education teachers and programs. They feel that the evaluation of special education should be the responsibility of someone who has been certified in special education.

Retention

The attrition rate of teachers continues to be a significant issue for school districts. The issue becomes very costly not only monetarily, but also to the teaching and learning process. Hence, states, and teacher associations have begun to reconsider alternative routes to certification. An example of an alternative route can be seen in a partnership developed between the University of Missouri at St. Louis and the St. Louis public schools—a cooperative effort to train elementary teachers, social studies teachers, and long-term substitute teachers as special education teachers. These teachers work in special education classrooms as they are earning certification in special education. They commit two to five years to the special education program and are remunerated $2,500 toward tuition (*St. Louis Post-Dispatch,* Jan. 6, 2000).

Governor George Pataki of New York has proposed a loan forgiveness plan for teachers who agree to work in areas of need. Arizona, Connecticut, Florida, Georgia, Illinois, Kentucky, and Missouri have similar loan forgiveness plans (*Jacksonville, FL Times-Union,* January 2000).

Other solutions to the retention issue are: better assistance programs for beginning teachers, incentives to lure retirees back into teaching by allowing them to keep pension payments at the same time they receive a salary, increasing the salaries of teachers in high-risk areas, and developing a future teachers program.

It is important to consider and build into the selection process an understanding of why staff members leave or transfer to other positions. Using this knowledge, the organization can establish an orientation and proactive retention program, which will prepare new hires for the inevitable problems associated with stress and burnout among special education teachers.

Regulatory Issues

The human resources function is shaped by internal and external controls. School district policy, federal and state laws, municipal laws, case law, attorney general opinions, arbitration decisions, and executive orders influence each aspect of the human resources function. This section of the chapter will focus upon external controls since internal controls may vary from district to district.

The United States Constitution does not directly address education, but there are provisions within amendments to the Constitution that affect school human resources administration:

- Article 1, Section 10: Contracts with employees, once agreed upon, must be honored.
- First Amendment: Personal protection of freedom of religion, speech, and assembly.
- Fifth and Fourteenth Amendments: Personal contracts are considered to be contract rights. Due process requirements include: the right to know what charges are alleged, the right to confront the accuser, to relate the accused's side of the issue, and to have representation.
- Fourteenth Amendment—Equal Protection Clause: Discrimination on the basis of race, sex, and handicap is prohibited.

In addition to provisions to the U.S. Constitution there are statutes and federal or state agencies that regulate the day-to-day operation of school districts. Examples follow.

Statute
- The Civil Rights Act is a statute that requires all employers to ensure that protected classes receive fair treatment. "Protected classes" are based on race, gender, age, disability, and veteran status.

Federal and State Agencies
- The Office of Civil Rights (OCR)
- The Equal Employment Opportunity Commission (EEOC)
- The U.S. Office of Education (USOE)
- The Occupational Safety and Health Act (OSHA)

The Office of Civil Rights (OCR) is an example of a federal agency that plays an important, but not always understood, role in regulating public schools. OCR is responsible for processing and resolving discrimination complaints dealing with: race or color, disability, sex, age, or national origin. The discrimination complaints cover issues dealing with student as well as district personnel. Anyone feeling that they have been discriminated against in any of the areas listed above is entitled to have his/her complaint reviewed by an OCR official.

If the OCR official feels that the complaint is justified, a remedy through negotiations will be sought. If the negotiations fail, the officer may either seek enforcement against the district or refer the case to the Department of Justice. The OCR may also defer new or additional federal funding as well as terminate existing funding, a very costly solution.

It is important for school administrators and teachers to be proactive in their efforts in dealing with the regulatory controls that shape the human resources function. The consequence of failing to follow various regulatory controls can be costly and embarrassing to a district.

SUMMARY

Each of the human resources functions that have been discussed in this chapter becomes more and more critical as the number of teachers in the labor pool continues to decrease. New approaches and incentives will be needed in the near future to train and retain staff in general and regular education.

Concluding this chapter are two case studies focusing on human resources issues in special education. After reading the case studies, you will discuss issues relating to problems dealing with recruitment, selection, orientation, staff development, evaluation, and retention of personnel.

CASE STUDY 7.1: "NEW TECHNOLOGY"

"I believe that you will not only be impressed by this presentation but you will leave today with a greater understanding of how this new technology will assist you in truly integrating regular and special education. You will see that the program has taken an approach that moves from traditional teaching techniques to the use of various technologies in presenting and reinforcing lessons to students with disabilities. We have utilized *Integrated Technology* successfully in pilot programs in urban, rural, and suburban school districts throughout the nation. Each time the results have been the same. An assistant superintendent from a large school district stated, '*Integrated Technology* is the type program that we have been looking for. It has helped us on the road to truly integrating the special education student into the regular education program.' Now let me begin the presentation by introducing the members of our staff."

Raphael Jackson introduced his staff to the administrators of the Washington Heights School District administration. He knew that the district had been seeking assistance in establishing a more inclusive special

education program. Parents and staff alike had been critical of the administration for its seeming lack of attentiveness towards students with special needs.

The presentation lasted for an hour. Raphael said, "I would like for us to take a break. We have provided refreshments for you. Let's take about fifteen minutes before we come back for the last part of the presentation."

The district's curriculum committee, administrators, a large number of special education teachers, and members of the human resources department had listened to the presentation. Typical to the comments that were heard during the break came from Gloria Ahmed, a staff member representing the Wolfbranch School. She said in an enthusiastic voice, "I can't believe how impressive the program is. Did you see how easily Mr. Jackson and his staff moved through each of the learning stations? Ms. Stein, although she is a paraplegic, easily manipulated the computer program."

There was a dissenting voice. Claire Musial, a long-time behavioral disorders teacher, remarked, "You must remember that the group that presented this program to us has this program down cold. They can do it in

(Continue)

CASE STUDY 7.1 (CONTINUED)

their sleep. How much time will we need to put into this program before we are as proficient as they are? Do you remember the last reading program we purchased a few years back? The teacher's edition must have weighed ten pounds. I have heard some of you say that even after two years you still don't know how to teach the program. There is a lot of glitz in the program. I don't think that we should just jump into anything without doing a great deal of study."

Mary Caster, assistant superintendent for human resources overheard Claire's comments. She wrote them down and later that night she began to think about what was best for the district. The board of education and the superintendent wanted a program that would put the district on the cutting edge of inclusion. Was this the program that she would push for? She called the assistant superintendent for special education services the next day and asked him to meet her to discuss the program adoption process and the merits of the *Integrative Technology* program.

Note to the reader: You will now be asked questions about this case. Before you read the Questions and Reflections section at the end of the book (Appendix A), you should fill out a case study analysis (Appendix C), then answer the questions and share your ideas with the class.

Questions

1. What aspects of staff development should be considered before accepting the *Integrative Technology* as a program for the district?
2. What are the implications for moving from the traditional teaching format currently in the program to this new technology for staff development?
3. What are the implications for the recruitment and selection of special education teachers?
4. Are there implications for the personnel appraisal process?

CASE 7.2: "THE OCR COMPLAINT"

Bill David always wanted to be an elementary special education teacher. He had worked very hard to graduate at the top of his class despite being in the initial stage of muscular dystrophy. Some of his undergraduate teachers tried to dissuade him from becoming a teacher because of the nature of his condition.

Bill was determined not to allow muscular dystrophy to stand in his way of becoming a special education teacher. He had interviewed for two positions but in both cases someone else was hired. On his third attempt the Park West School District hired him to teach in a cross-categorical classroom. He remembered telling Dr. Wilbur, the director of special education, "I wasn't trained to be a cross-categorical teacher. I wanted to work with students that have physical disabilities." "Bill, you will do just fine. We have an orientation program, which will answer all your questions. If the orientation program doesn't provide the information you need, we will help you by providing additional staff development," said Dr. James Wilbur.

The orientation program was less than Bill had expected. It covered mostly information dealing with insurance, the district's retirement plan, and the school calendar. There was a short meeting for "job alike" faculty. He met with two new faculty members and a tenured member of the school district. Bill told them of his concern about not being prepared but was told that he would be "just fine."

A week after the orientation program, Bill happened to meet Libbi So, who was also special education teacher. Libbi had been in the district for four years and had been teaching physically disabled students. When she was seven years old she was involved in a car accident, which confined her to a wheel chair. As they were about to part company Libbi said, "I know that you haven't been in the district long, but you need to know that I don't feel I receive the assistance that I need. Take for instance the orientation program. I went through the program four years ago and was disappointed by the lack of discussion concerning special education. Then, I asked my supervisor for a

(Continue)

CASE 7.2 (CONTINUED)

teacher assistant to help me, and was told that my classes were too small. It is difficult for me to do everything that I should to help my students because I am confined to the wheel chair." Bill looked at her and replied, "Libbi, you are right, I haven't been here a long time but I feel the same way. I am going to ask the principal for classroom assistance. Do you mind if I mention the fact that I had talked to you and that we both feel that we are entitled to help?" "Sure you can use my name. Just one more thing Bill, you do know that teachers in the regular education program receive additional classroom assistance when there is a specific need. I don't understand the differentiation, but I know it does happen."

The next morning Bill wrote a memo to the principal stating his needs. He also included in the memo that Libbi So was also having difficulty. A few days later Bill called Libbi and asked her if she felt any difference in the way she was being treated since he sent the memo to the principal. Libbi said that she had been treated coldly by the assistant principal during the last few IEP meetings.

Martha Colbert-Nelson, assistant principal, called Bill in for his first evaluation. She said, "After observing your classroom I have some recommendations. I think that you need to spend more time developing lessons that will meet the needs of your students. You need to spend more time with each individual student. I know you have muscular dystrophy but you can't let that be a problem." He explained to Ms. Colbert-Nelson that he had not been trained to work in a cross-categorical situation and that it was difficult for him to "get around to each student." He also mentioned that he had asked the principal for classroom assistance in the form of an aide. Ms. Colbert-Nelson looked at him and in very closely cropped words said, "I know about your memo."

Libbi had her first formative evaluation of the year a week later. She called Bill a day after the evaluation. "Bill, I waited a day to call you because I was so angry. Ms. Colbert-Nelson had scheduled a formative evaluation with me yesterday. My evaluations have been excellent for the last three years. But this one really bothered me. Colbert-Nelson didn't really have anything positive to say to me. It seems that I am not making the kind of advances toward tenure that she had hoped for. What is going on? I am going to ask a few of my friends what they think about all of this."

In October he read in the district bulletin that there was going to be an in-service meeting for the spe-

cial education staff. He immediately sent in a request for specific help in working in a cross-categorical classroom situation.

He met James Wilbur one day on his way to the parking lot and said, "Dr. Wilbur, how are you today? I am glad that I have the chance to see you. I wanted to know if you received my memo about the staff development day that is coming up. I hope that you will include training on cross-categorical techniques—I really need the help."

"I did get your memo. There is a possibility that a section can be put into the staff development day covering cross-categorical techniques. I won't promise anything," said Dr. Wilbur.

A day later he received the agenda. He was disappointed by what he read. The focus of the meeting was to be a review of IDEA and not on any of the issues he had asked to be included.

By the end of the first year his physical condition had deteriorated. He now pleaded for additional help from the director of special education and from the principal of his school. Both declined his request indicating that Bill's class load was too small to consider an aide. Libbi had also requested that an aide be assigned to her classroom. She was also told that an aide would not be assigned to her class.

Bill requested a meeting with the assistant superintendent of schools. Although the discussion was cordial Bill felt that he again had struck out. He was not tenured and began to feel that he never would be.

Libbi met Bill at a local coffee shop. She told him that she had also asked for a meeting with the assistant superintendent. "Bill, I can't believe how cold he was to me. After he said that he could not help me I went back to school and discussed the problem with some of the faculty. One of the teachers told me, "I have seen it all too many times. You probably won't be around here long. You 'rocked the boat' and asked for something that just won't be funded."

Bill was feeling that the only thing he could do was to file a grievance. The grievance was heard by the superintendent but he ruled that no additional assistance would be given. "We just don't have the money," he stated.

Bill began to hear via the grapevine that he was "persona non grata," and would not receive a contract for the next year.

Bill called the United States Office of Education—Office of Civil Rights and filed a discrimination complaint form (see Figures 7.2 and 7.3).   *(Continue)*

CASE 7.2 (CONTINUED)

FIGURE 7.2   *Discrimination Complaint Form*

1. NAME (Mr./Ms.): <u>Bill David</u>

    STREET ADDRESS: <u>19252 White Oak Valley Drive</u>

    CITY AND STATE: <u>West Park, IL</u>   ZIP CODE <u>63111</u>

    PHONE NUMBER (AREA CODE):   Home <u>618-650-6666</u>

    Work <u>618-656-3030</u>

    In the event this Office is unable to locate you to discuss this complaint, the following person will know where to contact you:

    NAME (Mr./Ms.): <u>Libbi So</u>

    STREET ADDRESS: <u>1515 Franklin</u>

    CITY AND STATE: <u>West Park, IL</u>   ZIP CODE <u>63111</u>

    PHONE NUMBER (AREA CODE):   Home <u>618-650-1234</u>

    Work <u>618-650-3030</u>

2. You were discriminated against on the basis of (please circle the appropriate basis):

    Race or Color   Disability   Sex   Age   National Origin

    If this complaint is based upon disability, please identify disability:

    <u>I have muscular dystrophy.</u>

    If you feel that you were discriminated against on more than one basis (for instance, disability and sex), this office will need to know why you believe that you were treated differently on each basis.

3. Who do you allege discriminated against you? Give the name of the institution (e.g., school district, vocational-technical school, university, college, etc.).

    NAME: <u>The Park West School District</u>

    STREET ADDRESS: <u>16 School Dr.</u>

    CITY AND STATE: <u>West Park, IL</u>   ZIP CODE <u>63111</u>

    PHONE NUMBER (AREA CODE):   <u>618-650-1111</u>

    ORGANIZATIONAL UNIT: <u>K–12 District</u>

CASE 7.2 (CONTINUED)

4. Have you filed this complaint with any other federal, state, or local agency or any federal or state court or administrative tribunal?

YES   NO

If yes, when was the complaint filed and with what agency, court, or administrative tribunal (include the address)? What are the issues of the complaint and what is the current status of the complaint?

_____
_____
_____
_____
_____

If no, do you intend to file with another agency, court, or administrative tribunal?   YES   NO

What agency, court, or administrative tribunal (include the address) and when?

_____
_____

5. Have you pursued resolution of your complaint through the internal grievance or due process procedures at your institution?

YES   NO

If yes, when did you initiate the action and what is the status of your complaint?

Yes I filed an internal grievance with the principal and the superintendent. The superintendent said that he could not do anything about the complaint.

6. When did each act of discrimination occur?

School year 99/2000

OCR will process your complaint only if it is filed within 180 calendar days of the last act of discrimination, except where the complaint alleges a continuing discriminatory policy or practice or where OCR grants a waiver of the 180-day filing requirement.

If the alleged discrimination occurred more than 180 days prior to your filing a complaint with OCR, please explain why you waited until now to file your complaint.

The violation occurred 20 days ago.

_____
_____
_____

(Continue)

CASE 7.2 (CONTINUED)

7. If you are filing this complaint on behalf of an injured party, provide the following information about the injured party.

NAME: _____

If injured party is a minor child, name of parent or guardian:

_____

STREET ADDRESS: _____

CITY AND STATE: _____ZIP CODE: _____

PHONE NUMBER (AREA CODE):_____

What is the injured party's race or color, national origin, disability, sex, or age?

_____

_____

8. Describe the alleged discrimination and provide the factual bases for your belief that discrimination has occurred.

I began teaching in the West Park School District this year. When I first came to the district I asked for help getting ready to teach a class that I had not been trained to teach. I was assigned to teach cross-categorical students. I was trained to teach physically handicapped students. An orientation program was scheduled for all new teachers. I was disappointed to discover that the agenda only covered benefits and district policy. I began teaching and soon was involved in a controversy. I sent a memo to the principal asking for an instructional assistant. I also asked that an upcoming curriculum day focus upon teaching techniques for those of us teaching out of our area of training. I met the director of special education and said that I hoped that the curriculum meeting would include a section that would be relevant to teachers like myself. I spoke to another teacher (she is confined to a wheel chair) who teaches physically handicapped students. She also asked for aide help in her classroom. Her request was denied.

I then requested a meeting with the superintendent. He sent his assistant over to meet with me. The answer again was no. The assistant said, "You would find this district very friendly if you learned how we do things around here." He listened to me, then said that the superintendent would not authorize an aide to my class.

(Continue)

CASE 7.2 (CONTINUED)

I then filed a grievance against my principal for not accommodating my disability. The superintendent heard my complaint. Two weeks later I received a note saying that the superintendent ruled against me. The other teacher, Libbi So, also requested a hearing. Her request for classroom assistance was denied.

For the past few weeks both Libbi and I have heard that our contracts would not be renewed because of our instance of classroom accommodations to meet our disability.

The meeting was held. The agenda basically dealt with IDEA and discipline. Soon after, the assistant met with me to review my progress and the in-class observation she completed. She made reference to the memo and said that there were no funds available for special education classroom, unless the classes became too large. I asked why regular education classrooms were still receiving new aides. She then asked what part of "no" I did not understand. The meetings between the two of us became contentious. My physical condition began to worsen.

(If more space is required, attach additional sheets.)

9. Please submit any written materials, data, or other documents which you think are relevant to your complaint. Please be aware that OCR procedures require all complaints to be signed.

_____Bill David_____	_____12/31/99_____
SIGNATURE	DATE

Early Compliant Resolution Process (ECR)

OCR has an ECR procedure in which OCR attempts to help the complainant and the institution to voluntarily resolve the issues of the complaint without an OCR investigation. OCR does not use ECR if class issues or systemic discrimination are alleged. In addition, both the complainant and the institution must voluntarily want to participate in the ECR process. The complainant, the institution, or OCR may end the ECR process if it appears that an agreement cannot be reached. If this happens, OCR will investigate the complaint. One of the primary benefits of the ECR process is that it may be possible to resolve your complaint quickly, without the need for an investigation. If OCR believes that ECR of your complaint is appropriate, are you interested in having OCR attempt to resolve your complaint through the ECR process?

_____ Yes   _____ No

CASE 7.3 (CONTINUED)

FIGURE 7.3   *Information About OCR's Complaint Resolution Procedures*

I. Complaint Evaluation

OCR begins by evaluating complaints. OCR's objective in complaint evaluation is to determine whether or not OCR can proceed to complaint resolution. OCR cannot proceed to complaint resolution under a variety of circumstances, for instance, where OCR has no jurisdiction; where a complaint is not timely; where another agency has already reached a binding decision; or where the person alleged to be injured declines to cooperate in OCR's investigation.

OCR will actively work with complainants and examine other sources of information to ensure that the agency has sufficient information to evaluate complaints appropriately. OCR staff will provide appropriate assistance to complainants who may need help in providing information OCR needs.

It is expected that complainants will also work actively with OCR to ensure that OCR has the information needed; OCR can initiate complaint resolution only for those complaints for which sufficient information has been provided.

Generally, OCR will take action only with respect to those complaints that have been filed within 180 calendar days of the last act of alleged discrimination, or where the complaint alleges a continuing discriminatory policy or practice. If a complaint is not filed in a timely manner, the complainant may request a waiver, which may be granted only under limited circumstances.

OCR is responsible for enforcing the following federal civil rights laws:

- Title VI of the Civil Rights Act of 1964, which prohibits discrimination on the basis of race, color, or national origin;
- Title IX of the Education Amendments of 1972, which prohibits discrimination on the basis of sex in educational programs;
- Section 504 of the Rehabilitation Act of 1973, which prohibits discrimination on the basis of physical and mental disability;
- The Age Discrimination Act of 1975, which prohibits discrimination on the basis of age; and
- Title II of the Americans with Disabilities Act of 1990, which prohibits discrimination on the basis of disability.

II. Complaint Resolution

OCR's primary objective in complaint resolution is to resolve the complainant's allegations of discrimination promptly and appropriately. OCR has a variety of tools for resolving complaints. These include: Early Complaint Resolution (ECR), agreements for corrective action, and enforcement. Any approach, or combination of approaches, may be initiated at any time and multiple approaches may be used to resolve any complaint.

a. Early Complaint Resolution (ECR)

Early Complaint Resolution provides the parties involved the opportunity to immediately resolve the allegations prompting the complaint. If the complainant and the recipient are willing to utilize this approach, OCR will work with the parties to facilitate resolution of the complaint. OCR does not sign,

CASE 7.3 (CONTINUED)

approve, or endorse any agreement reached between the parties; however, OCR will assist both parties in understanding pertinent legal standards and possible remedies.

OCR does not monitor any agreement reached between the parties in ECR, but if the recipient does not follow through on the agreement, the complainant may file another complaint with OCR.

b. Agreements

OCR's investigations continue until such time as OCR can determine an appropriate resolution of the complaint allegations under OCR regulatory standards. OCR may use a variety of fact-finding techniques, which may include informal fact-finding such as joint discussions with the complainant and recipient.

Any agreement for corrective action will specify the action, if any, to be taken by the recipient to resolve each complaint allegation. Implementation of such agreements will be monitored by OCR.

c. Other Ways Complaints Can Be Resolved

OCR may also consider a complaint resolved when any of the following occur:

- If the complaint has been investigated by another agency and the resolution of the complaint meets OCR standards;
- If OCR determines that the evidence is insufficient to support a finding of a violation;
- If the complainant withdraws his or her complaint;
- If OCR obtains information indicating that the allegations raised by the complaint have already been resolved.

III. Letters of Findings and Enforcement

If OCR determines that the recipient has violated one or more of the civil rights laws, and the recipient is unwilling to correct the violation(s), OCR will promptly issue a violation letter of findings specifying the factual findings and the legal basis for the violation(s). OCR will again attempt to negotiate a corrective action agreement. If OCR is still unable to obtain voluntary compliance, OCR will move immediately to enforcement by either initiating administrative enforcement proceedings or referring the case to the Department of Justice. OCR can also move immediately to defer any new or additional federal financial assistance to the recipient, and will begin administrative enforcement proceedings to terminate existing federal assistance.

IV. Additional Information for the Complainant

a. What to Do if You Disagree with OCR's Resolution of Your Complaint

OCR is committed to ensuring that every complaint is appropriately resolved. If the complainant has questions or concerns about OCR's resolution determination, he or she should contact the OCR staff person whose name appears in the complaint resolution letter. If the complainant believes OCR's resolution determination was based upon incorrect or inaccurate factual information, she or he should be encouraged

(Continue)

CASE 7.3 (CONTINUED)

to address these concerns with as much specificity as possible. Should the complainant continue to have questions or concerns, she or he should be advised to contact the regional director or his or her deputy. The regional director will verify the appropriateness of the complaint resolution.

b. Information About the Right to File a Separate Court Action

The complainant should be aware that a separate court action may be filed regardless of OCR's findings. It should be clear that, in resolving complaints, OCR cannot and does not represent the complainant in the way that a person's private attorney would. If the complainant wishes to file a court action, he or she may do so through an attorney.

c. Prohibitions Against Intimidation or Retaliation

A recipient may not intimidate, threaten, coerce, or engage in other discriminatory conduct against anyone who has either taken action or participated in an action to secure rights protected by the civil rights statutes enforced by OCR. If any individual believes that he or she is being harassed or intimidated by a recipient because of the filing of a complaint or participating in the resolution of it, a complaint alleging such harassment or intimidation may be filed with OCR.

d. Investigatory Uses of Personal Information

OCR processes complaints of discrimination and conducts compliance reviews on the basis of race, color, national origin, sex, disability, or age at institutions that receive federal financial assistance from the Department of Education. The resolution of such complaints may involve the collection and analysis of personal information, such as student records (including academic standing) and, in some cases, employment records. No law requires a complainant to give personal information to OCR, and no sanctions will be imposed on complainants or other individuals who do not cooperate in providing information requested by OCR in connection with its case resolution process. However, if OCR is unable to obtain information needed to investigate or to otherwise resolve allegations of discrimination, it may be necessary for OCR to discontinue its complaint resolution activities.

There are two laws governing personal information submitted to all federal agencies, including OCR: the Privacy Act of 1974 (Privacy Act), 5 U.S.C. § 552a, and the Freedom of Information Act (FOIA), 5 U.S.C. § 552.

The Privacy Act of 1974 protects individuals from the misuse of personal information held by the federal government. The law applies to records that are kept and can be located by the individual's name, social security number, or other personal identifier. It regulates the collection, maintenance, use, and dissemination of certain personal information in the files of federal agencies. Persons who submit information to OCR should know that the information that OCR collects is analyzed by authorized personnel with the agency and will be used only for authorized civil rights compliance and enforcement activities.

However, OCR may need to reveal certain information to persons outside the agency in the course of verifying facts or gathering additional information to develop a basis for resolving a complaint. Such details

(Continue)

CASE 7.3 (CONTINUED)

could include the physical condition or age of a complainant. Also, OCR may be required to reveal certain information to an individual who requests it under the provisions of the Freedom of Information Act (FOIA) (discussed below). OCR will not release information to any other agency or individual except in the 11 instances defined in the Department of Education's regulation at 34 C.F.R. § 5b.9(b), one of which is released under the FOIA.

Finally, the Office for Civil Rights does not reveal the name or other identifying information about an individual unless it is necessary for the completion of an investigation or for enforcement activities against an institution that violates the laws, or unless such information is required to be disclosed under the FOIA or the Privacy Act. OCR will keep the identity of complainants confidential except to the extent necessary to carry out the purposes of the civil rights laws, or unless disclosure is required under the FOIA, the Privacy Act, or otherwise by law.

THE FREEDOM OF INFORMATION ACT gives the public a right of access to records and files of federal agencies, including those of OCR. Individuals may obtain items from many categories of records of the federal government, not just materials that apply to them personally. OCR must honor requests under the FOIA with some exceptions. Generally, OCR is not required to release documents during the case resolution process or enforcement proceedings if the release could have an adverse effect on the ability of OCR to do its job. Also, any federal agency may refuse a request for records compiled for law enforcement purposes if their release could constitute an unwarranted invasion of privacy of an individual. Also, a request for other records, such as medical records, may be denied where disclosure would be a clearly unwarranted invasion of privacy.

e. Allegations Under the Age Discrimination Act

If you have made allegations under the Age Discrimination of 1975 (Act), under the regulation implementing the Act, OCR must inform you of the following: You may file a civil action under section 305(e) of the Act after administrative remedies are exhausted. Administrative remedies are exhausted if 180 days have elapsed since you filed the complaint with OCR or if OCR issues a finding in favor of the recipient, whichever comes first. This civil action can only be brought in a United States district court for the district in which the recipient is found or transacts business. If you prevail in the civil action, you have a right to be awarded costs of the action, including reasonable attorney's fees, but these costs must be demanded in the complaint. Before commencing the action, you must give 30 days notice by registered mail to the Secretary of U.S. Department of Health and Human Services, the Attorney General of the United States, the Secretary of U.S. Department of Education, and the recipient. This notice must state the alleged violation of the Act, the relief requested, the court in which the action will be brought, and whether or not attorney's fees are demanded in the event that you prevail. You cannot bring the civil action if the same alleged violation of the Act by the same recipient is the subject of a pending action in any court of the United States.

(Continue)

CASE 7.3 (CONTINUED)

Note to the reader: You will now be asked questions about this case. Before you read the Questions and Reflections section at the end of the book (Appendix A), you should fill out a case study analysis (Appendix C), then answer the questions and share your ideas with the class.

Questions

1. Review the agenda for the orientation meeting. What should an orientation program contain?

2. If Bill initially qualified for assistance, because of his disability, what should the district have offered him?

3. Was the human resources department proactive in its treatment of a teacher with a disability?

4. Does the treatment that Bill received warrant an OCR complaint?

5. In whose favor would the OCR rule? Why?

CHAPTER 8

Transportation Issues in Special Education

This chapter focuses on the legal and practical issues involved in transporting children with disabilities. Discussion of who must be transported, discrimination, least restrictive environment, and individual education planning teams form the foundation of understanding. Proactive planning issues are discussed and include personnel training and safety. Transporting children in and around schools is also addressed. After reading this chapter and analyzing the cases, you should be able to:

- Determine who and under what circumstances special transportation is required.
- Discuss what should be included in a student's individual education plan when transportation is necessary.
- Discuss the proactive planning issue of personnel training and safety in transporting children with disabilities.
- Discuss issues in transporting children with disabilities in and around the school building.

See semantic map detailing Chapter 8 on page 141.

Overview

Transportation has been and continues to be an important, and oftentimes, difficult, issue in the delivery of special education services. As a special education administrator, how would you respond to the following problem situations involving transportation? Would your school system be able to safely transport these children to and from school?

1. A junior high school principal made a telephone call to the special education director. He said, "John, one of our most difficult behavior disordered students threw a book on the bus and hit another student in the back of the head! He's suspended five days from the bus. You need to understand that he is always causing problems on the bus. He needs to be on a special bus now!"

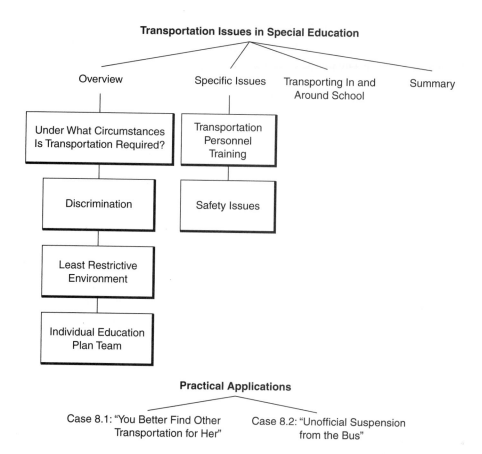

Transportation Issues in Special Education

Overview   Specific Issues   Transporting In and Around School   Summary

Under What Circumstances Is Transportation Required?

Transportation Personnel Training

Discrimination

Safety Issues

Least Restrictive Environment

Individual Education Plan Team

Practical Applications

Case 8.1: "You Better Find Other Transportation for Her"

Case 8.2: "Unofficial Suspension from the Bus"

2. A 3-year-old child enrolled in the special education early childhood classroom rode a special bus to and from school daily. Three days in a row he jumped out of his seat while the bus was moving and hit other students. The transportation supervisor contacted the special education administrator and requested a harness to contain the child on the bus immediately.

3. The IEP team met with the parent of a new student who just enrolled in the school district. The boy was a quadriplegic who was wheelchair-bound, had a feeding tube and required oxygen 24 hours a day. The parent asked the team how her child would be safely transported to school.

The statutory law addressing transportation for students with disabilities is brief. Administrators have long relied on interpretations of the law from the court system, the Office of Civil Rights, and the Office of Special Education Programs in the federal Department of Education to guide decision making. A survey of superintendents and school business managers of small rural districts and a review of rural education literature revealed that transportation was one major concern in special education (Freitas 1992). Following is a discussion of important issues to be considered in transporting students with disabilities, including legal issues, the role of the IEP team, training for transportation staff, safety issues, transportation in and around the school building, and emerging issues.

Under What Circumstances is Transportation Required?

One of the foundations of IDEA is that all children with disabilities have available to them a free appropriate public education (FAPE). FAPE includes access to individually determined special education and related services. Related services are defined as "transportation, and such developmental, corrective, and other supportive services as are required to assist a child with a disability to benefit from special education" (34 C.F.R. § 300.16 (a)). The service of transportation can be a related service for a child with a disability. It is defined in the regulations for IDEA to include the following:

(i) Travel to and from school and between schools,
(ii) Travel in and around school buildings, and
(iii) Specialized equipment (such as special or adapted buses, lifts and ramps), if required to provide special transportation for a (child) (34 C.F.R. § 300.13 (b)(13)).

The Office of Special Education Programs (1995) answered a question in a policy letter regarding a school district's obligations to provide transportation to students with disabilities. The interpretation stated that transportation was required for all students with disabilities in two situations.

1. If the school district provides transportation to the regular school population to and from school, the district must provide transportation to all students with disabilities, including transportation to any special education program where a child might be placed.
2. If the school district does not provide transportation to the regular school population, the transportation issues for students with disabilities must be decided on an individual basis. If it is determined that a student with a disability requires special transportation, it should be provided as a related service to the child on the IEP.

What is considered special transportation depends upon the individual needs of the child. To illustrate, consider the issues discussed in the following court cases involving transportation to and from a parochial school for special education purposes. In the first case, *Donald B. By Christine B. v. Board of School Commissioners of Mobile County*, 26 IDELR 414 (11th Cir. 1997), the court determined that a 7-year-old speech impaired student did not require special transportation service between the parochial school and the school district to benefit from the special education program. This was due to the age of the student, the short distance (three blocks) between the parochial school and the public school and the ability of the student to easily travel the distance. Conversely, the court in *Board of Education of the District 130 Public Schools v. Illinois State Board of Education*, 26 IDELR 724 (N.D. Ill. 1997) reached a different decision. In this case, the court held that the student required transportation between the parochial school and the district school to benefit from her special education program. The student was too young to walk the two miles between schools and the route was slightly dangerous. The 11-year-old student had attention deficit disorder and received resource services at the district school several times a week. Each of these cases, although involving parochial schools, demonstrates how individual differences and facts affect the outcome of school district responsibility to provide special transportation.

Other interpretations about the transportation obligations have helped school districts to determine the parameters of special transportation. They include the following:

1. A school district can't compel a parent to provide transportation for a student with disabilities even if the district offers to reimburse the parent for transportation expenses (see, for example, *Letter to Hamilton*, 1996). However, the school district can contract with the parent to provide special transportation if the parent is willing to provide the service.
2. The school district must provide transportation to and from extracurricular activities if the activity is required for the child to benefit from his/her special education program (see, for example, *Carmel (NY) Cent. Scho. Dist.* 1993).
3. The school district must provide transportation for a student with disabilities whose academic day extends beyond the typical day (see, for example, *Brent v. San Diego Unified Sch. Dist.* 1996).
4. Door-to-door transportation for a student with disabilities has been the subject of dispute. If the school bus must travel down a private road that is not well maintained to reach the student's home, the school district must find alternate transportation to the student's home (see, for example, *Kennedy v. Board of Educ.* 1985, and *Fort Sage Unified Sch. Dist. v. Lassan County Office of Educ.* 1995).

Discrimination

Discrimination has become an issue when transporting children with disabilities. Section 504 of the Rehabilitation Act of 1973, as a broad civil rights law, prohibits discrimination on the basis of disability in programs that accept federal funds. The Americans with Disabilities Act creates a high standard of nondiscrimination because it applies to agencies that don't accept federal funds.

As an example, consider the following case. In one school district, nondisabled students are transported to and from school. The bus ride does not exceed 45 minutes for any student. In the same district, students with IEPs attend the same schools and ride "special education buses." The transportation time for students with disabilities is 75 minutes in most cases. This case could be the basis for discrimination because students with disabilities are, as a category, riding only the special education buses. In addition, their bus ride exceeds the time used for nondisabled students just because these students are in special education.

Another example of discrimination might involve loss of instructional time for a student with disabilities. In this case, a student with behavior disorders is transported to a neighboring school district for special education services. The normal school day for students in the building is 9:00 A.M. until 3:30 P.M. However, the transporting school district must pick up the student with the behavior disorder at 2:45 P.M. in order to make other pickups on time. This, in effect, shortens the disabled student's day not because of his individual needs, but because of the convenience of the transportation.

A third example involves suspension from the bus. In one school district, a student with a disability is suspended from the bus because of inappropriate behavior on the bus. The parent can't transport the student to and from school during the suspension. Therefore, the student cannot attend school and is, in effect, denied access to school. The student is being denied the benefits of his special education program because of his disability and, therefore, being discriminated against by the school district. If this bus suspension exceeds ten school days in one year, the issue could be problematic for the school district.

Least Restrictive Environment

Least restrictive environment (LRE) is a founding principle of IDEA. The basic rule is that students with disabilities should be educated with children who are not disabled to the maximum extent appropriate. LRE is determined individually in an individual education plan meeting. The concept of LRE extends to all portions of a child's program, including the related service of transportation.

As more and more children are receiving special education services in regular school buildings, schools can expect to face the issue of combining regular and special transportation (Harrington-Lueker 1991). This trend might involve more expense, e.g., adapting existing school buses to accommodate wheelchairs, and training more bus drivers in the transportation of students with disabilities.

Transporting a child with disabilities with or without nondisabled children may be appropriate depending upon individual circumstances surrounding each child's case. For example, LRE requirements would be met if a child had to ride a special bus to attend a special education program in a school that was outside of the home school district or a considerable distance from the child's home. If a child required specialized equipment that could only be placed in a special bus, LRE requirements would also be met. Similarly, if a child required special transportation for safety reasons, LRE requirements would be satisfied.

Other factors might prompt an IEP team to consider regular bus transportation for a child with disabilities as a related service. For example, if a child with disabilities could benefit from language modeling or social interaction with nondisabled peers, regular transportation with nondisabled children might be necessary and would be included on the IEP as a related service.

Individual Education Plan (IEP) Team

IEPs must contain information about special education, related services, and supplementary aids and services to be provided to a child with a disability. In addition, the IEP must specify modifications or supports for school personnel that will be provided for the child. Because transportation can be considered a related service for some children, the IEP becomes an important document to specify transportation arrangements (Bluth and Hochberg 1994). Best practice suggests that transportation personnel should be involved in the IEP meeting for some children with disabilities for whom the regular bus is not appropriate (Linder 1991).

To illustrate the importance of transportation personnel involvement in the IEP process, consider this example. A child in fifth grade was recommended to attend special education classes in her home school. The child had many health problems, including the need for tracheal suctioning every hour. The parents visited the special classroom and were very pleased with the placement. At the IEP meeting, it was stated that the bus ride each way to and from school would be twenty minutes and this time was written on the IEP. This presented no problem with the required suctioning, as the nurse could provide the health service upon arrival at school. After the IEP meeting, transportation personnel were contacted. On the first day of school, the bus picked up five other children who lived in the same area and the child's one-way transportation time was close to fifty-five minutes. The parents were very upset because the IEP stated that one-way transportation would be twenty minutes. The parents threatened to request a due process hearing. If the transportation personnel had been involved in the IEP meeting, this problem could have been avoided.

When should transportation personnel be involved in IEP meetings? Obviously, it is not necessary or practical to involve transportation personnel in all IEP meetings. There are, however, three situations which necessitate the involvement of transportation personnel in an IEP meeting (Bluth 1991).

1. The child transported has significant health problems (e.g., medically fragile, infectious disease).
2. The child transported requires specialized equipment or services (e.g., wheelchair, bus aide).
3. The child transported displays significant behavior concerns.

To determine the extent of special services necessary during transportation, several states have drafted best practice documents which include guiding questions for IEP teams (Maryland State Board of Education 1991; Iowa State Department of Education 1992). These questions are outlined in Figure 8.1. After discussing the answers to these questions, IEP teams would be better prepared to draft a transportation plan in the IEP which would detail provisions on the IEP for special transportation. Although there are no statutory guidelines or specific requirements for this documentation, the Iowa State Department of Education (1992) provided parameters for best practice about what should be included on an IEP in terms of special transportation. These parameters are included in Figure 8.2.

One question that has sometimes been raised involves the need to include goals and objectives on the IEP for the related service of transportation. The Office of Special Education Programs (1995) provided guidance on this matter. In a policy letter, it was stated that if the sole purpose of transportation was to enable the student to travel to and from school, in and around school, and between schools, no goals or objectives were needed on the IEP. However, if, as a part of the student's instruction, transportation was provided to enable the student to increase his/her independence or improve social skills during travel, goals and objectives must be included in the IEP.

SPECIFIC ISSUES

Several professional organizations and states have developed best practice policy for transporting children with disabilities. These issues include personnel training and safety issues. Both topics are discussed below.

Transportation Personnel Training

It is generally considered best practice to provide bus drivers and aides with specialized training to safely transport students with disabilities (Carter 1992; Reed and Brazeau

Questions to Ask

1. How will the child be transported to school? Can regular transportation be utilized?
2. If not, can regular transportation be utilized if supplementary staff, equipment, and/or services are provided?
3. If not, what type of special transportation is necessary?
4. Can the child be safely transported to school without significant risk to the student or others?
5. How long will the child be in transit? What is the travel distance?
6. Does the child have significant health, physical, or behavioral concerns which could be a safety issue in transportation?
7. What necessary assistive or adaptive equipment will be transported with the child?
8. Can the equipment be safely secured and transported with the child?
9. Will someone need to accompany the child for medical intervention and/or safety reasons?
10. Who will accompany the child, if necessary?
11. Is the driver adequately trained to meet the needs of the child while in transit?
12. What are the procedures in the event of a medical emergency?
13. What are the routine procedures necessary during transit?
14. Is someone needed to help the driver at the school site?

Adapted from: "Supervisor's Guide for Transporting Children with Special Health Needs," Maryland State Board of Education (1991) and "Transporting Students with Disabilities: A Manual for Transportation Supervisors," Iowa State Department of Education (1992).

FIGURE 8.1   *To What Extent Are Special Services Necessary During Transportation?*

What to Include on an IEP When Special Transportation Is Necessary

1. Mode of transportation to and from school.
2. Length of time on the vehicle each way.
3. Equipment and/or adaptations necessary for transportation.
4. Evacuation procedures in the event of an emergency.
5. Emergency transportation options in the event of, for example, inclement weather.
6. Need for a bus assistant.
7. Protocols for on-board health care procedures, including a list of health facilities along the bus route.
8. Protocols for behavioral procedures and driver training.

Adapted from: "Transporting Students with Disabilities: A Manual for Transportation Supervisors," Iowa State Department of Education (1992).

FIGURE 8.2   *Best Practice*

1991; Maryland State Board of Education 1991; Raper 1990; Bluth and Hochberg 1994; Linder 1991; Iowa State Department of Education 1992). By providing training prior to transporting students with disabilities, school districts place themselves in a proactive position instead of in a reactive position and students can be safely transported. It is recommended that initial training include a comprehensive program for all drivers and aides. Follow-up training should occur annually for all drivers and aides reviewing safety issues and changes in procedures and/or practice. The following areas might be considered for inclusion in a driver/aide training program.

Characteristics of Children with Disabilities

This portion of training would provide a foundation of basic knowledge for drivers and aides transporting children with disabilities. Characteristics of various disabilities (e.g., autistic, health impaired, emotionally disturbed) would be presented as well as how to meet the transportation needs of these children. Drivers and aides would gain information on appropriate expectations for students with various disabilities, while developing an understanding that each child has unique characteristics and needs. It would also be important to summarize the identification and placement process in special education and confidentiality of records and information about students. This portion of training could be presented by the special education administrator.

Legal Mandates

Bus drivers and aides should have a general understanding of federal, state, and local mandates for providing transportation to students with disabilities. For example, if a student in regular education misbehaves on the bus three times, it may be local school policy to remove the student from the bus for one day. However, if a student with behavior disorders engages in similar behavior, the issue could be considered a placement issue and should be discussed in an IEP meeting. Bus drivers and aides would need a basic understanding of these issues and why students might receive different treatment for the same behavior. A special education administrator would be qualified to summarize legal mandates.

How to Operate Specialized Equipment and Assistive Devices

Each bus driver and/or aide should be thoroughly familiar with the safe transport and operational procedure for specialized equipment and assistive devices. These devices and equipment could include wheelchairs, occupant restraint systems, operation of hydraulic lifts or ramps, safe transport of oxygen, etc. The director of transportation, with assistance of other consultants, would be well qualified to present this portion of the training.

Transporting Medically Fragile Students

Due to medical advances, more medically fragile children attend school and must be transported. Many of these children will be technology-dependent. Case law (*Skelly v. Brookfield LaGrange Park Sch. Dist. 95*, 1997) suggests that if the child receives related health services at school and it is included in the IEP, the school district must provide the service during transportation.

One issue that has been debated by the courts revolves around what is a medical service (and not required by IDEA) and what is a related service (and required by IDEA). Courts in the past used a multifactor test which usually included the expertise required to provide the service, the physical burdens associated with providing the service, the relationship of the care to the child's overall welfare, and the expense of the service. Prominent cases included *Detsel v. Board of Education of the Auburn Enlarged City School District,* 1987, and *Tatro v. State of Texas,* 1984. The Supreme Court issued an important decision in this matter in the case *Cedar Rapids Community School Dist. v. Garret F.* (1999). In the case, a 12-year-old child had multiple health needs at school and at home, requiring nursing services during the school day. The Supreme Court affirmed the lower courts' decisions and determined that the health services were required to assist the child to benefit from special education and attend school, and the services needed could be provided by a nurse. Therefore, the health services were required as a related service under IDEA and should be paid for by the school district. The outcome of this case affects transportation because if a health-related service is required on the child's IEP, it will be required on the child's transportation.

An understanding and description of health care intervention necessary during transportation, including who will provide what services, should be addressed in a general training program. Follow-up training specific to individual children should occur for bus drivers and aides responsible for transporting medically fragile children. Bus drivers and aides should also know how to maintain appropriate records and how to file reports regarding a child's health and medical status. Training in this area should also include basic first aid and cardiopulmonary resuscitation. This training should be presented by a qualified nurse or medical personnel.

Communication Skills

Bus drivers and aides communicate daily with students and parents. They must be able to communicate at a level appropriate to each child's level of development and communicative status. They must also be able to communicate effectively with parents of children with disabilities. For example, if drivers ask students to inform them if they begin to feel ill and the students are unable to comprehend what the drivers are asking, problems could occur. In addition, if a parent complains about an occurrence on the bus, the driver must be able to use appropriate communication skills to clarify the parent's concerns and tell the parent to whom the complaint should be addressed. This portion of training could be completed by a special education administrator and/or transportation supervisor.

Knowledge of Behavior Management Techniques

Bus drivers and aides must have basic knowledge of techniques to develop appropriate behavior and manage inappropriate behavior to maintain safety on the bus. They also should be able to document behavior, complete appropriate reports, and have knowledge of local procedures for dealing with misbehavior on the bus. It is possible that problems could be averted if drivers and aides were proactive in encouraging appropriate behavior and appropriately reactive to problem situations.

For example, the following strategies could help prevent problems with inappropriate behaviors on buses (LRP Publications 1998):

1. Do not yell or scream at students.
2. Do not plead or beg.
3. Do not use the word "try." In other words, do not say, "Why don't you try to sit down?"
4. Start sentences with a directive and inform students what they should do, not what they shouldn't do.
5. Use verbal praise to reinforce good behavior.

Training in behavior management skills could be accomplished by utilizing a special education teacher or a school psychologist well versed in behavior management skills. Role playing might be used so that drivers and aides could practice skills.

Knowledge of Emergency Procedures

Should an emergency occur when transporting students with disabilities, bus drivers and aides must know how to react quickly. For example, if the bus is involved in an accident or if a child stops breathing, the driver and aide may only have minutes or seconds to react. The driver and aide should have immediate access to important medical information on each child, including emergency procedures, and be ready to act quickly should something happen to a child. Drivers and aides should also know conditions that might necessitate a bus evacuation and how the evacuation would be performed. Emergency evacuations can easily become complicated if the bus is transporting students in wheelchairs and/or who are medically fragile. It is recommended that drivers and aides practice emergency evacuations annually. This training could be accomplished by the transportation supervisor and other consultants, e.g., physical therapist, nurse, special education teacher.

Important in all training areas would be knowledge of local school district procedures in transporting students. It is good practice to develop board-approved policies and procedures in the transportation of students and to communicate these policies and procedures to school staff, bus drivers and aides, parents, and administrators. Well-thought-out policies and procedures are proactive in avoiding unnecessary problems involving safety and conflict when transporting students with disabilities.

Safety Issues

The major goal of transporting children with disabilities is to transport the children in a safe manner. There are no federally-mandated safety procedures for transporting children with disabilities. The task of regulating transportation of children with disabilities falls largely to state and local school boards.

In 1994, the American Academy of Pediatrics developed a policy on transporting children with special needs on the bus. Guidelines from this policy are outlined in Figure 8.3. In another document, the Council for Exceptional Children emphasized important safety procedures for transporting medically fragile children. Some of the major points are summarized as follows:

Transporting Children with Special Needs on the Bus

1. If a child who uses a wheelchair can be moved to a regular seat or a child car seat, the child should be moved. If possible, a child in a wheelchair should not be transported in the wheelchair.

2. Empty wheelchairs should be secured to avoid harming passengers in a sudden stop or crash.

3. Occupied wheelchairs should be secured with the child facing forward.

4. Wheelchairs should be secured with a four-point tie-down system attached to the floor.

5. Lapboards or trays attached to wheelchairs should be removed and secured separately during transport.

6. In accordance with state laws and regulations, a nurse with appropriate training can provide necessary on-board assistance and support to most children with tracheotomies who may require suctioning or emergency care during transport.

7. Bus transportation staff should be trained annually in special needs transportation.

8. Parents should be informed of the importance of incorporating appropriate and safe transportation in the IEP.

9. Schools should protect children by establishing a written plan that outlines procedures for emergency evacuation and that requires an annual evacuation drill.

10. Because children supported by technology may have increased potential for carrying infectious and communicable diseases, schools should develop a comprehensive infection control program to protect staff and children. Transportation staff should have training and supplies that allow them to carry out universal prevention practices.

Adapted from: "School Bus Transportation of Children with Special Needs" by American Academy of Pediatrics Committee on Injury and Poison Prevention, *Pediatrics,* 93 (1) 1994: 229.

FIGURE 8.3   *Guidelines*

1. Modifications of traditional transportation vehicles is encouraged.
2. Transportation personnel should be provided training in transporting students with special health needs.
3. All transportation vehicles should have an emergency card for each student transported to expedite appropriate procedures and contacts in case of emergency.
4. Written procedures for the transportation of students with special health needs should be developed and the procedures should be disseminated to all involved in the service delivery, including transportation (Council for Exceptional Children 1998).

Transportation of students in wheelchairs is an important area of emphasis in a training program. Sometimes, due to tradition and economics, schools have chosen side-facing wheelchair mounts on buses (Harrington-Lueker 1991). This means that wheelchairs face the side of the bus instead of facing the front of the bus. This is in direct conflict to guidelines from the American Academy of Pediatrics (1994). In 1991, 16 states mandated forward-facing wheelchair positioning on school buses, and other options were acceptable in other states (Linder 1991). Wheelchairs should be secured forward-facing and the wheelchair and student should be secured independently—the student by a torso and lap belt and the wheelchair by a four-point tie-down system. Schools should also look closely at the wheelchairs they transport. Some are built for mobility and comfort, but often they are not safe for transport in a moving vehicle according to the manufacturer.

Transportation In and Around School

IDEA regulations define transportation to include travel in and around school buildings. To carry out this obligation, the school district must maintain accessible buildings and provide students with the equipment to move around the building (LRP Publications 1998). The Americans with Disabilities Act of 1990 sets detailed standards for accessibility and the standards apply to classrooms, parking lots, bathrooms, playgrounds, and all other locations in the building (Americans with Disabilities Act of 1990, 42 U.S.C. § 12101 et seq.).

One issue that was clarified by the Office of Civil Rights involved a question about the school district's obligation to provide a wheelchair for a nonambulatory student. The affirmative answer stated that the standard for making this determination is whether the wheelchair is required to assist the child with disabilities to benefit from the special education program. In addition, because related services includes transportation in and around school buildings and can involve specialized equipment, a wheelchair can be required (see, for example, *Letter to Stohrer* 1989).

Summary

At the beginning of this chapter, three short problem situations were described. In resolving the problems, two issues must be emphasized. The first involves the importance of the IEP team in determining special transportation for a child with disabilities. The first situation's problem (the junior high principal requesting a special bus for a behavior disordered child) should be referred to the IEP team. At the IEP meeting, the team must determine if the child needs special transportation in order to benefit from special education. If so, a special bus might be appropriate. If not, the team might address how the child's behavior has been handled on the bus and, with a transportation staff person, devise an appropriate behavior management plan for the student on the bus. Likewise, the situation involving transporting the 3-year-old would be an issue to be addressed by the IEP team in a similar manner. The third situation, involving the boy who was a quadriplegic would also involve the IEP team. It is essential that no one person make unilateral decisions about transportation, but that any changes should be addressed by the IEP team.

The second issue to be emphasized in the three situations involves taking a proactive approach to avoid problems. This proactive approach would include appropriate training for bus drivers and aides, developing, implementing, and communicating board-approved policies and procedures concerning the transportation of students with disabilities, and involving transportation staff, when necessary, in IEP meetings. It is possible that some of the problem situations described could be avoided.

Transporting students with disabilities is a mandatory and necessary activity for many children with disabilities. With careful thought and planning, a school district can continue to provide safe, efficient transportation for children with minimal problems.

To assist you in developing proactive planning for the transportation of students with disabilities, two practical case studies follow.

CASE 8.1: "YOU BETTER FIND OTHER TRANSPORTATION FOR HER!"

When Dr. Rodriguez answered the telephone, an angry voice said, "This is Gail Richards. My daughter Melanie rides the bus to Forest City School District because of her physical disability. You know, she has to go to the neighboring school district because you don't have a program in our home town. I just want you to know that I am very unhappy about the bus service this year. Last year, Mr. Ryan transported Melanie in his van. It was air-conditioned and Mr. Ryan was so nice. I don't know why the bus service had to be changed! Anyway, this year some kids are on the bus over an hour. The bus can't turn around in my driveway and the driver won't come to my house. This might be OK today, but there will be a problem if it is hot or cold outside. You know Melanie cannot regulate her body temperature and it will be impossible to get her wheelchair from my front door up a hill 250 feet to the beginning of the driveway where the bus stops. I know Melanie deserves door-to-door transportation."

Dr. Rodriguez, a little surprised said, "Mrs. Richards, you and I have talked on many occasions. It seems that you're pretty angry about the bus situation. It's important that you know how the change happened. Every year, the school district takes bids on transportation routes and up until this year, Mr. Ryan made the only bid on the route to take physically handicapped students to Forest City School District. This year, Horizon Bus Company placed a bid on this route and it was the lowest bid. Therefore, the school board accepted the bid. Anyway, in terms of your concerns . . . "

Before Dr. Rodriguez could continue, Gail cut in and said, "I don't know why the school district has to always take the lowest bid, especially when the service is inferior. I've had it! Melanie said the driver was driving too fast. The bus service isn't personal any more. The bus is larger, is not maintained properly, and the air-conditioning isn't working all the time—and Melanie must have it cool on hot days. Dennis, from the bus company, said that the bus would come to the house and the driver isn't doing this! I can't send Melanie to school like this."

Dr. Rodriguez said calmly, "Mrs. Richards, I can assure you that we will provide safe transportation for Melanie. I know the service is different from last year. Mr. Ryan went above and beyond what was required by the contract. However, I made some notes about your concerns and I will contact the bus company to review them. We certainly will work out any problem areas."

Gail said reluctantly, "I certainly hope so. I will be watching daily. If something doesn't change immediately, I will not allow Melanie to get on the bus. By the way, could you give me the telephone number of a child advocate to advise me?"

After giving Mrs. Richards the telephone number, Dr. Rodriguez hung up the telephone. She pulled Melanie's file and began to review her IEP. The IEP, although appropriate, did not have much detail about transportation. It simply stated that Melanie was to receive special transportation to and from school. There were no notes concerning air-conditioning on the bus, although the IEP did indicate that the classroom had to be air-conditioned due to Melanie's inability to control her body temperature. There were no notes concerning emergency procedures if Melanie became overheated or too cold.

Dr. Rodriguez further reviewed the file. Melanie was in a wheelchair most of her day. She used special leg braces during a thirty-minute physical therapy session daily. She had to be catheterized three times daily and was also given various medications. Melanie was self-

(Continue)

CASE 8.1 (CONTINUED)

contained in a classroom for multiply-handicapped elementary students. According to her file Melanie's primary disability was "physically handicapped" and her secondary disabilities were "other health impaired" and "learning disabled."

Later that same day, Dr. Rodriguez spoke by telephone to Dennis Randle, the supervisor for Horizon Bus Company. Dr. Rodriguez carefully explained Mrs. Richards' concerns about the bus service. She concluded by saying, "You know, Dennis, part of the problem is simply that the school district changed bus transporters. Mrs. Richards was very pleased with the previous service."

Dennis replied, "We'll try to work through her concerns. There are five wheelchairs to place on and off the bus and it takes time for the driver to determine the most efficient way to place the wheelchairs. I will share the concerns with the driver and we'll do our best to work with all of the parents."

Dr. Rodriguez reviewed the situation with the superintendent so that he would be knowledgeable of the situation. Dr. Rodriguez assumed that the problems would be resolved after her intervention.

Two days later, Dr. Rodriguez received a frantic telephone call from Mrs. Richards.

Mrs. Richards cried as she said, "Melanie got sick with the heat today on the bus. I had to cool her off and she was crying. I'm so scared! Melanie is OK now, but I'm afraid it will happen again. You know, Dennis Randle's father, who owns the bus company, just got out of prison. That bus company can't be trusted."

Again, Dr. Rodriguez tried to detail exactly what happened. Apparently, it was a hot day and the air-conditioner did not function properly on the bus. Melanie became ill and her mother immediately moved her into the air-conditioned home. After an hour or so, Melanie recovered.

Dennis Randle was immediately contacted. He stated that the air-conditioner on the bus malfunctioned and the driver turned on two fans in the bus with the windows open. He apologized and said that the air-conditioner would be fixed.

Over the next week, several changes were made. Horizon Bus Company purchased an oversized van with air-conditioning. The driver changed the route to pick up Melanie last so she would have less time on the bus. Dr. Rodriguez contacted Dennis Randle every few days to assure that the problems had been resolved.

At the end of the week, Gail contacted Dr. Rodriguez again. She was hysterical on the telephone as she yelled, "That driver was driving too fast! Melanie had her braces on and she has bruises because of the bumpy bus ride. I don't want her riding on that bus. You better find other transportation for her! That driver doesn't care about these kids. I've done all I can do to be patient. I want this to change right now!"

Dr. Rodriguez replied, "Mrs. Richards, I think we need to arrange an IEP meeting to resolve this problem. We need to specify each problem and discuss possible solutions."

Mrs. Richards agreed and the IEP meeting was arranged for the following week. Dr. Rodriguez spoke to the bus driver, who said that Mrs. Richards was unreasonable. He said she screamed and cursed at him when he arrived to pick up Melanie daily. She questioned Melanie daily about the bus ride, then yelled at him.

Prior to the meeting, Dr. Rodriguez spoke to the superintendent again. She indicated that nothing short of a change in transportation would satisfy Mrs. Richards. She also felt that the bus company was partly at fault and that a due process hearing might be inevitable. Although the parent did not have the right to tell the district with whom to contract bus services, there were some concerns about the specificity of Melanie's IEP regarding transportation. Dr. Rodriguez proposed contracting with the previous bus transporter to transport Melanie and continue to use the current transporter for the other students. This would placate Mrs. Richards and the financial cost to the district would be less than entering into a due process hearing. After some discussion, the superintendent agreed to contract with the previous transporter to take Melanie to and from school.

Dr. Rodriguez contacted the previous transporter, Mr. Ryan, and he was able to accommodate Melanie on his van.

At the IEP meeting, Dr. Rodriguez explained to Mrs. Richards that the school district agreed to change the transportation for Melanie and that Mr. Ryan, Melanie's previous driver, would begin transporting Melanie. Mrs. Richards was very pleased with the change. Mr. Ryan attended the meeting and the team

(Continue)

CASE 8.1 (CONTINUED)

specified the transportation in detail and wrote an emergency plan for Melanie.

The IEP detailed that the type of transportation was a converted van and that the length of time one way to or from school would be fifty minutes. It was also specified that Melanie's wheelchair would be transported securely and that Melanie would sit in a regular van seat secured by the suitability. The bus driver, Mr. Ryan, would be trained in CPR and would have written instructions to take Melanie immediately to the hospital if she should turn blue from the cold or red and flushed from the heat. The IEP stated that the van would be air-conditioned and heated and that Melanie would be seated toward the front of the van. Mr. Ryan would be responsible for picking up Melanie in her driveway by the front door, would push her wheelchair up the manual ramp to the bus, then lift her to the van seat and secure the suitability. He would also transport her into the school.

Mrs. Richards contacted Dr. Rodriguez only one more time that school year to thank her for changing the transportation.

Note to the reader: You will now be asked questions about this case. Before you read the Questions and Reflections section at the end of the book (Appendix A), you should fill out the case study analysis (Appendix C), then answer the questions and share your ideas with the class.

Questions

1. Why did Dr. Rodriguez inform the superintendent of the situation?
2. What was wrong with Melanie's IEP initially? What should have been changed concerning her transportation?
3. Should Dr. Rodriguez have initiated the change in transportation? Why or why not?
4. Did the school district have an obligation to provide an air-conditioned vehicle? Why or why not?

CASE 8.2: "UNOFFICIAL SUSPENSION FROM THE BUS"

"Mrs. Allen? This is Ann Miller, principal of Lake View Elementary School. I'm calling about Kevin."

Mrs. Allen immediately felt a knot in her stomach. It was only 9:15 A.M. on Monday and already he was in trouble! She said, "Yes, This is Kim Allen. What has happened?"

Ann Miller continued, "Kevin has been disruptive on the bus again. On Friday he threw an eraser at another student. His BD teacher took away points on his behavior chart and gave him a warning. Today, however, he got out of his seat and hit another student on the head with a book. When the driver said something, he cursed at her. The driver brought Kevin into my office this morning. This situation is very unsafe for all students on the bus. I haven't talked to Kevin's BD teacher yet, but I'm sure there will be some consequences in the classroom. However, something has to be done to show Kevin that he cannot continue to act in this manner on the bus. I am taking him off the bus for one day."

Mrs. Allen asked, "Does this mean he can't ride the bus to and from school?"

Ann responded, "Yes. He won't be allowed on the bus tomorrow, but he will be expected to be at school. We will call this an 'unofficial' suspension from the bus, but it will not become part of his record. I assume you will be able to bring Kevin to school and pick him up at the end of the day."

Mrs. Allen said, "Yes, I will be able to transport him tomorrow. I'll certainly talk to Kevin about his behavior on the bus. He has been doing so much better in school lately and I hate to see him get into trouble on the bus."

Ann said, "Mrs. Allen, you have always been so supportive of Kevin and his program at this school. With us working together, I'm sure we can eliminate misbehavior on the bus. I have to consider the safety of all students on the bus."

(Continue)

CASE 8.2 (CONTINUED)

The next day, Mrs. Allen took Kevin to school. He seemed relaxed and talked all the way to school. He said he would improve his behavior on the bus.

Kevin returned to the bus on Wednesday, following the behavior incident on Monday. At 9:30 A.M., Mrs. Allen answered the telephone. Again, it was Mrs. Miller.

Ann Miller began by saying, "I'm sorry to call you again, Mrs. Allen, but Kevin had more problems on the bus today. He got out of his seat and hit another student while the bus was moving. Then he threw a pencil at a student. I simply cannot tolerate an unsafe situation on the bus. Again, I will not allow him to ride the bus to and from school for one day, Thursday. Kevin has to become responsible for his actions. We will consider this an 'unofficial' suspension from the bus and he will be expected to attend school, so you will have to bring him to school and pick him up tomorrow."

Mrs. Allen said, "I'm somewhat concerned about this punishment, Mrs. Miller. On Tuesday when I took Kevin to school, he seemed to enjoy riding with me. I think riding with me to school by himself is somewhat reinforcing to Kevin. When he misbehaves on the bus, he is rewarded by getting personal attention from me on the way to school the next day. I wonder if we could consider an alternative punishment. For example, Kevin hates to stay after school. Could he be assigned an after-school detention instead of a bus suspension?"

Ann Miller responded, "I cannot allow Kevin on the bus because he engaged in unsafe behavior. Could you try punishing him at home along with his removal from the bus—perhaps no TV? Anyway, I don't have any supervision after school for an after-school detention."

Mrs. Allen sighed and said, "I guess I could take away TV, but I still have a concern—that Kevin likes for me to take him to school. I think he would like to be removed from the bus all the time if I could take him to school. It's just impossible for me to do this every day. I can take him tomorrow, but it's difficult for me to do this because I have to rearrange my work hours."

"I understand, Mrs. Allen," said Ann, "I appreciate your cooperation. I'll talk to Kevin's BD teacher and see if she has any additional ideas."

The next week, Kevin got out of his seat on the bus and hit another child in the chest. Then he threw his backpack at a student. The driver pulled to the side of the road and Kevin cursed at her. The driver brought Kevin into the office to Mrs. Miller. Mrs. Miller talked to Kevin in an angry manner and told him she would

not tolerate his behavior on the bus. She telephoned Mrs. Allen and conveyed the incident to her. Mrs. Allen became rather upset when Mrs. Miller told her Kevin would be removed from the bus for three days. She also told Mrs. Allen that Kevin would have a substitute teacher on the fourth day and it might be better to keep him home on the fourth day because Kevin always had difficulty with substitute teachers.

Mrs. Allen said, "I can't do this, Mrs. Miller. It is impossible for me to rearrange my work schedule for four days. Kevin is a behavior disordered student. Although I don't condone his behavior, this is the reason he is in the BD class! I think we need to come up with an alternative plan to control Kevin's bus behavior."

Ann Miller was adamant about her position as she said, "I have to treat Kevin as I would all students in regard to safety on the bus. He is not allowed to ride the bus for three days. Again, it would be in Kevin's best interest to stay home on the fourth day because of the substitute teacher situation. I'm sorry, Mrs. Allen, but I won't change my position."

Mrs. Allen immediately contacted James Killday, the director of special education. She explained exactly what had occurred over the past few weeks and stated that if something didn't change she would contact her attorney and request a due process hearing. Dr. Killday listened carefully and suggested an IEP meeting the following day with Mrs. Miller and Kevin's BD teacher. Mrs. Allen readily agreed to the meeting. The notice of the meeting was to be delivered to Mrs. Allen by the end of the day.

Dr. Killday contacted Mrs. Miller to talk with her about the meeting and the situation. Mrs. Miller strongly stated her opposition to any change in her position. Dr. Killday stated that a child could not be removed from the bus as an 'unofficial' suspension. Mrs. Miller argued with him and said that Lake View Elementary School was her responsibility and she would do what she thought was best.

Dr. Killday also reviewed the situation with Jack Robinson, superintendent. Dr. Robinson appreciated the information and suggested that the problem might be settled at the IEP meeting the next day. Dr. Killday promised to update Dr. Robinson on the situation after the IEP meeting.

The IEP meeting was held in Ann Miller's office at 3:15 P.M. the following day. Mrs. Allen attended as well as Mrs. Miller, Dr. Killday, and Mrs. Jacobs, Kevin's BD teacher.

(Continue)

CASE 8.2 (CONTINUED)

Before Dr. Killday could begin the meeting, Mrs. Miller said, "I just cannot tolerate unsafe conditions on the bus. Kevin continues to create problems on the bus and this situation is just an accident waiting to happen. He will have to stay off the bus any time he misbehaves on the bus."

Mrs. Allen quickly said, "I worked with you the first few times Kevin misbehaved on the bus. I changed my work schedule so I could take Kevin to and from school. However, the last incident shows us that suspending Kevin from the bus doesn't change his behavior. I told you that I thought it was rewarding for Kevin to be suspended from the bus. He likes to drive with me to school. I cannot change my work schedule every time Kevin has problems. Kevin is a BD student and we should be able to come up with a plan within the school day to improve his bus behavior."

Dr. Killday quickly said, "The reason we are here is to discuss how we can help Kevin with bus behavior."

Mrs. Allen interrupted by saying, "I have contacted my attorney and she said if we can't settle this today, she will represent us in a due process hearing."

Mrs. Miller continued by saying angrily, "That is your *right*, Mrs. Allen."

The dialogue was very heated and angry voices continued until Dr. Killday stood up and said, "We will continue this meeting only if one person speaks at a time and the other persons listen. I will not continue with this angry dialogue. We are here to help Kevin and we are not helping him by arguing."

The group was then silent. Dr. Killday continued, "Mrs. Jacobs, Kevin has been your student for the past two years. Can you help us understand how he is progressing and what works behaviorally with him in the classroom?"

The meeting continued with each person allowed time to talk. If someone tried to interrupt, Dr. Killday provided a stern reminder that everyone would have a chance to state his/her side of the story.

After an hour, all agreed that no one condoned tolerating an unsafe situation on the bus. Dr. Killday stated that Mrs. Allen could not be expected to take Kevin to and from school each time he misbehaved on the bus. Kevin's teacher, Mrs. Jacobs, agreed with Mrs. Allen that Kevin was rewarded every time he was suspended from the bus and his mother took him to and from school. Mrs. Miller said that she had to have some type of consequence for misbehavior on the bus. The team drafted a behavior management plan that included immediate rewards for appropriate behavior on the bus. Mrs. Allen agreed to implement a reward system at home and communicate with Kevin's teacher on a daily basis. She also agreed to spend unqualified "alone time" with Kevin on a daily basis. The plan included an after-school detention with Mrs. Jacobs for thirty minutes if Kevin misbehaved on the bus. The team agreed to review the plan in six weeks to discuss its effectiveness. Dr. Killday stated that if the plan was unsuccessful, alternative transportation might be considered. Mrs. Allen left the meeting feeling relieved and satisfied.

After the meeting, Dr. Killday spoke sternly with Mrs. Miller. He said, "Ann, we could have had a serious problem by removing a student from the bus and calling it an 'unofficial' suspension. Mrs. Allen was asked to transport Kevin to school. However, it is the district's responsibility to transport him to school. If we were involved in a due process hearing, it would have been difficult to defend what happened."

Ann replied, "I don't care what would have happened at a due process hearing. I would tell a hearing officer the same thing I told you. This is my building and I will discipline students in a manner I think is appropriate and I will not tolerate unsafe behavior on a bus or in the school."

Dr. Killday continued, "Ann, if you face this type of situation in the future, please contact me and we will arrange an IEP meeting to discuss what to do."

Unhappy, Ann replied, "Whatever you say, Dr. Killday."

Note to the reader: You will now be asked questions about this case. Before you read the Questions and Reflections section at the end of the book (Appendix A), you should fill out the case study analysis (Appendix C), then answer the questions and share your ideas with the class.

Questions

1. Why would implementing an "unofficial" suspension from the bus be a problem legally?
2. If you were the director of special education, what position would you have taken with Ann Miller? Why?
3. Were correct procedures followed for resolving the problem? How do you know?
4. Would it have been correct procedurally for Ann to agree to an after-school detention the third time Kevin misbehaved on the bus? Why or why not?
5. What conflict resolution skills did Dr. Killday use to resolve the problem in the IEP meeting?

SCHOOL REFORM IN SPECIAL EDUCATION

Chapter 9 reviews the current state of school reform. The modern genesis for school reform is summarized as a means of understanding the forces involved in changes away from the status quo. After reviewing the chapter and analyzing the cases, the student should be able to:

- Describe the origins of modern school reform.
- Describe the various types of school reform.
- Understand the negative and positive aspects of each school reform.
- Describe how the IDEA relates to school reform.

See semantic map detailing Chapter 9 on page 158.

OVERVIEW

School reform is the current antidote for the ills that face public school education. Like any medication, it is necessary to understand the immediate effects and side effects that the regimen will have on the patient. What is school reform? What issues face special education in the era of school reform? Finally, will school reform eliminate the dual system that continues to separate regular education from special education?

Offering the community, parents, students, and educators options to restructure or completely reformat the governance of their schools, to rid the process of unneeded regulations and rules, to better meet the needs of local constituency, to transform old systems into more responsive systems is the alluring aspect of school reform.

What parent would not want programs that better meet the needs of his or her child? What parent has not complained about the lack of response on the part of the school or school district? What educator has not wished that useless "red tape" encountered on a day-to-day basis could be eliminated? In place of the word parent, insert "parent of a student with a disability." Then the allure of the reform takes on a greater meaning.

School reform has been part of the American educational scene for many years. The current reform movement began with the publication of *A Nation At Risk* (National Commission on Excellence in Education 1983). The publication spawned many news articles and debates that called question to the state of public education in the United States. The discussions that began in 1982 were responsible for proposed

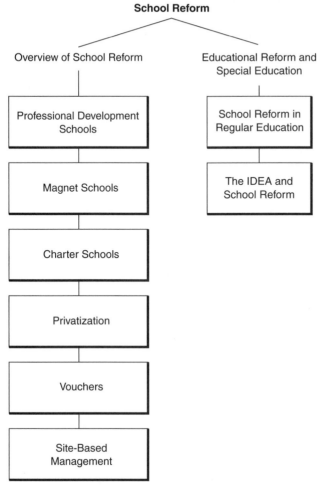

changes in approaches to public school governance and also in the assessment process states and schools now follow.

Besides *A Nation at Risk* (1983), three federal laws have promoted educational reform (Goals 2000 1994): Educate America Act, Improving America's Schools Act, and the School to Work Opportunities Act.

Goals 2000 set high standards for "all students" which included students with disabilities. The Improving America's School Act authorized funding for Title I (formerly Chapter 1). Like Goals 2000, the Improving America's Schools Act included all students.

The School to Work Opportunities Act helped schools combine classroom lessons and the workplace. The act also included children with disabilities. Before these three acts were approved, special education was evaluated in terms of compliance of the student's IEP, not in terms of student achievement.

Parents, teachers, administrators, and board of education members have many potential school reform options available to them. The school reform options frequently referred to in the literature are: magnet schools, charter schools, privatization, vouchers, and site-based management.

Although not usually considered a school reform option, the professional development school (PDS), offers an opportunity to alter preservice teacher education by forming a partnership between the local school district and the teacher training institution. In PDS, the instructional process is moved from the university to the school setting. Professors, school faculty, school administration, and preservice teachers center instruction within the confines of the classroom and the school. The PDS partnership mirrors actual teaching and learning by having each of the participants take part in the development and implementation of instruction within the classroom. Preservice teachers have an opportunity to observe school faculty and university faculty teach students. The PDS is cited here because it may be a reform movement that changes the way teachers are trained and subsequently changes the face of education in the United States.

Although the school reform momentum has continued and grown rapidly, a number of issues concerning the viability and success of these programs have surfaced, especially in the area of special education (Hess 1998). To illustrate, two situations are provided that are typical of the issues that face school districts and parents as they attempt to "customize" educational settings following school reform trends:

1. The White Oak Citizens for Excellence in Education Committee summarized their two-year study of restructuring by recommending that the school district develop a "high tech" magnet school. The committee's study pointed to a need for a technology curriculum, which would bring the district into the next century. The curriculum was to be based on computer software that was to be purchased or developed by the district. The board of education reviewed and approved the recommendation with an understanding that all excess school district expenses needed to be cut to pay for the new program. During its discussion the board determined that they would need to reduce the number of teacher assistants and increase the student-to-teacher ratio. In summarizing the decision the board president said, "Everyone must understand that we will need to eliminate this very important program, if for some reason the budget exceeds funding. This means that any vested faction will need to bend to the needs of the majority—we need to break new ground; we need to think out of the box." The local educational professional association was not in favor of the plan but agreed to accept the proposal. Five parents of children with disabilities requested that their children be included in the new magnet school. The board refused to place the children in the magnet school because they would "significantly alter the school's mission and create a funding problem."

As a second example, consider the following scenario:

2. Bill Ingram was delighted. He was the principal of a charter school developed by the parents of an inner city area of a large metropolitan school district. His school report card showed a dramatic increase in the reading scores of his students. When asked how he attained the increase, he pointed to the policy on homework and parent participation that was developed at the close of the last school year. Bill failed to mention that he had eliminated all special education students from the state testing program.

In the first situation, the school district had as its motivation the establishment of a specialized school. The concept, though laudatory, cannot be instituted if it would eliminate participation by any group that would normally attend a public school. "Bending to the majority" cannot be used to establish a program that eliminates qualified students.

The second situation appears to have a simple solution. It would appear that to meet the regulations established under federal law, persons with disabilities as a group could not be routinely excluded from testing or assessment. Disabled students must be tested, assessed, and receive the same benefits and services as other nondisabled students, unless individually excluded from assessment by the IEP team.

With the reauthorization of the IDEA, it is clear that there has been a strong reaffirmation that state education initiatives must fully include students with disabilities (PL 105–17). The team of parents and educators formulating the IEP must determine a student's participation in the assessment process. The amendments to the IDEA articulate the state's responsibility to include students with disabilities in reported data (PL 105–17, sec 101).

In this case, the principal was incorrect in eliminating students with disabilities from assessment without following statutory requirements.

RESTRUCTURING SCHOOLS

The restructuring of schools, and in some case school districts, is based on a belief that to meet diverse needs of students it is imperative to move away from current organizational patterns. The National Council on Disability (1993) reported that most of the educational reform initiated from 1990 to 1992 did not include programming for students with disabilities. Lipsky and Gartner (1996) reported that, "To a large extent, the national attention to educational reform has ignored students with disabilities." Examples may include:

1. It is not unusual for school districts to relegate special education classes to less than desirable classroom space or special education may be placed in classroom after all other aspects of the schools instructional space has been considered.
2. Special education faculty often cite lack of funding to support classroom instructional needs as a significant problem.
3. Special education administrators often feel that they do not have an opportunity to be part of the general education program.

From the reform movement, several types of reform have emerged and will be briefly reviewed.

Magnet Schools

Magnet schools, an extension of the public school, were established to offer parents and students a curriculum that focused upon a particular specialty. Schools dedicated to teach science, gifted, technology, the arts, or foreign languages are examples of magnet schools.

Magnet schools are a source of pride in many communities. The entrance requirements vary from stringent, accepting students with exceptional abilities in the magnet school's area of concentration, to accepting students with a desire to attend the magnet school in question.

There are criticisms associated with the magnet school concept. Central office administrators will point to a drain on district funds to establish and maintain a magnet school. Principals will suggest that the "cream of the crop," both students and teachers, tend to be attracted to these schools.

In the area of special education, magnet schools have had difficulty in dealing with the concept of the integration of disabled students. Schools with stringent entrance requirements and curriculum have an especially demanding time in creating a schooling experience for students with disabilities.

Charter Schools

Charter schools are one of the fastest growing forms in the school reform movement. In 1990 there were no charter schools in the nation. By the year 2005 it is estimated that there will be 2,500 to 3,000 charter schools in the United States (Borsa, Ahmed, and Perry 1998).

What is a charter school and what are the issues that face it? A charter school is an autonomous schooling unit that is created by and operated by an individual or group of individuals through the sponsorship of an entity such as, but not limited to, a local school board. A state board of education, a university or other public authority may also be a sponsor. A charter, or contract, defines the nature of the school, details the school's educational plan, reviews its assessment plan, and reviews compliance issues. One of the "selling" points of the charter school is that it is released from most, if not all, the rules and regulations that bind it to the local district.

In a study of charter schools Borsa, Ahmed, and Perry (1998) cited the following governance issues:

- Charter school management,
- Staff development,
- Principal/director experience and training,
- Supervisory/evaluation procedures,
- District support for the charter school,
- Assistance from the local district (legal assistance etc.),
- Discipline procedures, and
- Teacher certification.

In addition to the above stated issues, Borsa, Ahmed, and Perry (1998) noted a potential trend that may cause problems in the establishment of charter schools. The

Kansas City, Missouri school district has lost approximately 3,000 students to recently created charter schools. This loss of students, and the funding that follows the students, has caused the district to consider closing public schools and implementing a reduction-in-force policy. The Kansas City School Board is also considering requesting that the State of Missouri place a cap on the number of charter schools that can be established.

The authors summarized the state of the charter school process as "... a reform movement that has serious governance issues due to the ill-defined lines of authority between the charter school and its local school district. Within a very short period of time, there will be legal challenges to the charter school's inability to meet the needs of various groups of students, supervise the staff, and manage fiscal resources" (Borsa, Ahmed, and Perry 1998).

A study of Colorado charter schools (McLauglin, Henderson, and Ullah 1996) cited assistance from the local district to the charter school as a source of tension in the areas of fiscal planning, personnel policies, special education, and supervision of day-to-day classroom and school operations.

Charter schools have a great deal to offer the parent as a source of flexibility in meeting the needs of students with disabilities. Like all the reform movements, it will take time and an understanding of the issues that face charter schools before the potential of this reform movement can be met.

Privatization

A definition of private sector takeover of public school administration may be better understood by reviewing one of the largest privatization programs in the United States. In 1995 one of the most scrutinized privatization projects began with four schools. The Edison Project currently has contracted to carry out the schooling of children in 51 schools and four school districts in the United States. The project, developed by Christopher Whittle, began with a $25,000,000 grant from the Fisher Foundation. Its focus, as a for-profit corporation, was to apply business principles and structure to the organization, administration, and instructional process of the schools in the Edison Project.

What are the basic features of the project? The Edison Project has increased the number of hours and days a student is in school. One of the features touted by Christopher Whittle, the founder of the Edison Project, is to place a computer in the home of students attending project schools.

Some of the criticisms associated with the Edison Project deal with problems in educating special education students, difficulty in adapting to the educational complex design, and problems in the interpretation of test results.

Corporations like the Edison Project, have a distinct advantage over public schools. They have the ability to dismantle the administration and teaching staff without the restraints associated with state evaluation mandates and property right protections.

In the near future, the Edison Project plans to build their own schools developed around Edison specifications. These schools will include preschools. There are also plans to develop an Edison teacher's college.

Vouchers

The school voucher program empowers the consumer the ultimate in school choice. The voucher allows a parent to attend a school with a tuition grant paid for by the state. Under the voucher program the parent has a specific tuition amount to purchase education from a school other than the one his or her child currently attends whether it is another public school, a private school, or a parochial school.

The Supreme Court's refusal to hear the appeal in *Jackson v. Benson* (Case No. 98–376, 1998) upheld the Milwaukee voucher program. Supporters and opponents of the voucher concept took the refusal as a victory for their viewpoint. This issue began when opponents to the Milwaukee voucher program argued that inclusion of religious schools was prohibited by the 1973 Supreme Court ruling in *Committee for Public Education and Religious Liberty v. Nyquist* (Nyquist, U.S. 756 (1973). In June of 1998, The Wisconsin Supreme Court held that Nyquist did not preclude upholding what it saw as the neutral aid to religious schools provided under the Milwaukee plan.

There are problems associated with the voucher concept other than the religious issue. Many private schools cannot afford to accept a voucher student. The difference between the private school's tuition and the voucher payment is too great. For example, a private school might charge a tuition of $5,000 but the voucher grant is for $3,500. What school could afford to make up the $1,500 difference?

Special education is affected by the reluctance that a receiving school may have in accepting a student with a disability. Will private schools accept students with a disability? Can they afford the additional expense of instructing a student with a disability?

Site-Based Management

Brown (1990) defined school or site-based management as a practice by which a school is allocated money to purchase supplies, equipment, personnel, utilities, and other services deemed necessary to meet the needs of the school.

Definitions of site-based management differ. They can be as encompassing as Brown's definition or may be more restrictive as to the amount of empowerment the local school is allowed by the central office.

The groundbreaking work of Edmonds (1979) indicated that at-risk students were more likely to succeed in schools with site-based management than in traditional schools. His research found that site-based management afforded the principal an opportunity to be an instructional leader with the power to make instructional improvement without relying on the central office.

Comer (1988) found that schools that practice site-based management, shared decision-making, and never-ending improvement were more likely to be successful because they fostered:

1. Principals who provided instructional leadership.
2. School climates that are safe.
3. Positive parent involvement.
4. Faculty and staff that believed all children can learn.
5. Reading, writing, and arithmetic as high priorities.
6. Frequent evaluation of students and staff.
7. Staff development.

8. High student attendance.
9. Student high expectations of themselves.
10. Careful planning of special programs.

Site-based management is not a panacea, especially in the area of special education. As an example, the principal may want the special education staff to assist all children, even those children not in special education, but is thwarted by special education funding mechanisms and rules which do not allow for the flexibility.

Another problem area is staff development. Site-based management is a staff development intensive process that many districts fail to finance in funding and in the allocation of the time needed to adopt the procedures necessary to be successful.

EDUCATIONAL REFORM AND SPECIAL EDUCATION

In recent years, school reform in special education paralleled reform in regular education and included national and state legislation on student achievement goals, curriculum changes, assessment of student progress toward those goals, and accountability. In general, reform focused on shifting to a target on outcomes of students rather than inputs into the system.

Figure 9.1 summarizes school reform for regular education and special education. Regular education reform became a focus at the national, state, and local level in 1989, when President Bush and the nation's governors held a historic education summit. The results of the summit produced national education goals, which were legislated into law in 1994 and titled, "Goals 2000: Educate America Act."

The majority of states also enacted legislation specifying state goals that closely corresponded to the national goals (Thurlow 1994). For example, the State of Illinois adopted 34 "State Goals for Learning" in 1985. These were broad statements of what the State of Illinois expected its students to know and be able to do as consequence of their schooling. These goals were then reflected in standards or expectations for all students in Illinois. As a result of this process, local school districts aligned their curriculums with the standards. Illinois students were assessed at various grade levels by a state test to determine the number of students who met, exceeded, or did not meet these standards. The overall result was accountability with a focus on outcomes so that all children demonstrated they were learning.

In a similar manner several years later, school reform in special education developed. In 1997, the IDEA was reauthorized and included many aspects of regular education school reform. The IDEA specified that states must have goals for performance of children with disabilities that were consistent with goals for all children. Individual education plan goals, objectives, and special education services had to be tied to the child with a disability's involvement and progress in the regular education curriculum. The child with a disability had to participate in state and district-wide assessments. If the IEP team determined that the child could not participate, the child had to participate in an alternative assessment. As with regular education, the result was accountability with a focus on student outcomes. In the IDEA, there was a strong preference for including children with disabilities in movement toward school

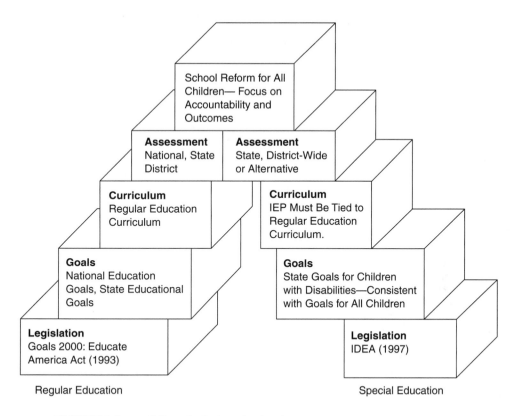

FIGURE 9.1 contents:

School Reform for All Children— Focus on Accountability and Outcomes

Assessment National, State District

Assessment State, District-Wide or Alternative

Curriculum Regular Education Curriculum

Curriculum IEP Must Be Tied to Regular Education Curriculum.

Goals National Education Goals, State Educational Goals

Goals State Goals for Children with Disabilities—Consistent with Goals for All Children

Legislation Goals 2000: Educate America Act (1993)

Legislation IDEA (1997)

Regular Education   Special Education

FIGURE 9.1   *Building Blocks for School Reform*

reform. The IDEA contained many regulations supporting school reform for all children. Some of these regulations are detailed in Figure 9.2.

With so many school reform possibilities, why are there still issues dealing with special education? As long as there is a dual system of training for teachers and administrators in the education of disabled and nondisabled, there is little chance that true educational reform will take place. If change is to be meaningful, it will be necessary to fade the lines between the disabled and the nondisabled in the nation's classrooms.

Campbell (1992, 15) described the basic way in which special education should be seen today: "People have to stop thinking of special education as synonymous with underachievement. Special education is not a place, it's not a remedial program, and it's not small group instruction. Instead, special education is specially designed instruction to meet the unique needs of individuals with exceptional needs. The ultimate educational outcomes for the child with a disability are the same for any other child."

Rockne and Weiss-Castro (1994) described a vision for the year 2000 as encompassing a unified education system. The system had the following components: a broader appreciation of diversity, school community collaboration, well-prepared personnel, a professional development system, appropriate policy, financing, specific accountability, effective systemic teaching and learning, and appropriate technology.

Lipsky and Gartner (1996, 26) stated, "The future work in educational reform remains extensive. Educational restructuring so that schools serve all students well

General

- . . . the term special education means specially designed instruction . . . specially designed instruction means adapting, as appropriate to the needs of an eligible child under this part, the content, methodology, or delivery of instruction—(i) To address the unique needs of the child that result from the child's disability; and (ii) To ensure access of the child to the general curriculum, so that he or she can meet the educational standards within the jurisdiction of the public agency that apply to all children (C.F.R. § 300.26).
- The State must have on file with the Secretary information to demonstrate that the State—(a) Has established goals for the performance of children with disabilities in the State that—(1) will promote the purposes of this part, as stated in § 300.1 and (2) are consistent, to the maximum extent appropriate, with other goals and standards for all children established by the State; (b) Has established performance indicators that the State will use to assess progress toward achieving those goals that, at a minimum, address the performance of children with disabilities on assessment, dropout rates, and graduation rates . . . (C.F.R. § 300.137).
- The State must have on file with the Secretary information to demonstrate that—(a) Children with disabilities are included in general State and district-wide assessment programs, with appropriate accommodations and modifications in administration, if necessary; (b) As appropriate, the State or LEA (1) develops guidelines for the participation of children with disabilities in alternate assessments for those children who cannot participate in State and district-wide assessment programs . . . (C.F.R. § 300.138).
- . . . In implementing the requirements of § 300.138, the SEA shall make available to the public, and report to the public with the same frequency and in the same detail as it reports on the assessment of nondisabled children, the following information: (1) The number of children with disabilities participating (i) in regular assessments, and (ii) in alternate assessments . . . (C.F.R. § 300.139).

IEP

- . . . The IEP for each child with a disability must include—(1) A statement of the child's present levels of educational performance, including (i) how the child's disability affects the child's involvement and progress in the general curriculum (i.e., the same curriculum as for nondisabled children); . . . (2) A statement of measurable annual goals, including benchmarks or short-term objectives, related to (i) meeting the child's needs that result from the child's disability to enable the child to be involved in and progress in the general curriculum . . . and (ii) meeting each of the child's other educational needs that result from the child's disability; (3) A statement of the special education and related services and supplementary aids and services to be provided to the child, or on behalf of the child, and a statement of the program modifications or supports for school personnel that will be provided for the child (i) to advance appropriately toward attaining the annual goals, (ii) to be educated and participate with other children with disabilities and nondisabled children in the activities described in this section; (4) An explanation of the extent, if any, to which the child will not participate with nondisabled children in the regular class and in the activities described in paragraph (a)(3) of this section; (5)(i) A statement of any individual modifications in the administration of State or district-wide assessments of student achievement that are needed in order for the child to participate in the assessment, and (ii) if the IEP team determines that the child will not participate in a particular State or district-wide assessment of student achievement (or part of an assessment), a statement of: (A) Why that assessment is not appropriate for the child; and (B) How the child will be assessed . . . (C.F.R. § 300.347).

Other Citations from the IDEA Regulations:

- C.F.R. § 300.532 Evaluation procedures.
- C.F.R. § 300.550 General LRE requirements.
- C.F.R. § 300.551 Continuum of alternative placements.
- C.F.R. § 300.552 Placements.
- C.F.R. § 300.553 Nonacademic settings.
- C.F.R. Appendix A to Part 300—Notice of Interpretation—I. Involvement and Progress of Each Child with a Disability in the General Curriculum (12470–12472).

FIGURE 9.2   *Regulatory Support for School Reform Under the IDEA (1997)*

does not mean 'fixing' of special education, increased 'mainstreaming,' or partial integration opportunities for students in special education programs. Rather, it is a challenge to the very nature of the dual system."

SUMMARY

The school reform movement is not a passing fad. The individual type of reform may pass, but the concept of reform will remain. The school administrator should take note of the strengths and weaknesses associated with each type of reform as one means of refining his/her school program. To assist the administrator in dealing with school reform issues, practical case studies follow this chapter.

CASE 9.1: "SCHOOL REFORM IS WITH US. WE NEED TO PREPARE FOR THE FUTURE."

"Hello, my name is Bill Freeman. I will be presiding over this National School Board Association's Pre-Conference Meeting. The speaker, Dr. Amy Poger, is a nationally known authority on school reform. She comes to us with exceptional credentials. She has been a principal, a superintendent, and currently is the Healey Distinguished Professor of Educational Administration at State University. Dr. Poger has written extensively on school reform. I have known Amy for many years and know that you will learn a great deal today. Dr. Poger may say some things that you do not want to hear, but listen and reflect on her comments. I am pleased to present to you Dr. Amy Poger."

Dr. Poger shook hands with Bill as she was walking up to the podium. She looked at the audience of 200 and said, "School reform is not a passing fad. If public schools are to survive, changes must be made to the basic way we approach schooling. If changes are going to be made school board members must take the lead and take the training necessary to understand school reform. Lasting changes will not come just because boards of education dictate change. Change will come because each board member will be trained in the programs that they want implemented. I know that the board members in the audience are saying, 'How in the world can we be expected to spend more time on school board work? We have full time jobs.' I understand your concern. I hope that in some way the issues that we discuss today will assist you in making some headway into the world that awaits all of us—educational reform."

"Now, please turn to the first page of the manual that you were given when you came into the conference room today. The first stage, understanding the nature of reform, lists an overview of my research. The data points to the charter school reform as the one concept that will, in the near future, make an impact on public education. The movement has seen unprecedented growth. Within the next few years it is projected that there will be from 3,000 to 5,000 charter schools in the United States. Charter schools will impact districts in the areas of finance and governance."

"I do believe though, that site-based management offers us the best opportunity to make changes, if carried out properly." She went on to review the research on site-based management.

A member of the audience raised her hand and asked, "Dr. Poger, I don't mean to interrupt but what would the effect of the various reforms have on special education?" "Thank you for asking that question. I will go into the relationship between special education and the reform movement later, but let me spend just a few moments answering your question. One of the areas within the reform movement that has intrigued me most is special education. I believe that before you take on the cause of school reform you should take on the cause of reforming your special education program. I hope that you will consider reforming education so that it will focus upon all children. I will go into an in-depth review of special education later this afternoon."

"Now, what do charter schools, vouchers, site-based management, and other school reforms have in

(Continue)

CASE 9.1 (CONTINUED)

common? They offer the parent empowerment. They offer the parent an opportunity to 'customize' a school, or help them to develop 'niche' programming. They offer the potential for parents to have a voice, what they believe is a true voice in their children's future."

Christopher Boyd, president of the Hill Town School District School Board, leaned over to the board's vice president and said, "Jack, Dr. Poger brought up some very interesting points. The issue of board training is something that has been one of my interests for a long time. She was right on the mark about parents beginning to demand changes. How do we begin to move our district into the twenty-first century?"

G. Jack Hall nodded and pointed to a word he had just written down, "Empowerment," he whispered. " Let me tell you about the discussion I had last week; I'll go over it at the break."

Dr. Poger spoke for another hour. She looked at her watch and said, "Let's take a fifteen-minute break. When we come back I would like for you to have thought about this question, 'What can I do to help all children to learn?' Notice that I said all."

As they were walking out of the conference room, Jack opened a can of soda and said, "Chris, when I was at the Lion's Club meeting last week I had a conversation with Mary Ann Weber. She believes that schools in our district should begin to look at various reforms that other districts are beginning to embrace. As a long-standing member of the community and president of the bank, she does have a great deal of influence. She is very concerned about special education. She wants to see more of the regular education teachers involved in working with the special education students. She has asked me if the board and the staff understands IDEA '97."

"Did you know that her daughter has a severe learning disability? I believe that she will begin to push the board and the community in the direction of change. I agree with Mary Ann. Our special education program needs to be studied in light of reauthorized IDEA and push-in programs. Our achievement scores need to improve. I want the board to be proactive in pushing the district to change."

Chris replied, "Jack, you are right. Change needs to take place with us or it will happen in spite of us. We have two charter school applications coming to us next month. How do we handle those applications? There are a number of questions with very few answers."

Dr. Poger came to the front of the room and asked that audience members be seated. She called for volunteers to answer the question that she had asked before the break. Many of the audience members had misgivings about the practicality of some of the reform movement, but there seemed to be consensus concerning the need for change in meeting the needs of all children.

Dr. Poger began the last two parts of the presentation. The first dealt with reform and special education. The last part of the presentation covered a board of education's responsibility toward the implementation of a program. At the conclusion of the presentation, Chris and Jack walked up to Dr. Poger and asked if they could have a few minutes of her time. They asked her questions about reform and about special education. Dr. Poger spent the next 20 minutes discussing the problems that faced districts that were implementing various reform initiatives. She also gave them the names of school districts that were changing their approach to special education programs.

Chris was seated next to Don O'Brien, the superintendent of the Hill Town School District, on the flight back. He shared his perceptions of the various meetings he attended, but spent most of the flight discussing change. He told the superintendent that he wanted a report on possible reform initiatives that the district might implement. He was especially interested in site-based management, charter schools, and IDEA '97.

Note to the reader: You will now be asked questions about this case. Before you read the Questions and Reflections section at the end of the book (Appendix A), you should fill out a case study analysis (Appendix C), then answer the questions and share your ideas with the class.

Questions

1. You are the superintendent of schools for the Hill Town School District. How would you organize your staff to prepare for a board of education work session?
2. You are the director of special education. Review some of the issues that may face you and your staff under site-based management.
3. What would be the effect of a charter school on the management of special education in your district?

CASE 9.2: " WE NEED TO DISCUSS SCHOOL REFORM AND SPECIAL EDUCATION."

Dr. Don O'Brien entered the office of the school district's attorney, Louis Beckmann. He had scheduled the meeting with the attorney to discuss a board of education work session that would take place in two weeks. The president of the Hill Town school board had requested that Don and his staff prepare a report on various school reforms. The board president also wanted to know the effect that reform would have on special education.

Dr. O'Brien was interested in what Mr. Beckmann had to say concerning the district's responsibility concerning various school reform initiatives. Mr. Beckmann had attended a preconference meeting of the Education Law Association (ELA). The preconference dealt with school reform, which was a particular interest of his.

During the meeting Mr. Beckmann reviewed for Dr. O'Brien his belief that with respect to each of these reforms, it would be beneficial for the district to take a proactive approach. He felt that anything that the district could do to assist the reform effort would only strengthen the district's position if litigation would ever be initiated. Like Don, he also believed that staff development and board development were the key to the success of any new program. He gave as examples the problems that he saw in the area of site-based management and in the implementation of charter schools. Since the district was either involved in, or was soon to be involved with both reforms, he felt that the board should concentrate on studying them.

When Don returned to his office, he called together his director of special education, director of human resources, and the assistant superintendents for elementary and secondary education. He reviewed what the attorney had said concerning school reform. Don was interested in hearing what each of his cabinet members had to say about the changes that were coming to the district. Each of the cabinet members had started their careers in the district. They had seen the district at its high point—at one time the district was considered a model district—and they saw its slow decline.

After the cabinet meeting Don called the board president, Christopher Boyd, and said, "Chris, if you have a few minutes I would like to review what our attorney and my staff had to say about the report that you requested. I am going to recommend that we have a board work session to in-service the board. Further, I am going to recommend that we incorporate a work session into each of our next four meetings. I don't think that in one meeting we can cover, in-depth, school reform."

Christopher pulled out the file he had started on school reform. He took out the notes that he had taken during Dr. Poger's presentation. He replied, "I agree with you. I don't think we will have problems with the rest of the board. I do have one request and a recommendation. Go ahead and schedule the meetings. Send out a draft copy of the material that you will cover the week before the work session. Since you have spoken to our attorney you need to include his comments in the report. I like the idea of an open board meeting to study this topic. I know that we will learn a great deal as will the general public that attends. Are you going to follow your usual format and have an executive summary for the media? Now I have a recommendation that I think you need to consider for the meeting. I think that you need to include a preliminary overview of IDEA '97. One of the National School Board meetings that I attended focused on our responsibility in making sure that it is properly implemented."

"Chris, I intend on having the material go out to the board at the end of this week. I will also have prepared an executive summary for the media. As usual it will be given to any member of the media that attends the board meeting, and sent out to those that cannot be at the session. I will make sure that IDEA '97 is part of the presentation. I don't have any additional matters to discuss, do you?" he asked. Christopher said, "No I don't, but I will need to see you about an issue dealing with the high school track."

"I will see you at the Chamber meeting next week," Don said as he ended the conversation.

Note to the reader: You will now be asked questions about this case. Before you read the Questions and Reflections section at the end of the book (Appendix A), you should fill out a case study analysis (Appendix C), then answer the questions and share your ideas with the class.

Questions:

1. As the director of special education what would you list as the key issues that the board members need to know about IDEA '97?
2. What can districts do to ensure that first-year teachers and experienced teachers understand their responsibility to develop the knowledge and implementation strategies necessary to meet the standards of IDEA '97?
3. What should a school district do to ensure that school reform initiatives meet special education requirements?

CHAPTER 10

❧

DISCIPLINE IN SPECIAL EDUCATION

This chapter addresses the difficult issue of discipline for students with disabilities. The IDEA regulations serve as a foundation for this chapter. Discipline is discussed from a systems perspective, presenting how the building level system, special education system and district level system must work together to provide FAPE. Procedures for addressing drugs, weapons, behavior likely to result in injury, and students not in special education are represented. Best practice issues are then addressed. After reading this chapter and analyzing the cases, you should be able to:

- Describe actions to be taken by the building level system, special education system, and district level system in a disciplinary situation involving a student with a disability or who may have a disability.
- Describe how the law applies to students who may have a disability.
- Develop a proactive, district-wide plan or approach-based best practice to effectively handle discipline for a child with a disability or who may have a disability.

See semantic map detailing Chapter 10 on page 171.

OVERVIEW

Discipline of students with disabilities has been and continues to be controversial in the field of education. To illustrate the controversy, consider the following scenarios.

1. A high school student has been caught with marijuana in his pocket. The student is labeled learning disabled under the IDEA. The student has never been a discipline problem in the past.
2. A sixth grade student has an unloaded pistol in his locker and has been caught by the principal trying to get the gun out of the locker. The student is labeled behavior disordered under the IDEA.
3. A first grader brings his father's one-inch pocket knife to school to show his friends. The student is not in special education, but is experiencing academic difficulties.
4. A junior high student ran down the hallway into a teacher, almost knocking her over. When confronted by the teacher, the student yelled obscenities and

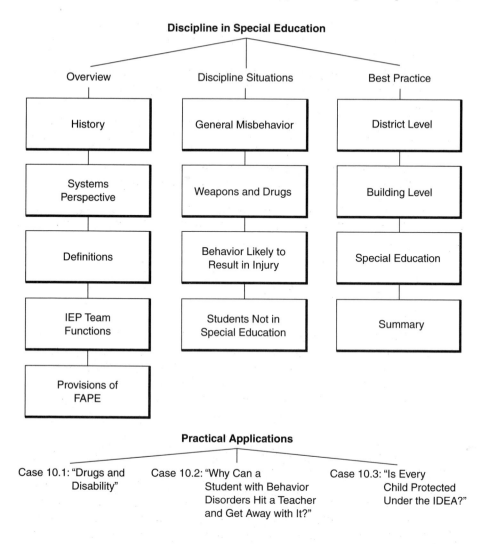

Discipline in Special Education

Overview	Discipline Situations	Best Practice
History	General Misbehavior	District Level
Systems Perspective	Weapons and Drugs	Building Level
Definitions	Behavior Likely to Result in Injury	Special Education
IEP Team Functions	Students Not in Special Education	Summary
Provisions of FAPE		

Practical Applications

Case 10.1: "Drugs and Disability"	Case 10.2: "Why Can a Student with Behavior Disorders Hit a Teacher and Get Away with It?"	Case 10.3: "Is Every Child Protected Under the IDEA?"

kept running. The student is labeled mildly mentally impaired in the special education program.

- What can or should happen in each of these cases?
- Should the building principal take action?
- What about the special education administrator or district superintendent?
- Should these students receive the same punishments as their regular education peers?

These real-life scenarios illustrate the importance of all administrators having current knowledge about how to discipline students with disabilities. By reading this chapter, the reader will be able to answer the questions posed about the scenarios.

History

Until the 1997 reauthorization of the IDEA, school districts looked to the court system to provide guidance in disciplining students with disabilities. The most prominent case, *Honig v. Doe,* was decided by the U.S. Supreme Court in 1988. In this case, two students with behavior disorders were expelled from school for violent and disruptive behavior. The Supreme Court ruled that the students' behavior was a manifestation of their disabilities and that expulsion would violate the students' right to a free appropriate public education. The Court essentially said that removals of students for disciplinary reasons will have restrictions, i.e., a principal cannot remove a student with a disability unilaterally more than ten days without an IEP meeting. In providing other school districts with guidance, the Court said that a student with a disability can be suspended for ten days, the school district can request a court injunction to remove the student from school for more than ten days if the parents and school district can't agree on an interim placement, and, if a due process hearing is requested, the student would remain in his/her then-current placement. This important case set the foundation for discipline of students with disabilities.

Systems Perspective

One useful perspective from which to view the discipline of children with disabilities is a systems perspective. Systems perspective, as applied to discipline, suggests viewing actions taken in a discipline situation in context and emphasizes a circular causality model (Becvar and Becvar 1982). Circular causality suggests that systems, people, events, and things reciprocally influence one another. In discipline, three systems are involved: the building level system, the special education system, and the district level system. All three systems are interrelated when the discipline of children with disabilities is involved. Figure 10.1 is a Venn diagram that shows the interrelationship between the three systems. An action within one system usually affects the other systems. As an example, consider the following situation:

> James, a ninth grade student with behavior disorders, places a note in his locker threatening to blow up the school, and the principal finds the note. The building level system, i.e., principal, is able to suspend James for 10 days, assuming there is not a previous pattern of suspensions. The building level system probably would also involve the police. If persons at the building level take further action, e.g., 20 consecutive days suspension, the action is not consistent with the IDEA. Depending on local district policy, the building level action following a 10-day suspension would probably lead to a request for an IEP meeting. The special education system would guide the situation through planning and carrying out a functional behavioral assessment (assessment of the antecedent and consequences of the behavior), planning a behavioral intervention plan (strategies and supports written as part of the IEP to address the problem behavior), making a manifestation determination (the IEP team determines if the problem behavior is related to the child's disability), and possibly a placement change. If the behavior is a manifestation of the disability, the school district system could not expel the student from school. If the behavior is not a manifestation of the disability, it is likely that the school district system would become involved in an expulsion hearing and decision.

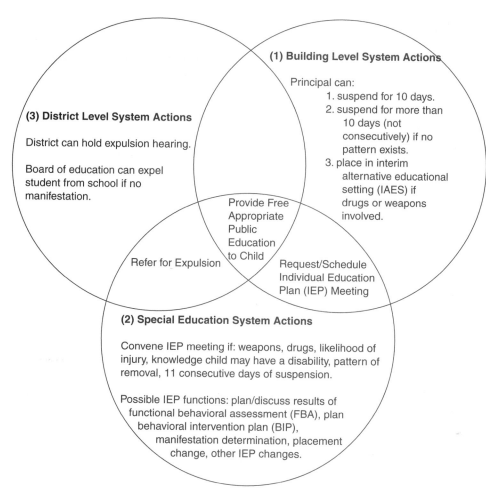

Note: Figure 10.1 is intended to provide an overview of how systems are interrelated in discipline, not specific procedures.

FIGURE 10.1   *Systems Perspective: Discipline for Children with Disabilities.*

The three systems—building level system, special education system, and district level system—are interrelated and must work together in a coordinated manner. If one system is not knowledgeable of its responsibilities, options for action, and limitations of action, the student in question will not be provided a free appropriate public education (FAPE).

Definitions

The reauthorization of the IDEA in 1997 and subsequent regulations provided specific mandates for the discipline of students with disabilities. To completely understand the provisions of the statutory law, it is essential that administrators understand and become familiar with specific terms used. These terms are listed and defined in Figure 10.2. It is important to note that two of the terms, functional behavioral

Change of placement Removal from school for more than 10 consecutive school days or a series of removals that constitute a pattern (must look at length of each removal, total amount of time removed, proximity of removals to each other) (C.F.R. § 300.519).

Interim alternative educational setting (IAES) An alternative placement that must be selected to enable the child to continue to progress in the general curriculum (in another setting) and to continue to receive services that will enable the child to meet IEP goals (C.F.R. § 300.522 (b)(1)); must include services to address the behavior which is the subject of the discipline and must be designed to prevent the behavior from reoccurring (C.F.R. § 300.522 (b)(2)).

Manifestation determination An IEP meeting whose purpose is to determine if a relationship exists between the behavior resulting in discipline and the child's disability; the IEP team must consider:

(1) all relevant evaluation data;
(2) observation of the student; and
(3) the student's IEP and placement (C.F.R. § 300.523(c)(1)(i–iii)).

The IEP team determines if the behavior is related to the disability by considering the following:

(1) Was the IEP appropriate?
(2) Did the disability impair the student's ability to *understand* the impact and consequences of the behavior?
(3) Did the disability impair the student's ability to *control* the behavior? (C.F.R. § 300.523(c)(2)(i–iii))

If the IEP was not appropriate, if the student could not understand the impact and consequences of the behavior due to the disability, or if the student could not control the behavior because of the disability, the behavior is a manifestation of the disability.

Functional behavioral assessment (FBA) Used in the IDEA Regulations, but not defined—could be considered as an assessment of the antecedent and consequences of the behavior that is subject to the discipline.

Behavioral intervention plan (BIP) Used in the IDEA Regulations, but not defined—could be considered as appropriate strategies and supports written as part of the IEP designed to address the problem behavior and to prevent it from reoccurring.

FIGURE 10.2   *Definitions of Discipline*

assessment (FBA) and behavioral intervention plan (BIP), are used in the IDEA Regulations, but are not defined. A functional behavioral assessment could be considered as an assessment of the antecedent and consequences of the behavior that is subject to discipline. For example, if a 9th grade student with learning disabilities was involved in a fight at school, the IEP team conducting a functional behavioral assessment might investigate what happened prior to and after the incident, and in what context. A behavioral intervention plan could be considered as appropriate strategies and supports written as part of the IEP designed to address the problem behavior and to prevent it from reoccurring. In the example cited above, the FBA might reveal that the fight occurred in the hallway during class passing time with two other students. The IEP team might include in the BIP peer mediation and conflict resolution training for this student. Defining these terms may present a challenge to the law as school districts and states strive to define them.

IEP Team Functions

The definitions in Figure 10.2 relate directly to the IEP meeting. A change in placement is triggered any time removal from school for disciplinary reasons exceeds 10 consecutive days or results in a pattern of removals. In this case, the IEP team, including the parent, must become involved and becomes pivotal in ensuring FAPE for the child. In a disciplinary situation, the IEP team could serve the following functions: determine the child's interim alternative educational setting (IAES) in cases involving drugs or weapons, plan or discuss the results of the child's functional behavioral assessment (FBA) and develop the child's behavioral intervention plan (BIP), conduct a manifestation determination, and/or make other changes to the child's IEP.

One function of the IEP team is to determine the nature of the child's proposed IAES. An IAES can be ordered by a principal if drugs or weapons are involved or by a hearing officer or judge if there is a likelihood that the child might harm him- or herself or others if returned to the previous placement. The IDEA Regulations state that the IAES must be determined by the IEP team and the placement must be selected to enable the child to continue to progress in the general curriculum and to continue to receive services that will enable the child to meet IEP goals. In addition, the IAES must include services to address the behavior for which the child is being disciplined and must be designed to prevent the behavior from reoccurring.

A second function of the IEP team is to plan the child's FBA, if the school district did not conduct one, or discuss results of the child's FBA. The FBA must be related to the behavior that resulted in the suspension. The IEP team's role is to develop an assessment plan and carry out the plan. As soon as the child is assessed, the IEP team must discuss the results and develop an appropriate behavioral intervention plan.

A third function of the IEP team in a disciplinary situation is to conduct a manifestation determination. In this meeting, the IEP team determines if a relationship exists between the child's behavior and his/her disability. The IDEA Regulations give guidance in how this determination is made. The IEP team must consider the following:

- All relevant evaluation data;
- Observation of the student; and
- The student's IEP and placement.

The manifestation determination is made by answering the following questions:

- Was the IEP appropriate? If it was not, the behavior is a manifestation of the disability.
- Did the disability impair the student's ability to understand the impact and consequences of the behavior? If the student did not understand, the behavior is a manifestation of the disability.

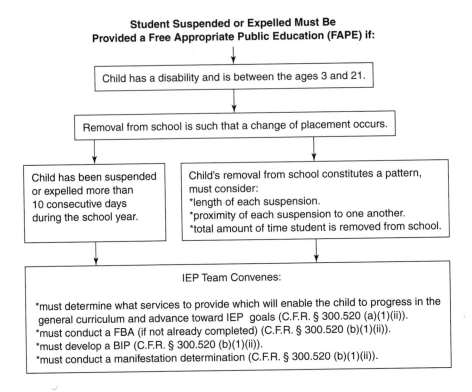

**Student Suspended or Expelled Must Be
Provided a Free Appropriate Public Education (FAPE) if:**

Child has a disability and is between the ages 3 and 21.

Removal from school is such that a change of placement occurs.

Child has been suspended or expelled more than 10 consecutive days during the school year.

Child's removal from school constitutes a pattern, must consider:
*length of each suspension.
*proximity of each suspension to one another.
*total amount of time student is removed from school.

IEP Team Convenes:

*must determine what services to provide which will enable the child to progress in the general curriculum and advance toward IEP goals (C.F.R. § 300.520 (a)(1)(ii)).
*must conduct a FBA (if not already completed) (C.F.R. § 300.520 (b)(1)(ii)).
*must develop a BIP (C.F.R. § 300.520 (b)(1)(ii)).
*must conduct a manifestation determination (C.F.R. § 300.520 (b)(1)(ii)).

FIGURE 10.3   *Discipline: When FAPE Must Be Provided*

- Did the disability impair the student's ability to control the behavior? If the student could not, the behavior is a manifestation of the disability.

If the behavior is a manifestation of the disability, the student cannot be expelled from school. However, the IEP team may change the student's placement and this placement could be outside of the regular school.

Provision of FAPE

The bottom line in discipline is that, regardless of the behavior or student involved, a school district must continue to provide FAPE to a child with disabilities. The IDEA Regulations state, "FAPE is available to all children with disabilities, ages 3 through 21, residing in the State, including children with disabilities who have been suspended or expelled from school" (IDEA Regulations, 34 C.F.R. 300.300 (a)). Figure 10.3 illustrates the general procedural provisions that must occur to assure that the student is provided with a FAPE.

DISCIPLINE SITUATIONS

The IDEA addresses discipline in four specific circumstances: (1) general misbehavior, (2) weapons and drugs, (3) behavior likely to result in injury, and (4) students not

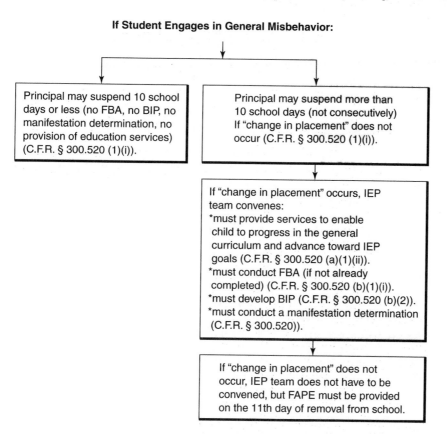

If Student Engages in General Misbehavior:

Principal may suspend 10 school days or less (no FBA, no BIP, no manifestation determination, no provision of education services) (C.F.R. § 300.520 (1)(i)).

Principal may suspend more than 10 school days (not consecutively) If "change in placement" does not occur (C.F.R. § 300.520 (1)(i)).

If "change in placement" occurs, IEP team convenes:
*must provide services to enable child to progress in the general curriculum and advance toward IEP goals (C.F.R. § 300.520 (a)(1)(ii)).
*must conduct FBA (if not already completed) (C.F.R. § 300.520 (b)(1)(i)).
*must develop BIP (C.F.R. § 300.520 (b)(2)).
*must conduct a manifestation determination (C.F.R. § 300.520)).

If "change in placement" does not occur, IEP team does not have to be convened, but FAPE must be provided on the 11th day of removal from school.

FIGURE 10.4   *Discipline: General Misbehavior*

eligible for special education. Each of these situations is addressed below to clarify how the three systems—building, special education, and district—must coordinate their actions to continue to provide FAPE to the child.

General Misbehavior

General misbehavior includes any behavior that isn't addressed by the IDEA under weapons and drugs. Examples of general misbehavior might be inappropriate language, stealing, tardiness, verbal abuse, or any other infraction in the school district disciplinary policy. The procedures for dealing with general misbehavior are outlined in Figure 10.4. Generally, the principal may suspend a student for 10 consecutive school days (or less) and not involve the special education system formally in an IEP meeting. No functional behavioral assessment, behavior intervention plan, manifestation determination, or provision of education services are required by the IDEA for suspensions of 10 consecutive school days or less.

The IDEA does suggest that a principal may suspend a student for more than 10 school days (not consecutively) if a "change in placement" does not occur. "Change in placement" is defined as suspending a child for more than 10 consecutive school days or where the removals constitute a pattern of removal from school. Although the IDEA does not define what is meant by a pattern of removal from school, it is suggested that the following be considered:

- Length of each suspension;
- Proximity of each suspension to one another;
- Total amount of time the student is removed from school.

If a child is suspended for more than 10 days and the principal thinks it does not constitute a pattern of removals from school, the child must be provided with education services on the 11th day of suspension, because the district is obligated to provide FAPE to each child with a disability. The nature of these services can be determined by the principal and special education teacher outside of an IEP meeting. As an example of general misbehavior, consider the following example:

> Jamil is a tenth grade student with learning disabilities. He continually taunts his peers in class until he disrupts the teaching process. His teacher warned him and applied appropriate consequences within the classroom. Because classroom intervention didn't seem to work, the special education teacher sent Jamil to the office and the principal suspended him for 3 days. This seemed to be effective. Later in the semester, Jamil became angry in a different class and used inappropriate language with the teacher. He was sent to the office and suspended for 5 days. A similar incident resulted in another 2-day suspension, making the total for the year 10 days. Jamil then seemed to be improving until the last month of school, when he was caught smoking in the bathroom. The principal consulted with Jamil's special education teacher and determined that a suspension for 3 additional days would not constitute a pattern of removal from school. The principal and special education teacher worked out a plan to continue Jamil's education for the 3-day suspension. No IEP meeting was held and Jamil was not suspended again that school year.

One must exercise extreme caution when suspending a child beyond 10 days in a school year. The law is not clear on when removals constitute a pattern. The law only gives general guidance on factors to consider when making that determination. In addition, the decision that removals do not constitute a pattern of removals is open to challenge and interpretation from parents, advocates, and attorneys. If it is determined that removals from school constitute a pattern, the special education system must become involved in convening an IEP meeting. If a student has already been removed for more than 10 days, it is too late to go back and provide the procedural protections of the law, i.e., IEP meeting. The most sound advice is for principals to suspend for only 10 days or less without involving the special education system. If more days are warranted, it is best practice to request an IEP meeting to determine what education services are necessary during suspension, conduct a functional behavioral assessment, develop a behavioral intervention plan, and conduct a manifestation determination. Although not required by law, it is better to be safe than sorry. In addition, it is wise for principals and special educators to consider any suspension from school as a "red flag" to review the student's program and services, even if the suspension is less than ten days. An IEP team might be able to prevent misbehavior by anticipating reoccurrence and conducting a FBA, developing a BIP, and/or changing services in the IEP.

> Weapon, device, instrument, material or substance, animate or inanimate, that is used for or is readily capable of causing death or serious bodily injury, except that such item does not include a pocket knife with a blade of less than 2 1/2 inches in length (18 U.S.C. § 930 (2)(g)).

FIGURE 10.5   *Definition of Dangerous Weapon*

Weapons and Illegal Drugs

The IDEA clearly indicates that weapons or drugs will not be tolerated in our schools. The language in the IDEA Regulations emphasizes the mandate to provide an appropriate education to all children with disabilities and, at the same time, reflects a zero tolerance philosophy adopted by many schools and society in general. Zero tolerance could have several meanings, but in this context it means that certain behaviors (e.g., bringing a gun to school) will not be tolerated under any circumstances and will result in a certain consequence (e.g., police contacted) regardless of who engages in the behavior.

If a student with disabilities engages in the following misbehavior, the three systems—building, special education, and district—should become involved.

- Carrying or possessing a weapon at school or at a school function.
- Knowingly possessing or using illegal drugs or selling or soliciting the sale of a controlled substance at school or at a school function.

The term "weapon" is defined in Figure 10.5.

Figure 10.6 outlines specific procedures to follow if a student with disabilities is involved in using drugs or carrying a weapon. To illustrate, consider the following example:

> Andy, a seventh grade student with learning disabilities, brings a loaded gun to school. At the building level, the principal can suspend the child for 10 days. In addition, he/she can order Andy to an interim alternate educational setting (IAES) for up to 45 calendar days. As local district policy dictates, the police could become involved and Andy could be arrested. Any action beyond these actions would be in violation of the IDEA. Because district policy often dictates that any student with weapons or drugs will be referred for expulsion and because an IAES is involved, the principal must involve the special education system. During the 10-day suspension, the IEP team would convene. The IEP team would determine what the IAES will be for Andy and would develop a plan for conducting a functional behavioral assessment (assuming one has not already been conducted). In addition, the team would develop a behavioral intervention plan based on the functional behavioral assessment, if one has been conducted, and conduct a manifestation determination. If the IEP team determines that Andy's behavior of bringing a gun to school is not a manifestation of his disability, Andy could be expelled from school by the board of education, but FAPE must continue to be provided. FAPE could be provided by placing Andy in an alternative school, for example. If it is determined that his behavior is a manifestation of his disability, he cannot be expelled from school. In that case, Andy would return to school on the 46th day after his IAES unless the school district and parents agreed to a placement change. If Andy and his parents disagreed with the 45-day IAES or expulsion from school,

If Student:

(1) carries a weapon to school or to a school function
(C.F.R. § 300.520 (a)(2)(i)); or

(2) knowingly possesses or uses illegal drugs or sells or solicits the sale of a controlled substance at school or at a school function (C.F.R. § 300.520 (a)(2)(ii)),

Principal can order the child to an IAES for up to 45 calendar days (C.F.R. § 300.520 (a)(2)(i)) and suspend for 10 days.

IEP team convenes:
* must determine what the IAES will be.
* must conduct a FBA (C.F.R. § 300.522).
* must develop a BIP (C.F.R. § 300.520 (b)(1)(i–ii)).
* must conduct a manifestation determination (C.F.R. § 300.523).

Day 46: Student returns to the previous placement unless parent and school district agree; otherwise, an IEP meeting or a court order extends the IAES.

FIGURE 10.6   *Discipline: Weapons or Drugs*

they could request an expedited due process hearing. During the hearing, Andy would stay in the IAES.

This case illustrates the complexities of discipline for students who become involved with weapons or drugs. The IDEA Regulations give more authority to school officials at the building level to immediately remove a student and make placement in an IAES in the case of drugs or weapons.

Behavior Likely to Result in Injury

Sometimes in a school setting, a student will engage in serious misbehavior for which the principal may not order the child to be placed in an IAES because drugs or weapons were not involved. Examples might include a student threatening to kill someone, a student destroying school property by cutting a teacher's car tires, or a student fighting with another student. These are often the most difficult cases for building principals because the student with disabilities can only be suspended for 10 consecutive days, but the incident is often serious enough to warrant more severe consequences. These kinds of situations illustrate the difficulty that exists when disciplining students in special education and students in regular education, i.e., the regular education student might be expelled for cutting the tires, but the student in special education whose behavior is a manifestation of his disability can only be suspended for 10 days, with a possible placement change determined by the IEP team.

If a student with disabilities engages in serious misbehavior likely to result in injury and the school district thinks that the student is too dangerous to return to

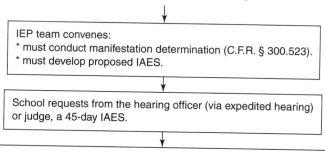

If Student Engages in Misbehavior Likely to Result in Injury and School Wants Student Removed Due to Dangerous Situation:

IEP team convenes:
* must conduct manifestation determination (C.F.R. § 300.523).
* must develop proposed IAES.

School requests from the hearing officer (via expedited hearing) or judge, a 45-day IAES.

Hearing officer or judge makes a decision on approval of the IAES by considering the following:
* Has the district provided substantial evidence that the child is substantially likely to injure him/herself or others? (C.F.R. § 300.521 (a)
* Is the current placement appropriate? (C.F.R. § 300.521 (b)
* Has the district taken reasonable steps to reduce the risk of harm in the current placement? (C.F.R. § 300.521 (c)
* Is the proposed IAES appropriate? (C.F.R. § 300.521 (d)

FIGURE 10.7   *Discipline: Misbehavior Likely to Result in Injury*

school, the building level system, i.e., building principal, must involve the special education system. The procedures to follow are outlined in Figure 10.7. If the school district wants to place the student in an IAES for 45 days, the school district must first convene an IEP meeting to conduct a manifestation determination and a proposed IAES. It would also be best practice to conduct a FBA and develop a BIP. Next, the district must request an expedited due process hearing. At the hearing, a hearing officer makes a decision on the proposed IAES by considering the following:

- Has the district provided substantial evidence that the child is substantially likely to injure him- or herself or others? Substantial evidence means beyond a preponderance of the evidence.
- Is the current placement appropriate?
- Has the district taken reasonable steps to reduce the risk of harm in the current placement?
- Is the proposed IAES appropriate?

To illustrate, consider the following situation:

Billy, an eighth grade student with behavior disorders and learning disabilities, became upset during a physical education class and hit the teacher. Billy was immediately suspended for 10 days. The special education administrator convened an IEP meeting where it was determined that Billy's behavior was a manifestation of his disability. The IEP team wanted to place Billy in a private day treatment facility for students with behavior disorders, but his mother objected. The district requested an expedited due process hearing to place Billy in the facility. The district also requested that Billy be placed in the facility as an IAES because he was likely to injure others if he returned to his current placement at the junior high school. The hearing officer ruled against the school district stating that Billy was not substantially likely to hurt himself or someone else, as this was the only incident in his school career where he had hit someone. The school district administrators were very unhappy, because Billy had to return to his previous placement after his 10-day suspension.

This case is an example of the double standard in discipline. If the student had been in regular education, the probable outcome would have been expulsion.

Students Not in Special Education

If a student not eligible for special education services violates a school rule, the student should be disciplined in accordance with the district's discipline policy and procedures unless the district had knowledge that the student may have a disability (IDEA Regulations, 34 C.F.R. § 300.527). If any of the following apply to the student, the district "has knowledge" that the student may have a disability.

- The parent of the child has expressed concern in writing (or orally if the parent cannot write) to the school that the child is in need of special education services.
- The behavior or performance of the child demonstrates the need for special education services.
- The parent of the child has requested an evaluation of the child in writing to school district personnel prior to the incident that prompted the disciplinary action.
- The child's teacher or other school personnel expressed concern about the behavior or performance of the child to district personnel responsible for the referral system in special education.

Not included in "having knowledge" that a child may have a disability would be if the child was evaluated for special education and found not eligible for services or if the child was referred for an evaluation and it was determined that an evaluation was not needed.

These regulations present a practical problem for educators because if the district has knowledge that the child may have a disability, the child is entitled to assert any of the protections provided for in the IDEA. To illustrate, consider the following example:

> Jill was an eleventh grade student in regular education who was found with marijuana in her possession. Jill said that she was given the marijuana by another student. The school district policy was to suspend for ten days any student with illegal drugs, then hold an expulsion hearing and possibly expel the student from school. Jill's mother objected to the suspension and possible expulsion. She asserted that Jill had a behavior disorder that was not recognized by the school district and was in need of special education services. Upon further investigation, it was found that two of Jill's teachers expressed concern in writing to Jill's counselor and parent about her progress in their classes. Jill was failing to complete assignments and skipped class frequently. One of the teachers even held a parent conference with Jill's mother prior to the marijuana incident. Ultimately, the school district conducted an expedited evaluation of Jill and found her eligible for behavior disorders services. It was determined that her disability was related to the behavior in question. An IEP was developed and Jill was placed in a behavior disorders program. Jill was not expelled from school.

If the school district has no knowledge that a child may have a disability, the same disciplinary procedures used with other children may be applied. If regular discipline procedures are applied and a request is made for a special education evaluation, the school district must conduct the evaluation quickly and apply procedural protections if the child is eligible for special education services.

BEST PRACTICE

Generally, school administrators should be proactive when approaching discipline of students with disabilities. It is far better to anticipate a possible problem and deal with it early than be surprised by a major problem and have to react quickly. Although it is not always possible to avoid problems in discipline, proactive thinking will decrease the number of problems in discipline. If districts, buildings, and teachers create a positive climate for learning, have caring and responsive teachers, and use appropriate curriculum for all children, it is likely that discipline concerns will be reduced. Creative approaches—like using wraparound services where the community, family, and school work together to remove barriers to success for individual students—could prevent discipline problems. Described below are some actions considered best practice and proactive.

District Level Best Practice

- Implement school board-approved policy and procedures for discipline that are consistent with state and federal law in special education.
- In-service administrators and teachers annually on policy and procedures in discipline.
- Set up a mentoring system for new administrators so that prior to making the decision, they can quickly get feedback on potentially serious decisions regarding students with disabilities.
- Board members should be in-serviced on special education law involving discipline with students who have or may have disabilities.
- Input from the IEP team should be considered in making decisions about possible expulsion from school.
- Consider and implement creative approaches to programming for students, e.g., peer mediation, wraparound programs, mentoring, after-school programs, parenting programs.

Building Level Best Practice

- The building principal should not suspend a student with disabilities for more than 10 days in one school year. If more than 10 days of suspension is warranted, the principal should request an IEP meeting.
- If a student is approaching 10 days of suspension in a year (i.e., 7 to 9 days of suspension), the principal or special education teacher should request an IEP meeting to conduct a FBA and possibly implement a BIP. This is a proactive approach to avoid having to react to serious problems.
- The building principal should establish a procedure for reviewing all short-term suspensions to ensure that a pattern does not exist, especially if the total number of suspensions during the year is approaching 10 days or if multiple suspensions of less than 10 consecutive days exist, but total more

than 10 days during the year. This review team could involve the special education administrator and/or teacher, as well as other building level personnel. This review should be documented in the child's temporary file.

- Consider and implement creative approaches to working with children, e.g., peer mediation, wraparound programs, mentoring, after-school programming, parenting programs.
- Use the IEP team as a problem-solving team, to think creatively about how to help an individual student with disabilities.

Special Education Best Practice

- All teachers should be in-serviced on how to refer a child for special education if they "have knowledge" that the child may have a disability.
- The special education administrator should make sure that parents are properly notified of all IEP meetings and outcomes of the meetings.
- If a special education teacher thinks that a child's behavior interferes with his learning or others' learning, consider this a red flag and hold an IEP meeting to conduct a FBA and implement a BIP.
- Annually, review with students in special education the school discipline code and consequences for misbehavior. This should be documented in the student's temporary record.
- If in-school suspensions are to be used with a student, the use of these removals should be documented in the student's BIP.

SUMMARY

Each case in the discipline of children with disabilities must be considered individually and all administrators must be knowledgeable of district policy and procedures, state law, and federal law.

After reading this chapter, the reader should be able to answer what can or should happen in each of the four scenarios described at the beginning of this chapter. The first two cases, a high school student with marijuana and a sixth grade student with a pistol, are similar in one aspect. The building principal may suspend the student up to and including 10 days and order each student into an IAES for 45 days. This option is clearly specified in the IDEA Regulations. Beyond those actions, the special education system, via the IEP team, must become involved. Expulsion from school will depend upon the outcome of the manifestation determination decided by the IEP team. In any case, expulsion or not, the students must continue to receive FAPE.

The third scenario involved a regular education first grader with a one-inch pocket knife at school. In this case, if the student did not threaten anyone, the knife would not be considered a weapon. It must be determined if the school district "had knowledge" that the student may have a disability because it was stated that the student was experiencing academic difficulties. If the school district did "have knowledge" as defined in the IDEA Regulations, the student would be entitled to the protections under the IDEA. The principal could suspend the student for 10 days or less, but further action could not occur until an IEP meeting was held. This action might include an expedited evaluation for special education.

In the fourth case, a student who was mildly mentally impaired ran into a teacher while running down the hallway and shouted obscenities. In this case, the principal could suspend the student for 10 days. The special education system probably would become involved by convening an IEP meeting. The IEP team might make a manifestation determination, conduct a FBA, and plan a BIP. Further action, if appropriate, at the district level, would be dependent upon decisions reached by the IEP team.

In all cases concerning discipline of children with disabilities, the three systems—building level, special education, and district level—must be coordinated and work together. The parent could become involved in the district and/or building level systems. It is mandated that the parent be a participant in the IEP meeting. A parent would likely be most active at the building level and special education systems. The three systems work together to ensure that each child is disciplined in a fair manner and that FAPE in ensured.

You will now be presented with three real-life cases involving discipline. These cases address the following issues: drugs, verbal threats, physical violence, weapons, and students who may not be eligible for special education services. For each case, questions are posed that illustrate how the building level system, special education system, and district level system must work together.

CASE 10.1: "DRUGS AND DISABILITY"

Carlos was walking down the hallway of the high school where he worked as a hall monitor. He turned a corner that morning and saw a student glance at him, then quickly put a small box, like a cigarette box, in his pocket. Carlos knew something was up. The other students standing there scattered and Carlos confronted the student. The student's name tag that hung around his neck read "Terrance Smith." Carlos didn't know Terrance.

Carlos said, "Terrance, what did you just put in your pocket?"

Terrance looked at the floor, hesitated, then answered, "Uh, nothing, just a box."

"Terrance, let me see what is in your pocket," said Carlos.

Terrance reluctantly pulled the box out of his pocket and handed it to Carlos. Carlos opened the box and saw ten hand-rolled cigarettes, which looked like marijuana.

Carlos said, "Terrance, come with me to the office," and he escorted Terrance to the principal's office.

The principal talked to Terrance and asked him to tell his side of the story. Terrance said it was marijuana and that someone gave it to him. When asked who, Terrance would not reveal any names.

The principal, Anna Kohl, had dealt with drug cases before and she knew how to proceed. The district had a zero tolerance policy when dealing with students who had drugs in school. She first called Terrance's mother and said that Terrance would be suspended 10 days pending the outcome of an expulsion hearing. She then called the police who field-tested the substance. After it was confirmed to be marijuana, Terrance was arrested and his mother followed him to the police station where he was soon released to her.

Anna checked the computerized discipline records on Terrance and found that the only discipline report was five tardies to a history class during his ninth grade year. Terrance was now in tenth grade. Upon further review of his records, Anna found that Terrance had passed all classes in ninth grade, with average grades.

(Continue)

CASE 10.1 (CONTINUED)

After speaking to the counselor, she discovered that Terrance had a learning disability and received special education services. She then talked with one of his special teachers who said Terrance had been no problem in class, but was a loner.

Anna's next telephone call was to the superintendent to inform him of the situation. Mr. Welch appreciated being informed of any serious discipline situation and he told Anna to proceed according to district policy and procedures. Anna knew that if a student was in special education, there were other procedures to follow, but she wasn't sure exactly what they were, as they were not part of the district policy or procedures. Therefore, she contacted Adriana Martinez, the special education director.

"Adriana," Anna began, "I have a problem here concerning one of your students in special education. Terrance Smith was caught with marijuana. He's been arrested and suspended 10 days. I'm going to set up an expulsion hearing in the next day or so. You know that the district has a zero tolerance policy on drugs, so it's likely he will be expelled. Is there anything I need to do since he's in special education?"

Adriana quickly said, "There are several things we need to do. First, we could place him in an interim alternative educational setting for 45 days, but we have to hold an IEP meeting to determine what the setting will be."

This sounded great to Anna and she said, "I just want him out of this school as quickly as possible."

Adriana said, "I'll arrange an IEP meeting in the next week. I know his mother and I know she will be cooperative about taking off work to attend a meeting. I've worked with this family for the past nine years and they have always been supportive. First, I will contact Terrance's mother, Mrs. Smith, to inform her of the meeting and to gain her consent for a functional behavioral assessment. We'll have to discuss this at the meeting. Also, there will be other issues we'll have to address at the meeting and I'll list those on the meeting notice. Would Thursday of next week at 2:00 P.M. be OK with you for the meeting?"

Anna said, "That will be fine. I'll make sure Terrance's teachers are released so they can attend. I'll see you next Thursday."

The IEP meeting was scheduled for the following Thursday. In attendance at the meeting were the following participants: Carlos Rodriguez, hall monitor; Adriana Martinez, special education administrator; Mrs. Smith, parent; Anna Kohl, principal; Linda Stein, special education teacher; Joe Wagner, regular education math teacher; and Charles Cattaneo, school psychologist.

Ms. Martinez opened the meeting by asking participants to introduce themselves, then stating the purpose of the meeting. She said, "Our purpose in this meeting today is to accomplish three tasks: determine if there is a relationship between Terrance's behavior and the discipline incident of having marijuana at school; develop a behavior intervention plan based on the recent functional behavioral assessment; and determine Terrance's interim alternative educational setting."

The hall monitor was asked to review the behavioral incident and the principal summarized what happened in her office. She said, "Terrance has never been involved in a significant discipline problem prior to this incident. I think he's a good kid, but he made a very poor choice."

The special education teacher, Ms. Stein, summarized Terrance's performance in her classes by saying, "Terrance is well liked by the other students in my classes. He always completes his assignments. His IEP goals center around reading and writing skills, which are far below average. He is a hard worker and pleasant to have in class."

The regular education teacher, Mr. Wagner, concurred by saying, "Terrance has average skills in math, but he always needs extra help if there is reading involved. I usually send him to the special education teacher for help with the reading. Otherwise, he's an average student with no behavior problems."

The school psychologist, Mr. Cattaneo, reviewed the most recent evaluations of Terrance. "Terrance," he said, "has average ability, but functions four grade levels below his peer group in reading, and writing is difficult for him. His math is average. There are no indications of impulsivity in his recent evaluation."

The functional behavioral assessment results were reviewed. The team determined that Terrance probably got the drugs from a friend and was going to give them to someone else. There was no indication that Terrance was involved in drugs.

Mrs. Smith, Terrance's mother, was quiet as she said, "Terrance knows better than to get involved in drugs. He's never been in trouble before. I think he made a poor choice."

(Continue)

CASE 10.1 (CONTINUED)

IEP team participants concluded that Terrance's IEP was appropriate, that he understood the impact of his behavior, and that he was able to control his behavior. They also determined that Terrance should receive an interim alternative placement for 45 days. His IAES would be carried out by the special education teacher, who would meet with him two hours per day after school at his home. She would coordinate all assignments from his regular education teachers and continue to work on his IEP goals in reading and writing.

Ms. Martinez concluded the meeting by saying, "It is the consensus of this group that Terrance's behavior of having marijuana is not related to his learning disability. Therefore, he can be disciplined just like any other student. He will also be placed in an interim alternative educational setting specified in his IEP for 45 days. A behavior intervention plan, including a drug awareness program, will be implemented. The next step is to provide a review of this conference at the expulsion hearing, scheduled for next week."

The expulsion hearing was held and it was recommended to the board of education that Terrance be ex-

pelled for the remainder of the school year. The Board, in a special session, considered the recommendation and voted unanimously to expel Terrance for the remainder of the year. After 45 days in the interim alternative educational setting at home, educational services for Terrance ceased.

Note to the reader: You will now be asked questions about this case. Before you read the Questions and Reflections section at the end of the book (Appendix A), you should fill out the case study analysis (Appendix C), then answer the questions and share your ideas with the class.

Questions

1. Was the board of education correct when it voted to expel Terrance? How do you know?
2. Was it correct for educational services to cease after the 45-day interim alternative educational setting? Why or why not?
3. Make an outline of the procedure followed during this case. Was the procedure correct? Would you have done anything differently?

CASE 10.2: "WHY CAN A STUDENT WITH BEHAVIOR DISORDERS HIT A TEACHER AND GET AWAY WITH IT?"

Mr. Kaleem walked briskly to his classroom on a beautiful day in October as he had for twenty-three years. He was an English teacher at Martin Luther King Jr. High School. He put the eighth grade students assignments on the board before class began. After the bell rang, students began filing into the room and sitting at their assigned seats. Mr. Kaleem was a very strict teacher and he always had work for the students to begin as soon as they entered his classroom. Today students were to copy four sentences from the board and edit them for correct punctuation, spelling, and grammar. As the second bell rang, Muhammad Brooks walked into the room and slammed his books on the desk.

Mr. Kaleem said, "Muhammad, the assignment is on the board. Please begin working."

Muhammad looked at his teacher and said, "I don't have to do this if I don't want to."

The other students, who were working quietly, looked up as Mr. Kaleem walked over to Muhammad. He put his hand on Muhammad's shoulder and started to speak to him when Muhammad yelled, "Get your hands off me!" Muhammad jumped up and pounded his fist into Mr. Kaleem's cheek. Mr. Kaleem backed up holding his face and Muhammad walked out of the room.

Mr. Kaleem sent a student to the office for the principal who ran quickly to the classroom. Mr. Kaleem was taken to the hospital and was later diagnosed with a broken jaw. While Mr. Kaleem was at the hospital, the principal, Ms. Belk, found Muhammad walking out of the front door. She ordered him to her office and he

(Continue)

CASE 10.2 (CONTINUED)

complied. She immediately called the police and Muhammad's mother. Muhammad was arrested and released to his mother pending a court hearing. Ms. Belk suspended Muhammad for 10 days.

Ms. Belk contacted the superintendent, Ms. Luther, to inform her of the situation, then called the special education administrator, Mr. Li. She arranged to meet with Mr. Li and Ms. Luther that afternoon to discuss the situation.

During the meeting, the discussion became heated. Ms. Belk stood up and said, "You mean we have to take this student back into the junior high? What will I tell my faculty? A student with behavior disorders hits a teacher, but you have to take him back in school after 10 days suspension because he's in special education? I don't think the faculty will accept that line of logic."

Mr. Li calmly said, "I think I know how you feel, but the law is clear about what we can and can't do. What we need to do right now is conduct an IEP meeting. At the meeting, we will determine if Muhammad's behavior is related to his disability. We could also discuss the possibility of changing his IEP to placement at our day treatment facility for students with behavior disorders. If everyone agrees, Muhammad might not have to return to the junior high."

Ms. Belk said, "If this student returns to the junior high, I think the teacher's union will file a grievance. Let's just hope we can make the change to another facility for Muhammad."

Mr. Li arranged an IEP meeting two days later at the junior high school. In attendance were the following persons: Mrs. Brooks, Muhammad's mother; Mr. Kaleem, English teacher; Mr. Jackson, special education teacher; Ms. Leiter, school psychologist; Ms. Belk, principal; and Mr. Li.

During the meeting, Muhammad's recent evaluation and IEP were reviewed. Muhammad was in special education for two classes per day, math and social skills. His evaluation included a functional behavioral assessment that indicated Muhammad had difficulty with anger control. Even though he usually understood consequences of his behavior, he was impulsive and often unable to control his behavior. The IEP goals addressed anger control and the IEP behavior management plan stated that Muhammad should never be touched because he viewed touch in a threatening way. The English teacher, Mr. Kaleem, knew that Muhammad was a student in the behavior disorders program, but had never viewed his IEP. The team also discussed observations of Muhammad at school. These observations suggested that Muhammad had improved greatly in his ability to control his anger and that he was passing all of his classes. Based on the information presented and discussed, the team decided that Muhammad's behavior of hitting the teacher was related to his disability.

The discussion then turned to Muhammad's placement. Mrs. Brooks, who had been quiet until now, said, "I don't think Muhammad would have hit Mr. Kaleem if he had not put his hand on his shoulder."

Ms. Belk said, "Hand on shoulder or not, he should not be allowed to return to this school. What kind of message would that send to the other students?"

Mr. Li led a discussion on the type of program that Muhammad might need to gain control of his anger. He explained that the district had a day treatment facility for students with significant behavior disorders and that Muhammad would be a candidate for the program. The teachers felt that Muhammad could benefit from the program and the administrators concurred.

Mrs. Brooks said, "I don't want Muhammad in a facility with only behavior disordered students. He is a follower and his behavior will become worse. He made a mistake. I want him to return to this junior high, maybe with a different English teacher after his suspension is finished next week."

Mr. Li stated that the school staff involved in the meeting thought that Muhammad needed a change in placement and if she disagreed, she could request a due process hearing. The team then revised Muhammad's IEP to provide his placement at the day treatment facility. Mrs. Brooks was told that the new placement would begin the day after Muhammad's suspension ended. Mrs. Brooks received notice of the change and a copy of Muhammad's new IEP.

The next day, the following letter was delivered to Mr. Li.

October 25

Dear Mr. Li:

I am requesting a due process hearing on behalf of my son, Muhammad Brooks, an eighth grader at the junior high school. I do not agree with Muhammad's new placement at the day

(Continue)

CASE 10.2 (CONTINUED)

treatment facility for students with behavior disorders. Muhammad is a follower and might pick up more severe behaviors from other students at the school. In addition, he would not have hit his English teacher if the teacher had not put his hand on Muhammad's shoulder. I discussed with his IEP team the fact that if Muhammad is touched in any way, he is likely to misinterpret and become angry.

I want Muhammad returned to his old placement at the junior high immediately following his suspension from school.

Sincerely,

Mrs. Raye Brooks

Upon receipt of the letter, Mr. Li first informed the superintendent and principal, then requested an impartial due process hearing officer from the state board of education. In addition, he requested an expedited hearing. After consulting the school board attorney, Mr. Li also requested that Muhammad be placed in an interim alternative educational setting for 45 days pending the outcome of the hearing. In the request, Mr. Li stated that Muhammad engaged in dangerous behavior and was likely to harm others. Mr. Li summarized the incident where Muhammad hit the teacher as evidence of his dangerous behavior. Mr. Li then attached Muhammad's revised IEP to the request.

Two days later, Mr. Li's request to the hearing officer for an interim alternative educational setting was denied and Muhammad was supposed to return to school the next day. The principal was furious and Mr. Li told him Muhammad had to return to his previous placement until after the hearing.

The next day, Muhammad did not return to school. In fact, he didn't return the whole week. When Mr. Li contacted Mrs. Brooks, she said she was moving out of the school district.

Note to the reader: You will now be asked questions about this case. Before you read the Questions and Reflections section at the end of the book (Appendix A), you should fill out the case study analysis (Appendix C), then answer the questions and share your ideas with the class.

Questions

1. Did the IEP team make a procedurally appropriate manifestation determination? How do you know?
2. Why did the hearing officer deny the district's request for a 45-day interim alternative educational setting?
3. Why did Muhammad have the right to return to his previous placement after his 10-day suspension?
4. What problems could Muhammad's return to his previous placement cause in the school district?

CASE 10.3: "IS EVERY CHILD PROTECTED UNDER THE IDEA?"

Lakisha sat in her third grade classroom in late September and took out a pencil. The third grade class was getting ready to take a standardized group achievement test this week and today was the first day of testing. Lakisha looked around and then got up to sharpen her pencil. The teacher, Mrs. Bush, told Lakisha three times to sit at her desk. Mrs. Bush explained what to do on the first section of the test, then set the timer for ten minutes. As she glanced up from her desk, she noticed that Lakisha was playing with something. She walked over to her desk and asked Lakisha to give her what was in her hands. Lakisha handed Mrs. Bush nail clippers which had a nail file of about 1 1/2 inches extended. When the timer went off, students' papers were collected and the class went outside for recess. Mrs. Bush took Lakisha to the office to see the principal.

Lakisha moved into the district at the beginning of the school year in late August. Her mother was very concerned about her progress in her previous school, a private school. Tabitha Jones, Lakisha's mother, met with the principal in August and requested that Lakisha be tested for special education services. Mrs. Jones was

(Continue)

CASE 10.3 (CONTINUED)

told that an evaluation would be completed, and until then, Lakisha would be placed in the third grade. Lakisha struggled with reading and math during the first few weeks of school. She also was very inattentive and impulsive. The teacher, Mrs. Bush often had to call Lakisha back to task and remind her again and again to sit at her desk. Mrs. Bush was pleased that Lakisha would be evaluated for possible special education services.

Mrs. Bush took Lakisha to the principal's office. Latoya Daniels, a first-year principal, asked Mrs. Bush and Lakisha to sit down in her office.

Mrs. Bush said, "Ms. Daniels, Lakisha had this in her hands during our test this morning and the blade was out." She handed the nail clippers to Ms. Daniels.

Ms. Daniels asked, "Was Lakisha threatening anyone with this? What exactly was she doing with it?"

Mrs. Bush said, "She had it in her hands and was trying to clip her nails."

Ms. Daniels turned to Lakisha and said, "Lakisha, what were you doing with this?"

Lakisha looked at the floor as she said, "I wasn't doing anything. I was just trying to cut my nails."

Ms. Daniels said, "Do you know that someone could have been hurt with this blade?"

Before Lakisha could respond, she continued, "Lakisha, this is a knife blade. We have a rule in this district forbidding weapons and this looks like a weapon."

Lakisha didn't respond.

Ms. Daniels continued, "Lakisha, you are going to be suspended out of school for 10 days. You may sit in the outer office until I can contact your mother to come and get you."

Coincidentally, Lakisha's mother, Mrs. Jones, walked into the building about ten minutes later. Ms. Daniels explained the situation to her and informed her verbally that Lakisha couldn't come back to school for 10 days. Mrs. Jones was upset, but took Lakisha home.

Later that morning, Ms. Daniels explained the situation to Mr. James Wykoff, superintendent. He reviewed the policy on weapons with Ms. Daniels and arranged an expulsion hearing.

A week later, an expulsion hearing was held concerning Lakisha. Mrs. Jones did not attend the hearing, but the hearing was held anyway. Evidence was presented and a recommendation was made to expel Lakisha for 45 days because she had a weapon at school. The following Tuesday, the board of education voted to ex-

pel Lakisha for 45 days. Mrs. Jones was informed by certified letter of the meeting's outcome.

Mrs. Jones was very confused about what was happening. First she thought that Lakisha was suspended for 10 days. Then she received a letter that said she would be expelled for 45 days! All of this because Lakisha was clipping her nails in school. Mrs. Jones looked at a parents' rights booklet she received when Lakisha was referred for an evaluation in August. In the back of the booklet was a listing of low-cost legal services. She contacted the agency closest to her home and made an appointment with an attorney. Mrs. Jones also contacted the local newspapers and television stations.

The attorney, Mr. Thomas, immediately took the case and requested an expedited due process hearing. Before the hearing, two local newspapers carried the story with headlines like, "Girl Punished for Clipping Her Fingernails at School" and "State Board Will Review Suspension." Television news teams tried to interview school administrators. Mrs. Jones and her daughter appeared on the local television news.

The hearing was held two weeks later in the central office of the school district. The hearing was open to the public at the request of the parent and newspaper, and television reporters were in the audience. The hearing lasted three hours, with several witnesses testifying for both the school district and the parent. At the end of the hearing, both sides were asked to give closing statements.

Mr. Thomas began testimony by saying:

"This child, Lakisha Jones, has been wrongly removed from school. The school district alleges that she had a weapon at school. My witnesses showed that what she had was a fingernail clipper and that she did not threaten anyone. The blade was actually a fingernail file and it was only one inch long, hardly a weapon by legal standards. The school district unlawfully expelled Lakisha for 45 days because of the alleged weapon. The witnesses demonstrated that the school district had knowledge that Lakisha might be a student in need of special education services. Mrs. Jones testified that she referred Lakisha for a special education evaluation in August. Lakisha's teacher testified that Lakisha was having serious academic difficulties in school. Because the school district had knowledge

(Continue)

CASE 10.3 (CONTINUED)

that Lakisha might be a student with a disability, she was entitled to all protections of the Individuals with Disabilities Education Act. This means that she should not have been removed from school for more than 10 consecutive days without an IEP team considering her case. This did not occur. In addition, Mrs. Jones testified that she was not properly notified of the initial suspension from school. She was verbally told not to bring Lakisha back to school for 10 days. Mrs. Jones was never notified of an expulsion hearing. She only received the results of the school board's decision to expel Lakisha for 45 days after the decision was made. This child, a third grader, has been out of school for 35 days! We are requesting relief in the following way:

- We want Lakisha immediately returned to school.
- We want Lakisha's evaluation for special education completed in one week, with any possible placement in special education immediately planned and implemented.
- We want Lakisha to receive compensatory education during the summer to help her catch up after her loss of school during these 35 days.

Thank you for you consideration."

The school board attorney made a strong plea to the hearing officer in his closing statement. He said, in part, "This child, Lakisha Jones, was found with a weapon at school. The school board policy specifies what will occur if any child of any age has a weapon at school. This policy was followed. The school board ultimately expelled Lakisha for 45 days. This child was not

a child with a disability, as she had not been evaluated for special education. We request that the hearing officer uphold the school board's actions concerning this child. Thank you."

Three days later, the school district and parent received the hearing officer's decision. The school district was ordered to immediately return Lakisha to school and complete her evaluation for special education in 10 days. They were also ordered to provide compensatory education to Lakisha in the form of summer school for six weeks, four hours per day. Mr. Thomas, the parent's attorney, also requested from a federal court that Mrs. Jones receive reimbursement for all of her attorney's fees. The school district was ordered by a judge to pay the fees. The local media interviewed Mrs. Jones and newspapers carried lengthy editorials lauding the decision.

Note to the reader: You will now be asked questions about this case. Before you read the Questions and Reflections section at the end of the book (Appendix A), you should fill out the case study analysis (Appendix C), then answer the questions and share your ideas with the class.

Questions

1. Why was Lakisha entitled to protections under the IDEA if she had not been evaluated for special education?
2. How should the principal have reacted?
3. If you were the special education administrator, how would you make sure this did not occur again?
4. Do you think Lakisha had a weapon?

APPENDIX A

Questions and Reflections

Case 2.1: "The Citizen's Statement"

1. What Are Mrs. Taylor's Concerns?

Mrs. Taylor has summarized a host of issues that confront the district. One of the major issues revolves around her belief that special education is not a priority of the district. She cites numerous examples of the district's lack of commitment. Mrs. Taylor points to the problems in staff development, funding, communications between parents and central office administrators, and the proper use of the IEP (individual education plan).

2. What Are the Special Education Issues Confronting the District?

If Mrs. Taylor's allegations are true, the district has concerns that have implications for not only special education but for strategic planning, the curriculum, the supervision function, the organizational chart, the budget, and the legality of some of the practices.

3. Is It Usual for a Parent to Be So Well Versed in the Issues Related to Special Education?

It is not unusual for a parent to be as well versed in the issues related to any aspect of a school district's operations. In this case Mrs. Taylor has had an opportunity to be involved in a number of special education programs. School districts often make a very serious error in underestimating the "singleness of purpose" that a parent(s) has in investigating a particular program. In this case, the seriousness of the student's future creates an energy in a parent that is unyielding.

An additional resource for the parent of a special education student is the advocate. The advocate has an opportunity to tap into local, state, and national information databases that can aide a parent in dealing with special education issues.

4. If You Were the Director of Special Education How Would You Approach the Problem? Should You Approach Mrs. Taylor Immediately After the Board Meeting to Defend the Program?

Information that is presented during a citizen's statement can significantly alter the way a board views a program. It is important to understand that the information that is given may not be factual. Whenever a statement is made by a board member or in this case a citizen, take careful notes. Item-by-item react to the issue. Is the statement fact or is the data misleading? If it is fact, review what has been done to rectify the issue. If it is not fact, refute it with fact. Generally administration is overly defensive about its programs. It is often difficult to remain objective but it is critical to do so.

A proactive superintendent will expect a report detailing the program director's reaction to critical statements. A practical recommendation in this case would be for the director of special education to bring together teaching staff, parents, and administrators to study the issue and make recommendations. It may also be appropriate for the district to have an outside consultant audit the special education program.

Mrs. Taylor has made negative statements about your program. It would not be prudent to approach her immediately after the meeting. More often than not it would lead to a confrontation. You may consider asking the superintendent to schedule a meeting with Mrs. Taylor and the two of you.

5. As the Director of Special Education You Are to Meet with the Reporter from the Dispatch. What Will You Say?

Hopefully the district has a procedure for dealing with the media. If the district does not have a procedure it is imperative that you meet with the superintendent to discuss the approach to take with the reporter. In any event someone must meet with him. Oftentimes it helps to have a written statement prepared that represents the district viewpoint.

6. If You Were the Superintendent, How Would You Approach the Issue?

The superintendent is faced with challenges like this on an all too frequent basis. In this case you should review the special education director's report and determine what your next action should be. Hopefully you have a strategic planning committee that can incorporate the needs of special education into the district's planning cycle. By proactively approaching this issue you will take an important step in developing a program that will begin to meet the needs of all children.

7. Can This Situation Be Salvaged?

Yes, this situation can be salvaged. The superintendent has admitted to the president of the board of education that there are problems with the current special education program. It is time for her to develop a process that will concentrate on rectifying problems with procedures, policy, and staff development. It may be helpful to initiate an association for the parents of students with disabilities to assist the district in developing an appropriate special education program.

Case 2.2: "If It Isn't Broken . . ."

1. What Problems Face Richard As He Works Through the Steivs' Complaint?

Richard is faced with a host of problems: the culture, his ethical responsibility to follow federal and state laws, and a school district that doesn't follow appropriate governance standards.

Although it is unusual to find administrators and teachers who do not always follow the rules, they do exist. In this case Richard must continue to work with his supervisors to help them understand the gravity of the situation. Richard must also determine if the practices that are being carried out at Fern Meadow are also being used in other district schools. Richard should recommend that the district carry a special education program audit, conducted by someone from outside the district.

The issue of performance evaluation should also be discussed with Randy's supervisor. It is obvious that he is not following federal, state, and district rules and regulations concerning special education. This should be noted in his yearly evaluation.

2. Is the District Responsible for Randy's Actions?

The district is ultimately responsible for Randy's actions. The potential ramifications of the Steivs' complaint could be costly and embarrassing to the district. If, for example, other parents heard about the complaint, it would not be unusual for a class action complaint or multiple individual suits to be filed.

3. What Recourse Does the Steiv Family Have in Dealing with the Approach That Is Being Taken with Their Son's IEP?

The Steiv family has a number of options. First they should work through Richard Elliott. It is important for them to let the district mediate the issue internally. If Richard's attempts fail they should file a complaint with the superintendent and the school board. Mr. and Mrs. Steiv should ask for a meeting with the superintendent and Randy's supervisor. If that does not succeed they need to exhaust each of the potential remedies available under special education law. The case may also be brought before the Office of Civil Rights (OCR) in the form of an official complaint.

Case 3.1: "Basketball Player or Special Education Student?"

1. What Were the Important Issues Concerning Corey's Eligibility for Special Education Services?

The primary issue in the eligibility decision was that the data, i.e., evaluation results, had not changed since the last evaluation. The only change was the availability, via the basketball coach, to provide supplementary aids and services within the regular education system.

2. Was the Outcome, i.e., Discontinuing Eligibility for Special Education Services, in the Best Interest of the Child? Why or Why Not?

A case could be made that discontinuing eligibility for special education services might be in the best interest of the child. In the case, Corey was discontinued as eligible for special services. Corey still had a disability and special needs resulting from the disability, i.e., difficulty in reading and spelling, but those needs could be met within the regular education system, via the coach's plan for intervention. It is possible for a child to have a disability and not need special education services, therefore not be eligible as disabled under IDEA. The unanswered question might involve whether Corey continued to learn at least at the same rate as he did when he was in special education. One might presume that he continued to make progress as evidenced by his passing grades. It was clear from the case that both the parent and Corey supported discontinuing eligibility for special education.

3. What Was the Motive of Coach Fisher? Did His Motive Have An Adverse or Positive Effect on the Outcome?

It appeared that the coach's motive was to develop a talented basketball player. If Corey had not been talented as a basketball player, it seemed unlikely that Coach Fisher would have taken a strong interest in Corey. In that respect, one might question the ethics of the coach and sports in general. Regardless of the motive, the coach's efforts seemed to have made a positive difference in the child's life. One might, however, be concerned about what might happen if for some reason Corey was unable to continue playing basketball. Would the coach continue coordinating supplemental services for Corey? Probably not.

4. Did the Special Education Administrator Proceed Appropriately When Faced with the Request from the School Board Member? How Do You Know?

The special education administrator appeared to proceed appropriately. Rather than make a "deal" with either the school board member or the coach, the administrator relied upon the results of a reevaluation and the IEP team to make an appropriate individualized decision. It is always appropriate to proceed in this manner when there is a question of significant placement change rather than make a unilateral decision.

5. Describe a Different Outcome for This Case.

A different, and reasonable, outcome for this case might have been to continue eligibility for special education services based on the continued need for special education intervention in reading and spelling. If this had occurred, the coach probably would have been unhappy. In addition, the parent, if unhappy with the decision, might have exercised her right to request a due process hearing. It is possible that a hearing officer might uphold the district's right to continue special education services based on past progress in school with the services and on the apparent motive of the coach to provide services. If this occurred, the student might not be motivated to continue progressing in school because he did not want special education services.

Case 3.2: "I Know What's Best for My Child!"

1. Was It Proper to Change Will's Placement Three Times to Placate Mrs. Brown? Why or Why Not?

No, it is never proper to change a child's program or placement to placate the parent. According to the IDEA, the child has rights and the school district's responsibility is to protect the child's rights. Placating the parent is not doing what is in the best interest of the child or protecting the child's rights. In the short term, doing what the parent requests may be easy, but if placating the parent does not coincide with what is best for the child, there may be a problem in the future. Even though it is difficult to do something disagreeable to the parent, an administrator can always defend the decision if it was done to protect the child's rights or in the child's best interest.

2. What Is the Systemic Issue That Needs to Be Addressed to Avoid Future Problems? How Should This Issue Be Addressed by the Special Education Administrator?

The main issues involve changing a child's IEP because the parent insists on a change and changing an IEP unilaterally without a properly convened IEP meeting. One way to address this issue would be to make sure policies and procedures for changing IEPs are in written form and to communicate these procedures to all professional staff throughout the school district. An inservice would emphasize proper written notice in advance of any meeting, the importance of team consensus in making decisions, and the importance of documenting any changes in a child's program in his/her IEP. In addition, inservice should address the issue of the school district's responsibility, i.e., to provide a free appropriate public education and to assure that the child's rights are being observed. Teachers would also be told that when not sure if an IEP meeting should be held, it would be better to err on the side of holding a meeting.

3. How Should the IEP Be Changed Procedurally? Describe What Should Have Happened.

After receipt of a verbal request for a change in the IEP, the department chairperson should have arranged an IEP meeting at a mutually agreeable time and place. The purpose of the meeting and persons attending would then be confirmed in writing, with parents' rights accompanying the letter of confirmation. Participants would include a special education teacher(s), the department chairperson (as one who could commit services), a regular education teacher(s), and the parent. The requested change would then be discussed by the team and consensus reached on the appropriateness of the change. If the team decided not to change the IEP and the parent disagreed, the parent could request mediation or a due process hearing. If the team decided to change the IEP, all changes and the rationale for making the changes would be documented on the IEP. The parent would then be informed in writing (or given a letter at the conclusion of the meeting) of the specific changes to be made.

4. Was the Parent Correct When She Said the Child's Program Wasn't Appropriate? Why or Why Not?

It was possible that the child's program was not appropriate based on the procedural errors made in making the changes. The decision to make changes was unilateral and not based on the child's best interest, no IEP meeting was held, and changes apparently were not reflected in the IEP.

5. Was Mrs. Dust Correct in Saying That She Would Not Accept Responsibility if Will Did Not Do Well in the Regular Social Studies Class? Why or Why Not?

Mrs. Dust was not correct in making this statement. As a representative of the school district, Mrs. Dust was charged with the responsibility of providing an appropriate education to each of her students. She could not abdicate this responsibility and allow another person, i.e., the parent, to make a decision that she felt was not in the best interest of the child.

Case 3.3: "I Will Not Include This Child in My School!"

1. If a Similar Student Transferred to Your Building Tomorrow, How Would You, As Building Administrator, Prepare for the Student?

It would be important to gather pertinent information about the child and to form a support team to plan and implement a program for the child. First, an evaluation on the child should be requested. Current information would be essential in formulating a plan. It would also be important to gather pertinent records from previous placements. Second, it would be important to begin an open communication system with teachers by talking to the sixth grade teacher and scheduling a follow-up meeting with the school staff after the IEP meeting. An IEP meeting should then be held with all persons who may work with the child in attendance. The meeting should be scheduled during the day with substitutes for teachers so that full attention can be given to planning. During the meeting, a plan should be formulated with the child's best interest in mind. It is possible that team participants would not formulate a plan for full inclusion because it would not be appropriate for the child. If this was the case, the parents might not agree and request a due process hearing. The administrator would then prepare a case to defend the LEA's actions.

Whatever the plan, it should be based on current data and provide appropriate support for the child. It would be important to detail special education services, related services, accommodations and supports for the regular class teacher (as appropriate), and a detailed behavior management plan. It might also be useful to plan a follow-up IEP meeting in three weeks to review the program. If the team planned an inclusion program, the administrator would want to check with teachers on a regular basis (perhaps daily) to provide support. Overall, the administrator should approach the situation in a systematic manner,—that is, follow procedures for determining a placement, be as objective as possible, and lead the team to make an individualized plan.

2. Was Mr. Brolin's Behavior Acceptable in the Superintendent's Office? Why or Why Not?

No, Mr. Brolin's behavior was not appropriate in the superintendent's office. He allowed his emotions and his feelings about including a child with behavior problems to rule his behavior. A better approach would have been to express concerns about the child, to request information, and to ask questions. Mr. Brolin could have expressed his disagreement with the decision and still maintained his respect for the position and decision of the superintendent.

3. Did the Program, As Implemented, Provide a Free and Appropriate Public Education? Was the Program in the Least Restrictive Environment? How Do You Know?

If the IEP was procedurally correct (e.g., contained all components) and was determined to provide educational benefit, then the IEP was appropriate (see *Board of Education of the Hendrick Hudson Central School District v. Rowley*, 458 U.S. 176 (1982)).

If the IEP team truly considered supplemental aids and supports within the regular education classroom setting (e.g., inclusion planning process detailed in text), if he was receiving educational benefit from the placement, and if his behavior did not have an adverse effect on other students in the class, his program probably would be considered as the least restrictive environment. In addition, Jake also attended his home school with age and grade peers and the team determined that this placement configuration was the most appropriate plan.

Case 4.1: "Once You're in Special Education, You Never Get Out!"

1. What Was Mrs. Smith's Position Initially? Likewise, What Was the School District's Position Initially?

Mrs. Smith focused on her definition of the concept "special education" and what it might mean for her son. Her definition reflected what she saw as her husband's shortcomings and his past unsuccessful involvement in special education. The school district also focused on the definition of special education and what it might mean for Mrs. Smith's son. School district personnel viewed special education as a positive service, one that might help David learn to read and be successful in school. Although both focused on "special education" and what it might mean for David, the definitions were very different. Therefore, the opinions of whether special education services were useful were opposite one another.

2. If the Two Parties, Mrs. Smith and School District Personnel, Had Stayed with Their Positions, What Might Have Occurred?

It would have been difficult, or impossible, to resolve the resulting conflict if both parties had maintained their positions focusing on the concept of "special education" because there was no common ground or common definition to which both agreed. It is likely that further conflict would have resulted, perhaps even a due process hearing.

3. What Happened During the Second Meeting That Resulted in Conflict Resolution? What Steps of the Negotiation Process Can Be Identified?

The foundation of the second meeting was good communication skills. Several steps in the negotiation process can also be identified.

- Mr. Turner began the meeting by requesting agreement on some basic ground rules, including an agreement to cooperate and taking turns listening and talking.
- Mr. Turner then engaged in gathering points of view by asking the question, "What is your understanding of David's progress in school?" Mr. Turner led

the discussion and focused on using empathic listening skills. It is assumed that Mrs. Smith and school personnel felt that their positions were heard and understood.

- Mr. Turner then led the discussion to find common interests. It was noticeable that he tried to avoid discussing their original positions, which resulted in conflict. Common interests for David included helping him learn to read and ultimately graduating from high school.
- The discussion then focused on creating win-win options. The first grade teacher agreed to provide extra reading assistance for the remainder of the school year. The learning disabilities teacher explained what she thought might help David next year in second grade, i.e., 30 minutes of extra reading help daily as well as special assistance in the regular classroom. Although this was special education, the focus was not the concept or term, but David's needs and how they could best be met.
- The evaluation of options and creation of an agreement culminated in writing an IEP for David.

4. How Was the Communication Different During Each of the Two Conferences?

Good communication formed the foundation of resolution for this conflict situation during the second meeting and was noticeably absent during the first meeting.

During the first conference, Mrs. Smith adamantly stated that she didn't want David in special education and Mr. Turner responded by not hearing or listening. He said, "We'll discuss special education after we review the evaluation, Mrs. Smith." When Mrs. Smith again stated her opposition to special education, school personnel defended the option of special education for David and Mrs. Smith angrily walked out of the meeting.

During the second meeting, after ground rules were established, Mrs. Smith was asked about her perception of the problem. School staff listened and reflected her feelings, summarized, and clarified. Mrs. Smith appeared to feel that school personnel heard and understood her concerns. School personnel seemed to feel that Mrs. Smith heard and understood their concerns about David. The focus of the second meeting centered around agreed-upon goals for David, not the original positions of both parties.

Case 4.2: "I Went to School to Teach Fifth Grade, Not Work with Behavior Disorders Students!"

1. How Should Ms. Kowalski, Special Education Director, Address Conflict with the Following: King Elementary Staff? King Elementary Principal? District Superintendent? Board of Education? Parents?

To address conflict with the King Elementary staff, a meeting with faculty (and perhaps staff) should be scheduled. The meeting could be conducted by the special education administrator (in this case Anna Kowalski). The administrator would gather points of view (e.g., "What is your understanding of the problem?"), gather descriptions of actual incidents involving BD students, determine the frequency of any incidents, and clarify staff feelings and concerns. The special education administrator should practice good communication skills because it is essential that staff concerns are heard and validated, whether a change occurs or not. It is important for the special education administrator to realistically consider staff input and to follow up with staff on the outcome of the meeting.

It is important for the special education administrator to inform the superintendent of the meeting's content (for communication to the school board). Ultimately, the superintendent would be involved in any changes in the makeup of the building. The board of education would be kept informed by the superintendent.

The special education administrator might attempt to develop a good working relationship with the principal to improve the principal's "team playing" skills. The principal probably had concerns about the BD program, but did not express these directly to the special education administrator or superintendent. A meeting with the principal using the negotiation process discussed earlier in this chapter could result in resolution of conflict.

It is not useful to write a letter to all parents, it is better to handle this situation as a building and district concern at this time. However, if parents expressed concern about any incidents in the building, the special education administrator and principal should address them individually as they occurred.

2. What Issues of Programming for Elementary BD Students Are Related to This Conflict? How Might These Issues Be Addressed?

Issues of programming for elementary BD students should be reviewed. Placing all BD students in one building legally is allowed, but may overload one small elementary school. Case law has generally upheld the fact that children do not have to attend their home school to receive an appropriate education—for example, see *Murray v. Montrose County School District,* 51 F. 3d 921 (10th Cir. 1995) and *Schuldt v. Mankato Independent School District #77,* 937 F. 2d 1357 (8th Cir. 1991). The special education administrator and superintendent could discuss the possibility of moving one or two of the BD classes to other buildings.

3. How Should the Special Education Administrator Approach the BD Teacher(s) About How the Student in the Case Was Managed (i.e., Force the Student Down the Hall, Kicking and Screaming)?

The special education administrator might wish to meet directly with the BD teachers in the building to discuss the following: how children are disciplined; BD teacher concerns with programming; and suggestions for improvement in the program. Again, good communication skills coupled with the structure of the negotiation process would be essential. It is possible that staff inservice, (e.g., conflict resolution and nonviolent crisis intervention) could help improve the program. Issues of liability (e.g., if a BD student was hurt) could also be addressed.

4. What Issues About Line of Authority Are a Concern?

The board of education's role in a school district is primarily one of making policy. The superintendent's role is chief executive officer of the district. He or she is ultimately responsible for day-to-day operations in the district, as well as maintaining fiscal responsibility, making recommendations for employment and dismissal of personnel, and assuring that children in the district are receiving the best education possible given the resources of the district. The role of director of special education is to assure that children with disabilities are receiving an appropriate education and to make recommendations to the superintendent to that end.

In this case, the superintendent and director of special education were not informed of a potential problem situation in a building that could affect the education of children. It would have been appropriate for the building principal to inform the superintendent and the director of special education of the teachers' concerns. It is possible that the issue could have been resolved at the administrative level without involving the school board. The superintendent probably would have informed the school board of the issues. The practical issue is that no one likes "surprises." Teachers like to be informed of a potential problem situation in their classes so that they have the opportunity to address the issues, and principals like to be informed about potential problems so they, too, can adequately address the issues. In the same manner, directors and superintendents like to be informed about potential problem situations in the district. Knowing about a potential problem situation may not result in a solution, but it allows the administrator and/or teacher involved to be proactive and search for a solution before the situation escalates.

Case 5.1: "Parent Involvement in the Assessment Process"

1. How Would You Involve Parents in the Assessment Process?

The superintendent has asked his administrative council to assist him in developing a parent awareness program dealing with school district accountability in the area of the assessment of students with disabilities.

One of the first discussions should revolve around current programs that deal with parent involvement in all aspects of the special education. Is there a general orientation process for parents? If there is, does it present a plan that shows a progression of school district and school assistance from preschool through transition?

If there is not a general orientation program for parents in the general education program and special education available, the district may want to consider developing one rather than dealing with only one aspect of an informational process. Websites, videos, and face-to-face presentations may be used to develop parent understanding of the entire special education program.

Some of the areas that may be covered under the section dealing with assessment for parents with students in a special education program might be:

- What is assessment? What is accountability?
- How would assessment help my child?
- How do I know if my child should participate in the general assessment?
- What assessment accommodations are available for a student with a disability?

Another program that may foster understanding and a sense of belonging for the parent of a student with a disability is the use of an ombudsman. An ombudsman is someone with the authority and responsibility to cut through problems to develop equitable solutions.

Whatever a school district can do to assist parents and students early in the process will result in dividends through the families' involvement in the special education program.

Case 5.2: "Movement to a Noncategorical System"

1. You Are the Assistant Superintendent of Schools Responsible for Special Education. What Would You Say About Moving into a Noncategorical Program?

As the assistant superintendent for special education it is important for you to review the issue in terms of the viability of the concept but also the matter of the time needed to implement the program. Chad made a sweeping generality in saying that by moving to a noncategorical process that the district would now be able to evaluate the special education program. The assistant superintendent for special education should review the entire process of program evaluation. If the district does not employ a staff member responsible for research and assessment then it should seek assistance from a local university.

2. What Do You Believe Would Be the Best of All Settings for the Students in the Special Education Programs?

There is no best program for all children unless it is one that offers a continuum of services. It would be naive to believe that children with various disabilities could be taught in the same setting, unless there were a great deal of staff development. If the district decided to move in the direction of establishing alternative noncategorical classrooms then it is suggested that sufficient lead-in time be allocated to implement the program.

3. How Should the President of the Board of Education Deal with the Request from the Former Board of Education President?

The president of the board of education deals with requests as a routine part of the position. This request has with it a number of elements that should cause concern. The former president of the board would have considerable power in the community, which could cause problems. But to move into a noncategorical system should be treated as any other major change in the school district. If there is a strategic plan then it should become part of the plan and follow the district's decision-making process.

Case 6.1: "Why Should I Keep the District's Worst BD Students in the Community?"

1. If You Were a Superintendent on This Board, What Questions Might You Ask the Special Education Director?

Potential questions might focus on cost factors and possibly on personnel. Questions might include the following:

- What will be start-up costs if we have 5 students? 10 students? 20 students?
- How many students do we anticipate during the first year?

- In my district, how many students do I have who potentially could be placed in the program?
- What is the history of private school placements for BD students in my district?
- If I don't currently have students who are potential candidates for the program, does that mean my district will pay start-up costs?
- What if all students move out of the cooperative during January except one student from my district. Does this mean my district will pay the entire cost of the program for the remainder of the school year?
- Will these students attend summer school?
- Will we have difficulty locating qualified staff?
- We currently employ clerical, noncertified personnel, psychologists, and social workers. Will these new personnel be placed on the same salary scale?

2. What Were the Barriers That Might Have Prevented the Superintendents from Supporting the Proposal? What Were the Advantages of the Local Program?

The major barrier appeared to be the cost of implementing a local program. Not only would school districts have to pay for start-up costs, they would pay more per student in comparison to the private school. Another barrier involving cost might be the fluctuating cost per district of the program if the student population fluctuated, e.g., students that moved in and out of the cooperative.

The major advantage was that districts would exert more local control over the education of these children. It also might have appealed to superintendents to educate these students in the local communities so that the possibility of successful transition would be greater. The reduced transportation cost would also have been an advantage. In addition, it was unlikely that significant behavior problems would be exhibited on the buses because of the close proximity to each student's home. Not stated would be the ease of placing a student in the program because the program was part of Longman Cooperative. Unlike the private school, which would have its own entry requirements, Longman Cooperative could determine its entry requirements.

3. What Type of Reimbursement Would the Districts Receive for the Local Public School Program and What Placement Incentive Is Inherent?

The districts would receive pupil reimbursement, which appears to be a resource-based formula. The state would reimburse the district $2,000 above the per capita tuition cost. The district would provide the resources to educate the child, e.g., teacher, classroom, materials, etc. The state would recognize the additional high cost necessary to provide this child's education by reimbursing an additional $2,000. As illustrated in this case, the reimbursement of excess costs in no way covers the entire cost of educating students with severe behavior disorders in a local public school program. The incentive, then, would be to avoid setting up high cost placements locally and place these students in private facilities where the reimbursement is greater.

4. How Were Start-Up Costs Going to Be Funded? Why Do You Think They Were to Be Funded in This Manner?

The member districts of the cooperative would be charged an assessment based on the costs for setting up the program. This means that the total start-up costs would be divided evenly among the member districts. The rationale for this division could be the potential for any member district to use the program. In other words, all member districts could access the program at any time.

5. Describe a More Neutral Funding Formula That Would Support Placing Students in Local Public School Programs.

One possible funding alternative would be a pupil weight formula, where students with severe disabilities are assigned more weight than children with mild disabilities. This formula would generate more reimbursement for the program serving students with severe disabilities (public or private).

Another alternative would be a variation of the resource-based funding formula. If the state reimbursed the district the same amount above two per capita tuition costs as it did private schools, the reimbursement would be equal to that of the private school, eliminating the fiscal incentive for private school placement.

A third possibility would be the flat grant formula, where reimbursement for all placements, public and private, were made using the same amount. Again, this would eliminate the fiscal incentive to place a child in a private school.

Case 6.2: "Generating Additional Funding Using Medicaid"

1. How Well Did the Special Education Director Answer the Speech and Language Therapists' Questions?

Although Joan, the special education director, acknowledged how overwhelmed the therapists felt about additional paperwork, she didn't really address the issue in terms of possible supports needed. For example, one therapist asked if additional clerical assistance would be available, and Joan didn't address this question. It might have been helpful to determine what supports were necessary to assist the therapists, and take these suggestions under consideration.

When asked how the funds generated from Medicaid reimbursement would be used, it was evident that Joan did not have definite plans. She gave examples of how the funds could be used (e.g., to renovate a building, purchase additional materials for the therapists) but did not commit to using the funds for a specific activity. It might have been helpful for Joan to have more definite plans for the use of funds generated.

In response to the moral issue of billing Medicaid for school services, Joan's answer was not complete. She indicated that Medicaid would have to pay someone to provide speech therapy services and it might as well be the local school district. This rationale was not specific enough. It might have been useful to provide a short historical summary on the use of other funding sources for providing special education services and the support within the school district for pursuing this funding source.

2. Were There Other Supports the Special Education Director Could Have Implemented to Gain the Support of the Speech Therapists?

Joan could have provided a sound rationale for using Medicaid as a source of funding. As stated above, she could have been more definite about how the funds generated would be used. She could also have generated a discussion on specific supports needed by the therapists to complete more paperwork. It might have been useful to ask the therapist from the neighboring school district to attend this meeting instead of a future meeting.

3. Should Medicaid Reimbursement Be Used to Employ Another Speech and Language Therapist? Why or Why Not?

Employing another therapist with Medicaid reimbursement funds probably would not be an appropriate use of the funds. The major concern would be that the dollars generated would not be constant from quarter to quarter or year to year. Therefore, local funds would have to make up for a possible lack in Medicaid funds to support such a position. This would cause a problem in budgeting and recordkeeping.

Case 7.1: "New Technology"

1. What Aspects of Staff Development Should Be Considered Before Accepting Integrative Technology As a Program for the District?

Claire Musial's observation was accurate. Too often school districts approve a program without going through a two-stage process which includes determining individual and group needs and monitoring where the group is in relationship to desired changes to instructional programming. The *Integrative Technology* program may indeed be what the faculty needs but how long will it take to implement it? Has the district contacted other districts using the program to determine how successful it has been? Is a new program needed?

The answers to these questions could have been answered through a needs assessment of the special education staff and an evaluation of the current programs.

2. What Are the Implications for Moving from the Traditional Teaching Format Currently in the Program to This New Technology for Staff Development?

There are a number of implications associated with moving from the traditional methods to the new technology. The first deals with the change process itself. Change is difficult. A decision or recommendation to change a program has a better chance for success if the people that will implement the program initiate the change process. In this case the recommendation for change is coming from the superintendent.

Little consideration was given to the time needed to implement the program. Are special education faculty and regular education faculty ready to meet the demands of the new technology in the time given to assimilate the new program? The time needed for implementation is often misjudged.

3. What Are the Implications for the Recruitment and Selection of Special Education Teachers?

The school district must consider the new educational program as it recruits and selects personnel. In this case the district is moving towards a new way of delivering special education. New staff may or may not be familiar with the new program. It is essential that the new program be part of an in-depth orientation.

4. Are There Implications for the Personnel Appraisal Process?

The appraisal process is utilized to judge a person's performance against a standard. In this case a program is being reviewed that will create a standard that faculty may or may not be able to reach in the initial phase of implementation. It is important that if the program is adopted administrators receive training to better understand the implications of the new technology upon the school district's special education program.

Case 7.2: "The OCR Complaint"

1. Review the Agenda for the Orientation Meeting. What Should An Orientation Program Contain?

An orientation program should consist of two parts. The first part of the orientation is general in nature. As an example, all new employees should receive information dealing with benefits, district organization, strategic planning goals, and a tour of the district's facilities. The second part of the orientation should center on the needs of the individual or group of individuals sharing the same position or having similar needs. The district should have developed a short-term and long-term plan to assist Bill David to teach a cross-categorical class, a class he was not trained to teach.

2. If Bill Initially Qualified for Assistance, Because of His Disability, What Should the District Have Offered Him?

Bill should have been offered the assistance necessary to carry out his function as a teacher. The district should have been proactive in its approach to help him whether this was in the form of staff development or the in-class assistance of an aide.

3. Was the Human Resources Department Proactive in Its Treatment of a Teacher with a Disability?

No, the human resources department was not proactive in meeting the needs of a teacher with a disability. The human resources department should have developed a program that accommodated for Bill's disability.

The district should have initiated a program to assist Bill as soon as he indicated that he had a disability. The program of accommodation should have been shared with the central office and the administration of Bill's school. Referring back to Figure 7.1 you will see that information should flow to and from the central office administration and the schools.

4. Does the Treatment that Bill Received Warrant an OCR Complaint?

The issue should not have been elevated to a point where an OCR complaint was required. The district was bound by ADA (Americans with Disabilities Act) and Section 504 of the Rehabilitation Act to assist Bill. Since they did not offer him the assistance necessary to be successful, an OCR complaint was warranted. In addition the question of retaliation must be considered. Was Bill evaluated as less than satisfactory because he was not an effective teacher or because he complained about his need for accommodations?

5. In Whose Favor Would the OCR Rule? Why?

The Office of Civil Rights would approach the issue brought about by Bill's OCR complaint by reviewing not only Bill's complaint but also whether the district had a history of discriminating against faculty with a disability. The Office of Civil Rights would begin its discovery by assigning an investigator. The investigator would contact the complainant and the district to discuss the accusations of discrimination.

There is a secondary issue in the complaint form. Bill is claiming that the district has not only discriminated against him but also retaliated against Libbi. If the OCR felt that Bill was justified in his complaint they would try to remedy the situation through negotiations. If the negotiation process failed OCR could either initiate administrative enforcement proceedings or refer the case to the Department of Justice. The OCR can also move to defer any new or additional federal financial assistance and can move to terminate any existing federal assistance.

Case 8.1: "You Better Find Other Transportation for Her!"

1. Why Did Dr. Rodriguez Inform the Superintendent of the Situation?

Simply stated, superintendents do not like surprises. It was possible that Mrs. Richards would take her concerns to the superintendent. If Dr. Rodriguez had not informed the superintendent of the situation, he would have had no knowledge of what had occurred and would have been caught by surprise. It is always good practice to inform one's superiors, superintendent or board, of possible problem situations. The superintendent or board is then well-informed from the beginning and better able to make final decisions and offer support to the administrator. It was also likely that the superintendent would mention the problem to school board members for the same reason.

2. What Was Wrong with Melanie's IEP Initially? What Should Have Been Changed Concerning Her Transportation?

It appeared from the information given that there was not enough detailed information concerning one of Melanie's related services, transportation. It was noted on the IEP that Melanie needed an air-conditioned classroom on hot days because she was unable to control her body temperature. This condition was not specified in the transportation on the IEP. There were no other details about transportation, including transporting her wheelchair and an emergency plan in case Melanie became overheated. The IEP at the end of the case detailed Melanie's transportation so that her needs could be met.

3. Should Dr. Rodriguez Have Initiated the Change in Transportation? Why or Why Not?

No, the transportation should not have been changed. The correct procedure would have been to conduct an IEP meeting to specify transportation necessary to meet Melanie's needs. The IEP meeting should have included a representative from the bus company, along with related service staff, the special and regular education teachers, the parent, and the special education administrator. At a minimum, the IEP should have included the following:

1. Mode of transportation,
2. Length of time on the van,
3. Equipment needed during transport,
4. Emergency procedures,
5. Specification for driver training,
6. Environmental controls (e.g., air conditioning).

The school district would then arrange appropriate transportation to carry out the IEP. The school district had the right to contract with any bus company providing that the child's needs, as specified in the IEP, were met.

It would have been good practice to provide the original bus driver with training in the transportation of children with physical and health disabilities. Given the training specified in the chapter and a detailed IEP, problems with the parent might not have occurred. Melanie would have been transported on an appropriate vehicle in an appropriate manner. If the parent was still unhappy because the bus company had changed, the special education administrator could have communicated with the parent that the transportation was safe and appropriate and that an IEP meeting could be arranged to discuss concerns. The special education administrator would have placed the school district in a defensible position.

Dr. Rodriguez felt that nothing short of a change in transporters would satisfy Mrs. Richards. The role of the special education administrator is not to satisfy the parent in this case, but to provide safe, appropriate transportation. However, the change implemented satisfied Mrs. Richards and resolved the problem, at least in the short term. It is quite possible that Mrs. Richards might find fault with the new bus arrangement and want another change. Where would efforts to placate Mrs. Richards end? In the short term, it was easier to placate the parent, but in the long term the problem might not have been resolved.

4. Did the School District Have an Obligation to Provide an Air-Conditioned Vehicle? Why or Why Not?

The school district was obligated to provide an air-conditioned vehicle. Courts (see, for example, *Skelly v. Brookfield LaGrange Park Sch. Dist. 95*, 1997) have held that if a related health service was included in a child's IEP, the service should be included in the child's transportation. In this case, an air-conditioned classroom was included in Melanie's initial IEP and should have been included in her transportation.

Case 8.2: "Unofficial Suspension from the Bus"

1. Why Would Implementing An "Unofficial" Suspension from the Bus Be a Problem Legally?

Suspending a child from the bus could be considered a form of functional exclusion from school. If Mrs. Allen had been unable or unwilling to transport Kevin to and from school, he probably would have missed school. In essence, Kevin would have been excluded from attending school or wouldn't have been afforded FAPE. If he was excluded from school for more than ten consecutive school days (which he wasn't), his placement would have been changed without following proper procedures.

In addition, the courts have been adamant about giving students who would be suspended rudimentary rights (see, for example, *Goss v. Lopez,* 419 U.S. 565 (1975)). "Unofficially" suspending Kevin from the bus (and possibly functionally excluding him from school) does not provide for these procedural protections.

2. If You Were the Director of Special Education, What Position Would You Have Taken with Ann Miller? Why?

After discussing the situation with the superintendent and gaining his support, it would be useful to discuss the situation with Ann in a planned meeting. Ann should be told that her actions were not legal and that a due process hearing based on that issue would be difficult to defend. School district policies and procedures for disciplining students with disabilities should be reviewed with the principal. In the same meeting, it would be conveyed that the building principal was in charge of the day-to-day operation of the building and the director of special education had no intention of interfering with that responsibility. Overall, Ann Miller would need to be directly informed what was legal, what was school district policy, and the possible consequences of making decisions that were not legal or part of district policy. It would be Ann's decision, as building principal, to follow or not to follow the director's recommendations and school district policy.

3. Were Correct Procedures Followed for Resolving the Problem? How Do You Know?

The problem can be defined as follows:

1. The principal made unilateral decisions regarding a student's behavior and related service, transportation.
2. The student was functionally excluded from school and was not afforded FAPE.

The director of special education adequately resolved the first problem by arranging an IEP meeting to discuss transportation and behavior. The IEP was revisited and revised based on input from the team.

The second problem was addressed by the director as he informed the principal of the problems in excluding Kevin from school, via bus suspension. Ultimately, it would be Ann's decision to follow the recommendations of the director and school district policy for disciplining students with disabilities.

4. Would It Have Been Correct Procedurally for Ann to Agree to an After-School Detention the Third Time Kevin Misbehaved on the Bus? Why or Why Not?

If Kevin had a behavior management plan as part of his IEP and it did not include after-school detention, it would not have been appropriate for the principal to deviate from the plan.

Absent a behavior management plan, it might have been acceptable for Ann to agree to an after-school detention the third time Kevin misbehaved on the bus. However, after three somewhat serious incidences of misbehavior on the bus, holding an IEP meeting would have been the more appropriate next step. IDEA states that if a child's behavior interferes with his/her learning or the learning of other children, the IEP team should consider a functional assessment of the behavior with positive behavior supports considered. In addition, any change in transportation, i.e., related service, must be addressed within an IEP meeting.

5. What Conflict Resolution Skills Did Dr. Killday Use to Resolve the Problem in the IEP Meeting?

After the parent and principal began to argue and disagree about Kevin's punishment for misbehaving on the bus, Dr. Killday stood up and stopped the debate. He refocused the meeting on meeting Kevin's needs and on the problem at hand, i.e., how to help Kevin. He focused on implementation of a behavior management plan and transportation as part of Kevin's IEP. Overall, Dr. Killday refocused the meeting on how to meet Kevin's needs as opposed to arguing about who was right or wrong in terms of the bus suspension. It also might have been useful to conduct a functional behavioral assessment and revise the behavior management plan based on the results.

Case 9.1: "School Reform Is with Us. We Need to Prepare for the Future."

1. You Are the Superintendent of Schools for the Hill Town School District. How Would You Organize Your Staff to Prepare for the Board of Education Work Session?

The superintendent cannot assume that his or her staff has a great deal of knowledge about site-based management, charter schools, or the effect that either of the reforms would have on special education. The superintendent should establish ground rules for the meeting, in effect, a work session to prepare for the board work session. It is imperative that the superintendent schedules the board of education meeting far enough in advance to allow for a complete study of the various reforms. But it must be understood that when a board of education asks for information, there is usually not a great deal of lead time to complete the assignment. The superintendent needs to work closely with the board president to assure that the staff has enough time to prepare for the meeting. It is important that the board of education receive information in a format that would be informative, concise, and correlates with the overall district strategic plan.

Planning for the School Board Study Session

1. The superintendent needs to organize the planning meeting with a realistic approach to timelines. Can the planning meeting accomplish its goals in a day, two days? If the staff assisting on this project has other responsibilities, how will those responsibilities be covered? Should the planning group meet during the day, evenings, or Saturdays?

2. He or she should be specific as to the responsibilities that each staff member has in gathering the information for the board meeting.

3. The format for gathering and preparing the information should be the same for each member of the team. The same software package, same font, and the same formats should be used.

4. It is important that the team includes not only central office staff but should also include teachers, and when possible, parents.

5. The information gathering process should not be limited to a review of the literature, but should include visitation of districts currently using site-based management or charter school formats.

6. Any recommendation should be reviewed with reference to the district's strategic planning process.

7. Prepare the board document so that it reflects both the positive and negative aspects of the reforms being studied.

8. Assign administrators, teachers, and when possible, roles in the board presentation.

9. Preview the information for the board president.

10. Send a copy of the report to the board of education at least a week before the presentation.

2. You Are the Director of Special Education. Review Some of the Issues That May Face You and Your Staff in Moving into Site-Based Management.

It is important to understand the concept of change as it is reflected in staff development. The director needs to spend a great deal of time preparing everyone, including him- or herself, for the realities of site-based management. A change of this magnitude will not come easily. It would be beneficial to visit sites that are currently utilizing a site-based management approach. In visiting various programs the director would see site-based management that range from the principal being allowed to make limited decisions to a system that allowed the principal the complete responsibility to manage the budget, hire personnel, and develop the curriculum. It is important to understand that the site-based managed school differs from charter schools in that the site-based managed school continues to be part of the school district.

As the director of special education you could be faced with a serious dilemma. If the site-based process is not developed correctly a district could have each of its schools making decisions that may be at odds with rules and regulations.

3. What Would Be the Effect of a Charter School on the Management of Special Education in Your District?

The charter school concept has many facets and differs in part from state to state. It is difficult to generalize unless one is familiar with the specific rules and regulations of a particular state. In theory, the charter school offers an opportunity to develop a school that creates its own curriculum, organization, budget, and governing board. The charter school in effect becomes a school district unto itself.

The funding in a majority of the states comes from the local school district. Unfortunately, the funding that establishes the charter school may not necessarily cover the total cost of special education and the issues that surround it. Although bound by IDEA, does a charter school have the staff, funding, curriculum, and staff development program to meet the needs of the student with a disability? There are other potential issues that need to be carefully scrutinized with respect to special education. Some charter schools are not bound by the same certification standards that apply to the local school district. Although the charter school has a mandate that allows it to become a separate entity from the local district, it still must conform to the laws that govern special education. This could mean that noncertified teachers might bear the full responsibility of carrying out an IEP. Who becomes responsible for the special education student if the charter school fails to fulfill the mandates of the IEP? Only time and case will determine this aspect of special education and the charter school.

Case 9.2: "We Need to Discuss School Reform and Special Education"

1. As the Director of Special Education What Would You List As the Key Issues That the Board Members Need to Know About IDEA '97?

- It is important to understand the IDEA '97 encourages everyone involved in education to think of special education not as a place, but as a way of helping students to learn.
- General curriculum is a major focus of IDEA '97. Everyone begins at that point. IDEA '97 makes it very clear that if a student cannot be successful in a general curriculum, it is mandated that the details of any changes must be listed in the IEP.
- A revision to IDEA includes the assumption that "all" students will be given regular assessment unless the IEP determines otherwise. The assessment results are to be reported in school district reports.
- Regular education teachers are accountable for student performance including students in special education.
- IDEA '97 called for changes to the discipline policies afforded to special education students. The changes call for the development of a behavior plan that is built upon information gathered from a behavior assessment. The plan was to be part of the IEP.
- Parent involvement is an essential part of IDEA '97.
- IDEA '97 calls for general and special education collaboration in IEP development, implementation, and documentation.

2. What Can Districts Do to Ensure That First-Year Teachers and Experienced Teachers Understand Their Responsibility to Develop the Knowledge and Implementation Strategies Necessary to Meet the Standards of IDEA '97?

If school organization, teaching, and learning are to meet the schooling needs of "all" children, it is important that the issues be attacked from both ends: in the universities, where future teachers are prepared for their profession, and in the classroom where teachers and students interact. A model is needed that will not only strengthen teachers and administrator's knowledge base but will make a difference to future teachers and administrators. The model would allow for a partnership to be developed between a school/school district and a university. The professional development school (PDS) model brings together teacher training, teacher accreditation, and the school district as partners. The Hill Town School District would best serve its future needs by forming a partnership with the local university to in-service current staff and to develop a PDS.

For the present the district should establish mandatory staff development that assists classroom teachers in understanding their responsibility for a student with a disability.

3. What Should a School District Do to Ensure That School Reform Initiatives Meet Special Education Requirements?

To ensure that a school reform meets special education requirements it is essential that every aspect of the school reform in question be studied carefully. The charter school will be used as an example here because unlike other reforms the charter school is not the responsibility of the local school district. The courts will decide if a charter school fails to meet its special education responsibility, does the local district become responsible? It is sound advice to be proactive to offer certain services to the charter school.

A district might assist the charter school in assessing its programming and in staff development. As an example: A district might offer to assist the charter school by carrying out an audit to determine if the school is meeting its responsibility in the area of special education. If there are problems, the district may offer to act as a consultant to the charter school. This cooperative approach, although not mandated by law, would be appropriate in protecting the rights of the student with a disability.

It might also benefit both the local district and the charter school to establish a shared staff development program, especially in the area of special education. The prudent superintendent and board of education should also offer staff development opportunities and assistance whenever possible to the initiator of the charter school, the administrator, and the staff of the school.

Case 10.1: "Drugs and Disability"

1. Was the Board of Education Correct When It Voted to Expel Terrance? How Do You Know?

Yes, the board of education could expel Terrance. The IDEA states that if determined through a manifestation determination that the child's behavior was not a manifestation of the child's disability, discipline procedures applicable to children without disabilities may be applied.

2. Was It Correct for Educational Services to Cease After the 45-Day Interim Alternative Educational Setting? Why or Why Not?

It was incorrect to cease to provide educational services to Terrance. Although a school district may expel a student if the student's behavior is not a manifestation of his/her disability, the district must continue to provide a free appropriate public education (FAPE). School districts must provide services that will enable the student to appropriately progress in the general curriculum and advance toward achieving the IEP goals. The decision to terminate educational services for Terrance was a major legal problem for the district.

3. Make An Outline of the Procedure Followed During This Case. Was the Procedure Correct? Would You Have Done Anything Differently?

Building Level Actions

- Child had drugs at school and was brought to principal and interviewed by principal.
- Child's parent contacted and police contacted.
- Child suspended 10 days, with possibility of expulsion.
- Principal reviewed discipline records and other school records, where it was discovered that the child was not a discipline problem and received learning disabilities services.
- Principal contacted special education administrator, where an agreement was made to place the child in an interim alternative educational setting for 45 days.

Special Education Administrator Actions

- Special education administrator arranged IEP meeting and gained consent from the parent for a functional behavioral assessment.

(*Note:* If the FBA consisted of a review of existing data, parental consent was not necessary.)

IEP Team Actions

- Considered relevant evaluation data, student observations, IEP, and student's placement.
- Conducted manifestation determination.
- IEP was appropriate, student understood the impact of the behavior, student was able to control the behavior.
- Therefore, behavior was not a manifestation of the disability.
- Team determined behavioral intervention plan and interim alternative educational setting.

School District Actions

- Expulsion hearing held.
- Recommendations from expulsion forwarded to board of education.
- Board of education voted to expel child for remainder of school year.
- Educational services terminated after 45-day interim alternative educational setting.

The procedure followed, assuming it was in agreement with district policy, appeared to be correct, with one major exception. The district should have continued to provide educational services to Terrance during his expulsion from school. Terminating services for a student expelled from school is a major violation of the zero reject premise of the IDEA.

Case 10.2: "Why Can a Student with Behavior Disorders Hit a Teacher and Get Away with It?"

1. Did the IEP Team Make a Procedurally Appropriate Manifestation Determination? How Do You Know?

In making a manifestation determination, the IEP team must consider all relevant evaluation data, observations of the student, and the student's IEP and placement. Evidence in the case suggests that these factors were considered. To determine if a student's behavior is related to his disability, the IEP team must ask the following questions:

- Was the IEP appropriate?
- Did the disability impair the student's ability to understand the impact and consequences of the behavior?
- Did the disability impair the student's ability to control the behavior?

The discussion at the IEP meeting clearly indicated that Muhammad was able to understand the consequences of his behavior, but was impulsive and unable to control his behavior. In addition, the team decided to revise Muhammad's IEP to a new placement. It could be assumed that the IEP was not appropriate because the team made a significant change. Based on this information, the team made a procedurally appropriate manifestation determination.

2. Why Did the Hearing Officer Deny the District's Request for a 45-Day Interim Alternative Educational Setting?

If a student engages in misbehavior that is likely to result in injury, the school district may request from a hearing officer (via expedited hearing), a 45-day interim alternative educational setting. In making the decision to grant the placement, a hearing officer must consider the following:

- Has the district provided substantial evidence that the child is substantially likely to injure him- or herself or others?
- Is the current placement appropriate?
- Has the district taken reasonable steps to reduce the risk of harm in the current placement?
- Is the proposed interim alternative educational setting (IAES) appropriate?

The only evidence submitted to support the supposition that Muhammad was very likely to injure himself or others was the recent incident of hitting the teacher. As serious as this incident was, one incident probably was not enough to convince a hearing officer that the student was substantially likely to injure himself or others if returned to his current placement. The current placement was not appropriate, as the IEP team proposed changing it to the day treatment facility. The district did not address whether reasonable steps were proposed to reduce the risk of harm in the current placement. The district obviously thought the interim alternative educational setting was appropriate as this was the placement sought by the district.

3. Why Did Muhammad Have the Right to Return to His Previous Placement After His 10-Day Suspension?

The district proposed changing Muhammad's placement at the end of his 10-day suspension. His mother disagreed and requested a due process hearing. This request caused Muhammad to "stay put" in his current placement pending the outcome of the hearing. The only action the district could take was to request from the hearing officer placement in an interim alternative educational setting for 45 days. The district made this request, but it was denied. If the parent and school district could not agree on another setting for Muhammad, he had to return to his current placement until the outcome of the hearing.

4. What Problems Could Muhammad's Return to His Previous Placement Cause in the School District?

Returning Muhammad to his current placement could cause several conflicts with students, staff, and the community. The unwritten message to students and staff was that a student in special education could hit a teacher, break his jaw, and return to school after a 10-day suspension. Many students and staff members might think this was unfair. If a student in regular education engaged in the same behavior, that student would likely be expelled. The incident highlights the double standard when disciplining students with disabilities.

Teachers and other staff probably would be very upset when forced to take Muhammad back in their classes after the 10-day suspension. Teachers might have protections built into bargaining agreements specifying safe work conditions. Therefore, one outcome might be a grievance filed by the teacher's organization. Teacher morale might also be a consequence of this incident.

The general community might be very upset at the outcome of this situation, given the fear for safety in schools in light of recent school shootings. The media could reflect the community's concern in newspapers, television, etc. This might exert pressure on the school board and administration to "get tougher" with violence in schools.

Case 10.3: "Is Every Child Protected Under the IDEA?"

1. Why Was Lakisha Entitled to Protections Under the IDEA If She Had Not Been Evaluated for Special Education?

The IDEA clearly specifies that any child has the procedural protections of the IDEA in discipline cases if the school district had knowledge that the child was a child with a disability before the behavior that precipitated the disciplinary action. The IDEA further clarifies under what conditions a school district might have this knowledge. The school district has knowledge that a child might have a disability if any of the following occur:

- The parent of the child has expressed concern in writing to the school district that the child is in need of special education services. If the parent cannot write or is unable to write, this concern can be expressed orally.
- The behavior or performance of the child demonstrates the need for these services.
- The parent of the child has requested an evaluation of the child.
- The child's teacher, or other staff of the school district, have expressed concern about the behavior or performance of the child to the special education administrator or other personnel in accordance with the district's referral process.

Based on this information, Lakisha was clearly entitled to the protections of the IDEA. The teacher expressed concern about Lakisha's performance and the parent requested an evaluation for special education.

2. How Should the Principal Have Reacted?

Ideally, the new principal would have had knowledge of the IDEA and district policy to implement the IDEA. Unfortunately, this was not the case. In the case of a possible weapon and a new principal, it might have been a good idea to contact the superintendent, special education administrator, or other veteran principal for advice on how to proceed. It is possible that, after consultation, the principal would have suspended the child for fewer than 10 days, completed the special education evaluation immediately, and avoided a costly due process hearing where the district did not prevail.

If the principal had been directed to proceed with possible expulsion, Lakisha should have been afforded the protections under the IDEA. The principal could have suspended Lakisha for 10 days without convening an IEP meeting. Any days in excess of 10 consecutive days in this case would have been a change in placement, which triggers the IDEA protections. The principal, in consultation with the special education administrator, would have convened an IEP team to do the following:

- Determine what services would be needed beyond 10 days suspension which would have enabled Lakisha to progress in the general curriculum.
- Conduct a functional behavioral assessment.
- Develop a behavior intervention plan based on the functional behavioral assessment.
- Conduct a manifestation determination.

The special education administrator would have assured the completion of Lakisha's evaluation promptly and an IEP team would have been convened to discuss the results and plan a program for her, if appropriate.

3. If You Were the Special Education Administrator, How Would You Make Sure This Did Not Occur Again?

It would be important to provide ongoing inservice for all principals on special education law and its implications in the school district. All new principals should be inserviced on basic provisions of special education law and district policy for carrying out the law. In addition, when provisions of federal and/or state law change regarding students with disabilities, it would be important to draft local policy and procedures for implementing the law. After policy and procedures were approved by the board of education, it would be essential to disseminate them to all district staff.

Since new principals are in a particularly vulnerable position, the special education administrator could arrange for a mentor so the new principal would have someone with whom to consult on difficult issues. This system might prevent difficult situations from "snowballing" into costly due process hearings.

4. Do You Think Lakisha Had a Weapon?

The IDEA uses the same definition of weapon that is found in 18 U.S.C. § 930 (g)(2). The term is defined as a weapon, device, instrument, material, of substance, animate or inanimate, that is used for, or is readily capable of, causing death or serious bodily injury, except that it does not include a pocket knife with a blade of less than 2 1/2 inches in length. According to this definition, Lakisha did not have a weapon. She had nail clippers with a file that could be construed to be a knife blade, but the blade was only 1 1/2 inches long. Technical definitions aside, one must look at how the alleged weapon was used. In this case, Lakisha did not threaten anyone or use the clippers to hurt anyone. Defining nail clippers as a weapon might have been an overreaction.

Appendix B

Issues Addressed in Case Studies
(** indicate primary issues)
(* indicates secondary issues)

Chapter/ Case Number	Governance/ Organization	Identification/ Placement	Conflict	Program Evaluation	Fiscal	Personnel	Transportation	School Reform	Discipline
Sample			**			**			*
2.1	**		*						
2.2	**		*						
3.1		**	*						
3.2		**	*						*
3.3		**	*			*			*
4.1		*	**						
4.2	*		**	*		*			
5.1		*		**				*	
5.2		*		**				*	
6.1	*			*	**		*		
6.2			*		**	*			
7.1			*			**			
7.2			*			**			
8.1		*	*			*	**		
8.2			*			*	**		*
9.1					*	*		**	
9.2					*	*		**	**
10.1		*							**
10.2		*	*			*			**
10.3	*	*	*			*			**

APPENDIX C

Case Study Analysis Form

Primary Issue:

Secondary Issue:

Tertiary Issue:

Audiences:

Decision Makers:

Influential Groups/Individuals:

Inclusive Activities:

Answers to Questions:

REFERENCES

Abbott, M., C. Walton, Y. Tupia, and C. Greenwood. 1999. Research to practice: A "blueprint" for closing the gap in local schools. *Exceptional Children* 65 (3): 339–52.

Ahearn, E. M. 1993. *Re-examining eligibility under IDEA: A background paper prepared for the policy forum re-examining eligibility under IDEA.* Alexandria, VA: National Association of State Directors of Special Education.

Ahearn, E. M. 1997. *Due process hearings: An update. Final report.* Alexandria, VA: National Association of State Directors of Special Education.

Algozzine, B., S. Christenson, and J. E. Ysseldyke. 1982. Probabilities associated with the referral to placement process. *Teacher Education and Special Education* 5:19–23.

Allington, R., and P. Johnston. 1986. The coordination among regular classroom reading programs and targeted support programs. In *Designs for compensatory education: Conference procedures and papers,* ed. B. I. Williams, P. A. Richmond, and B. J. Mason, 3–40. Washington, DC: Research Associates.

American Academy of Pediatrics Committee on Injury and Poison Prevention. 1994. School bus transportation of children with special needs. *Pediatrics* 93 (1): 129.

Americans with Disabilities Act of 1990, 42 U.S.C. § 12101 et seq.

Ammer, J. 1984. The mechanics of mainstreaming: Considering the regular educator's perspective. *Remedial and Special Education* 5: 15–20.

"A Nation at Risk," *Richmond Times-Dispatch,* Holland, Robert Sept. 30 1998.

Ascham, R. (1517) The Schoolmaster, London, England.

"As Students Return, Schools Cope with Severe Shortages of Teachers," *New York Times,* 31 August 1999, p. A1.

Baker, J., and N. Zigmond. 1995. The meaning and practice of inclusion for students with learning disabilities: Themes and implications from five cases. *The Journal of Special Education* 29:163–80.

Baruch Bush, R. A. 1992. *The dilemmas of mediation practice: A study of ethical dilemmas and policy implications.* Washington, DC: National Institute for Dispute Resolution.

Bay, M., T. Bryan, and R. O'Conner. 1994. Teachers assisting teachers: A prereferral model for urban educators. *Teacher Education and Special Education* 17 (1): 10–21.

Becvar, R., and D. Becvar. 1982. *Systems theory and family therapy.* Washington DC: University Press of America, Inc.

Belcher, T. 1997. *Assessment and equity.* Yearbook: National Council of Teachers of Mathematics. Reston, VA: H. W. Wilson.

Berg, B. D. (1994). *Educational burnout revisited. Voices from the staff room.* The Clearinghouse, 67 (4) 185–190.

Board of Education of the District 130 Public Schools v. Illinois State Board of Education, 26 IDELR 724 (N.D. Ill. 1997).

Board of Education of the Hendrick Hudson Central School District v. Rowley, 458 U.S. 176 (1982).

Bladen County (NC) Sch. Dist. 22 IDELR 253 (OCR 1994).

Bluth, L. F. 1991. *Transportation: The individualized education program process.* Paper presented at the National Association for Pupil Transportation Conference and Trade Show, Baltimore, Maryland.

Bluth, L. F., and S. N. Hochberg. 1994. Transporting students with disabilities: Rules, regs and their application. *School Business Affairs* 60 (4): 12–13, 15–17.

Bodine, R., D. Crawford, and R. Schrumpf. 1993. *Creating the peaceable school.* Champaign, IL: Research Press.

Bodine, R. J., D. K. Crawford, and F. Schrumpf. 1994. *Creating the peaceable school: A comprehensive program for teaching conflict resolution. Program guide.* Champaign, IL: Research Press.

Boe, E., Cook, L., and Kaufman, M. J. 1996. Special and general education teachers in public schools: Sources of supply in national perspective. *Teacher Education and Special Education* 19 (1): 1–16.

Borsa, J. C., M. Ahmed, and K. Perry. 1998. Paper presented at National Council of Professors of Educational Administration, 1998 conference.

Borsa, J. C., and J. Klotz. 1998. *Utilizing distance learning and the case study method to enhance instruction between two universities.* ERIC Document ED 429470.

Brent v. San Diego Unified Sch. Dist., 25 IDELR 1 (S.D. Cal. 1996).

Brown, D. 1990. *Decentralization and school-based management.* Bristol, PA: Falmer Press.

Campbell, P. 1992. *The Connecticut symposia on special education in the 21st century: Final report and executive summary.* ERIC document ED 345466.

Carmel (NY) Cent. Sch. Dist., 20 IDELR 1177 (OCR 1993).

Carter, J., and G. Sugai. 1989. Survey on prereferral practices: Responses from state departments of education. *Exceptional Children* 55: 298–302.

Carter, M. 1992. *Transportation: The neglected related service.* Paper presented at the annual convention of the Council for Exceptional Children, Baltimore, Maryland.

Casey, T. J. 1991. Special education transportation update and forecast. *School Business Affairs* 57 (4): 8–11.

Cedar Rapids Community School Dist v. Garret F. by Charlene F., 67 U.S.S.W. 4165 (1999).

Chalfant, J., M. V. Pysh, and R. Moultrie. 1979. Teacher assistance teams: A model for within-building problem solving. *Learning Disability Quarterly* 2 (3): 85–96.

Chalfant, J., and M. Van Dusen Pysh. 1989. Teacher assistance teams: Five descriptive studies on 96 teams. *Remedial and Special Education* 10 (6): 49–58.

Christensen, C. R. 1987. *Teaching the case study method.* Boston: Harvard Business School.

Christenson, S., and J. Ysseldyke. 1989. Assessing student performance . . . an important change is needed. *Journal of School Psychology* 27: 409–426.

Cincinnati Enquirer, 15 October 1999.

Comer, J. 1988. *Quantitative methods for public administration: Techniques and applications.* Fort Worth, TX: Harcourt Brace.

"Coping with Teacher Shortages," 11 January, 2000, *New York Times,* p. A24.

Council for Exceptional Children. 1998. *IDEA 1997: Let's make it work.* Reston, VA: Council for Exceptional Children.

Council for Exceptional Children. 1998. *Report of the council for Exceptional Children's ad hoc committee on medically fragile students.* Reston, VA: Council for Exceptional Children.

Crawford, D. K., R. J. Bodine, and R. G. Hoglund. 1993. *The school for quality learning: Managing the school and classroom the Deming way.* Champaign, IL: Research Press.

Crowner, T. T. 1985. A taxonomy of special education finance. *Exceptional Children* 51: 503–508.

Dempsey, S., and D. Fuchs. 1993. Flat versus weighted reimbursement formulas: A longitudinal analysis of statewide special education funding practices. *Exceptional Children* 59 (5): 433–43.

Detsel v. Board of Education of the Auburn Enlarged City School District, 637 F. Supp. 1022 (N.D. N.Y. 1986), aff'd., 820 F. 2d 587 (2d Cir. 1987), cert. den. 484 U.S. 833, 108 S. Ct. 495, 98 L. Ed. 2d 494 (1987).

Dewey, J. 1933. *How we think* (1st ed). Boston, MA: D.C. Heath.

Dobbs, R. F., E. B. Primm, and B. Primm. 1991. Mediation: A common sense approach for resolving conflicts in education. *Focus on Exceptional Children* 24 (2): 1–11.

Donald B. by Christine B. v. Board of School Commissioners of Mobile County, 26 IDELR 414 (11th Cir. 1997).

Dworkin, A. G. 1985. *When teachers give up: Teacher burnout, teacher turnover, and their impact.* Austin, TX: Hogg Foundation of Mental Health.

East Windsor Bd. of Educ., 20 IDELR 1478 (SEA CT 1994).

Edmonds, R. 1979. Effective schools for the urban poor. *Educational Leadership* 37 (1): 15–24.

Education Week. 1998. Quality Counts. Education Week (17) 17, 1–270.

Engiles, A. 1996. *Team-based conflict resolution in special education. Conciliation program.* Washington, DC: Office of Special Education and Rehabilitative Services.

Fisher, R., W. Ury, and B. Patton. 1991. *Getting to yes: Negotiating agreement without giving in* (2nd ed.). Boston, MA: Houghton Mifflin.

Florida State Dept. of Education 1992. *Mediation in special education. Technical assistance paper.* Tallahassee, FL: Florida State Dept. of Education.

Flugum, K. R., and D. J. Reschly. 1994. Prereferral interventions: Quality indices and outcomes. *Journal of School Psychology* 32: 1–14.

Fort Sage Unified Sch. Dist./Lassen County Office of Educ., 23 IDELR 1078 (SEA CA 1995).

Freitas, D. 1992. *Managing smallness: Promoting fiscal practices for rural school district administrators.* Charleston, WV: ERIC Clearinghouse on Rural Education and Small Schools, Appalachia Educational Laboratory.

Ginott, H. G. 1965. *Between parent and child.* New York: Avon.

Glasser, W. 1984. *Control theory.* New York: Harper & Row.

Goals 2000: Educate America Act, 1994 (Public Law 103–277).

Goertz, M., (1996). Bumpy road to education reform. Consortium For Policy Research in Education. University of Pennsylvania.

Goldberg, S. S., and J. D. Huefner. 1995. Dispute resolution in special education: An introduction to litigation alternatives. *West's Education Law Quarterly* 4 (3): 534–42.

Goor, M. B. 1995. *Leadership for special education administration: A case-based approach.* New York: Harcourt Brace.

Goss v. Lopez, 419 U.S. 565 (1975).

Graden, J., A. Casey, and D. Bonstrom. 1983. *Prereferral interventions: Effects on referral rates and teacher attitudes.* (Research Report No. 140). Minneapolis: Minnesota Institute for Research on Learning Disabilities.

Graden, J. L., A. Casey, and S. L. Christenson. 1985. Implementing a prereferral intervention system: Part I. The model. *Exceptional Children* 51: 377–84.

Greer, J. G., C. E. Wethered. 1984. Learned helplessness: A piece of the burnout puzzle. *Exceptional Children* 50 (6): 524–30.

Gutkin, R. B., M. Henning-Stout, and W. C. Piersel. 1988. Impact of a districtwide behavioral consultation prereferral intervention service on patterns of school psychological service delivery. *Professional School Psychology* 3: 301–308.

Harrington-Lueker, D. 1991. Special buses. *The American School Board Journal* 178 (4): 27–28, 43.

Hartman, W. T. 1992. State funding models for special education. *Remedial and Special Education* 13 (6): 47–58.

Hasazi, S. B., A. P. Johnston, A. M. Liggett, and R. A. Schattman. 1994. A qualitative policy study of the least restrictive environment provision of the Individuals with Disabilities Education Act. *Exceptional Children* 60 (6): 491–507.

Hess, F. 1998. *As the policy churns: Toil and trouble for urban school reform.* Ann Arbor, MI: The Educational Digest.

Heibert, B., B. Wang, and M. Hunter. 1982. Affective influences in learning disabled adults. *Learning Disabilities Quarterly* Vol. 5 #4 334–365.

Hocutt, A. M. 1996. Effectiveness of special education: Is placement the critical factor? *The Future of Children* 6 (1): 77–102.

Hollowood, T., C. Salisbury, B. Rainforth, and M. Palomboro. 1994. Use of instructional time in classrooms serving students with and without severe disabilities. *Exceptional Children* 61 (3): 242–53.

Honig vs. Doe, 479 U.S. 1804 (1988).

Idaho State Board of Education. 1996. *Special education mediation in Idaho: Managing parent and school conflict through effective communication.* Boise, Idaho: Idaho State Board of Education.

Illinois State Board of Education. 1997. *Illinois learning standards.* Springfield, IL: Illinois State Board of Education.

Improving America's School Act (PL 103–382).

Individuals with Disabilities Education Act Amendments of 1997, Pub. L. No. 105–17, 105th Cong., 1st sess.

Individuals with Disabilities Education Act Regulations, 34 C.F.R. § 300 (1999).

Iowa State Dept. of Education. 1992. *Transporting students with disabilities: A manual for transportation supervisors.* Des Moines, IA: Iowa State Dept. of Education.

Jackson County (AL) Sch. Dist. EHLR 353:346 (OCR 1989).

Jacksonville, FL Times-Union, Jan. 5, 2000. Incentives for teachers who transfer.

Johnson, L. 1998. *Program evaluation in special education: An examination of the practices utilized by local educational agencies.* (ERIC Document Reproduction Service No. TM 029 174).

Joyce, B., B. Showers. 1988. Student achievement through staff development. Educational Leadership, V46 #3 pp. 90–98.

Karlin, R. "States Search for Ways to Recruit New Teachers," *Albany, NY Times Union,* 10 January 2000.

Kennedy v. Board of Education, EHLR 557: 232 (W. Va. 1985).

Kreb, R. A. 1991. *Third-party payment for funding special education and related services.* Horsham, PA: LRP Publications.

Kreidler, W. J. 1984. *Creative conflict resolution: More than 200 activities for keeping peace in the classroom.* Glenview, IL: Good Year Books, Scott Foresman and Co.

Kreidler, W. 1990. *Elementary perspectives: Teaching concepts of peace and conflict.* Cambridge, MA: Educators for Social Responsibility.

Laycock, V. K., R. A. Bable, and L. Korinek. 1991. Alternative structures for collaboration in the delivery of special services. *Preventing School Failure* 35 (4): 15–18.

Letter to Hamilton, 25 IDELR 520 (OSEP 1996).

Letter to Stohrer, EHLR 213: 209 (OSEP 1989).

Lieb, S. "Kentucky has more 'emergency' teachers: Shortage crucial in special ed," *Cincinnati Enquirer,* 15 October 1999.

Linder, D. 1991. Special education transportation: An eight-point tune-up. *School Business Affairs* 57 (7): 26–28.

Lipsky, D. K., and A. Gartner. 1996. Inclusive education and school restructuring. In *Controversial issues confronting special education: Divergent perspectives* (2nd ed.), ed. In W. Stainback and S. Stainback, pp. 3–15. Boston: Allyn & Bacon.

Lipsky, D., and A. Gartner. 1996. *Inclusion, school restructuring, and remaking of American society.* Cambridge, MA: Harvard Educational Review.

Lloyd, J., J. Kauffman, T. Landrum, and D. Roe. 1991. Why do teachers refer pupils for special education? An analysis of referral records. *Exceptionality* 2 (3): 115–126.

Lombardi, R., and B. Ludlow. 1996. *Trends shaping the future of special education. Fastback 409.* Bloomington, IN: Phi Delta Kappa Educational Foundation.

Lombardi, T., and B. Ludlow. 1997. *Special education in the 21st century.* ERIC document ED 406086.

LRE Project. 1990. *Collaborative teams in inclusive-oriented schools.* Topeka, KS: Kansas State Board of Education.

LRP Publications. 1998. *The road to compliance: Legally transporting students with disabilities.* Horsham, PA: LRP Publications.

Male, M. 1991. Effective team participation. *Preventing School Failure* 35 (4): 29–35.

Malon, F., and E. Schiller. 1995. Practice and research in special education. *Exceptional Children* 95: 414–424.

Maloney, M., and B. Shenker. 1995. *The continuing evolution of special education law: 1978 to 1995.* Danvers, MA: LRP Publications.

Malouf, D. B., and E. D. Schiller. 1995. Practice and research in special education. *Exceptional Children* 61 (5): 414–424.

Maryland State Board of Education. 1991. *Supervisor's guide for transporting children with special health needs.* Baltimore, MD: Maryland State Board of Education.

Masoner, M. 1988. *An audit of the case study method.* New York: Praeger.

May, H., "Utah Battling a Teacher Shortage," *The Salt Lake Tribune,* 27 September 1999.

Mayer, L. 1982. *Educational administration and special education: A handbook for school administrators.* Boston: Allyn & Bacon.

McLaughlin, M., R. Henderson, and M. Ullah. 1996. *Charter schools and students with disabilities.* Alexandria, VA: Center for Policy Research on the Impact of General and Special Education Reform.

McLaughlin, M., and M. Owings. 1993. Relationships among states' fiscal and demographic data and the implementation of P. L. 94–142. *Exceptional Children* 34: 247–61.

McLeskey, J., D. Henry, and M. Axelrod. 1999. Inclusion students with learning disabilities: An examination of data from reports to Congress. *Exceptional Children* Fall 1999.

McLoughlin, J. A., and R. B. Lewis. 1994. *Assessing special students* (4th ed.). New York: Merrill Publishing Co.

Meyers, J., L. Gelzheiser, and G. Yelich. 1991. Do pull-in programs foster collaboration? *Remedial and Special Education* 12 (2): 8–9.

Miller, S. 1994. *Kids learn about justice by mediating the disputes of other kids.* Chicago, IL: American Bar Association Special Committee on Youth Education for Citizenship.

Murray v. Montrose County School District, 51 F. 3d 921 (10th Cir. 1995).

NASBE (National Association of State Boards of Education) Study Group on Special Education. 1992. *Winners all: A call for inclusive school.* Alexandria, VA: National Association of State Boards of Education.

NASP/NASDE/OSEP. 1994. *Assessment and eligibility in special education: An examination of policy and practice with proposals for change.* Alexandria, VA: National Association of State Directors of Special Education.

National Center for Educational Restructuring and Inclusion (1995). Graduate School and University Center of City University of New York.

National Commission on Excellence in Education. 1983. *A nation at risk: The imperative for educational reform.* Washington, DC: U.S. Government Printing Office.

National Council on Disabilities. 1993. *Serving nation's students with disabilities: Progress and prospects 1993.* Washington, DC: National Council on Disabilities.

Nelson, J. R., D. J. Smith, L. Taylor, J. M. Dodd, and K. Reavis. 1991. Prereferral intervention: A review of the research. *Education and Treatment of Children* 14: 243–53.

Nevada State Dept. of Education. 1995. *Nevada mediation system for early intervention and special education.* Revised. Reno, Nevada: Nevada State Dept. of Education.

New York Times, August 1999.

New York Times, January 2000.

Newman, H. 1955. *Teaching management; a practical handbook, with special references to the case study method.* London: Routledge & Paul.

NIDR Community Justice Task Force. 1991. *Community dispute resolution manual: Insights and guidance from two decades of practices.* Washington, DC: The National Institute for Dispute Resolution.

Occupational Outlook Quarterly, 1998 Summer.

Office of Special Education Programs. 1995. *OSEP letter offers disabilities transportation guidelines.* Washington, DC: Dept. of Education.

Olson, J., and A. Goldstein. 1997. *The inclusion of students with disabilities and limited English proficient students in large scale assessments: A summary of recent progress* (NCES 97–487). Washington DC: U.S. Department of Education; Office of Educational Research and Improvement.

Olson, J., and P. V. Matuskey. 1982. Causes for burnout in SLD teachers. *Journal of Learning Disabilities* 15 (2): 97–99.

O'Reilly, F. E. 1995. *State special education funding formulas and the use of separate placements for students with disabilities: Exploring linkages* (Policy Paper No. 7). Palo Alto, CA: Center for Special Education Finance, American Institutes for Research.

Osborne, A. 1993. *Effective management of special education programs: A handbook for school administrators.* New York: Teachers College Press.

Osborne, A., Di Mattia, and Curran. 1993. *Effective management of special education programs.*

Parrish, T. 1993. *State funding provisions and least restrictive environment: Implications for federal policy* (Policy Brief No. 2). Palo Alto, CA: Center for Special Education Finance, American Institutes for Research.

Parrish T. 1994. *Fiscal issues in special education: Removing incentives for restrictive placements* (Policy Paper No. 8). Palo Alto, CA: Center for Special Education Finance, American Institutes for Research.

Parrish, R. 1996. *Special education finance: Past, present, and future* (Policy Paper No. 8). Palo Alto, CA: Center for Special Education Finance, American Institutes for Research.

Parrish, R., and J. Chambers. 1996. Financing special education. *The Future of Children* 6 (1): 121–38.

Pazey, B. 1995. An essential link for the administration of special education: The ethic of care. *Journal for a Just and Caring Education* 1 (3): 296–311.

Podemski, R., G. Marsh, T. Smith, and B. Price. 1995. *Comprehensive administration of special education* (2nd ed). Englewood Cliffs, NJ: Prentice Hall.

Popham, W. J. 1993. *Educational evaluation* (2nd ed). Needham Heights, MA: Allyn and Bacon.

Position Paper of National Joint Committee on Learning Disabilities (Jan., 1993).

Raper, R. 1990. Two roads diverged in the woods and I took the bus: Rural transportation for exceptional students. *Rural Special Education Quarterly* 10 (2): 11–14.

Roach, V., D. Dailey, and Z. Goert. 1997. *State accountability systems and students with disabilities.* Alexandria, VA: The Center for Policy Research on the Impact of General and Special Education Reform.

Reed, P., and K. Brazeau. 1991. *Transporting students with special needs: A resource manual for school district administrators.* Salem, OR: Oregon Department of Education.

Reschly, D. 1980. School psychologists and assessment in the future. *Professional Psychology* 11: 841–48.

Reschly, D. 1996. Functional assessment and special education decision making. In *Controversial issues confronting special education: Divergent perspectives* (2nd ed.) In W. Stainback and S. Stainback, pp. 115–28. Needham Heights, MA: Allyn & Bacon.

Rockne, J., and R. Weiss-Castro. 1994. *The national agenda for achieving better results for children and youth with disabilities.* ERIC document ED 373530.

Rogers, B., and A. Ensign. 1996. *Your child on the bus: Transporting students with special needs.* Lansing, MI: Michigan State Board of Education.

Office of Educational Research and Improvement (1986). Educational Programs That Work. A Collection of Proven Exemplary Educational Programs and Practices (12th ed.) Washington, DC: Author.

Sage, D., and L. Burrello. 1994. *Leadership in educational reform: An administrator's guide to changes in special education.* Baltimore, MD: Paul H. Brookes Publishing Co.

"Finding and Keeping Teachers Is a Challenge," *St. Louis Post-Dispatch,* Aug. 22, 1999.

Salt Lake Tribune, 27 September 1999.

Salvia, J., and F. Ysseldyke. 1995. *Assessment* (6th ed). Boston: Houghton Mifflin.

Sarason, S. B. 1979. *Educational handicap, public policy, and social history: A broadened perspective on mental retardation.* New York: Free Press.

Savoury, G., H. Beals, and J. Parks. 1995, May-June. Mediation in child protection: Facilitating the resolution of disputes. *Child Welfare LCCIV* (3): 743–62.

Saver, K., and B. Downes. 1991. PIT crew: A model for teacher collaboration in an elementary school. *Intervention in School and Clinic* 27 (2): 116–22.

Schrag, J. 1996. *Mediation and other alternative dispute resolution procedures in special education: Final report.* Washington, DC: Office of Special Education and Rehabilitative Services.

Schrag, J. 1996. *Mediation in special education: A resource manual for mediators.* Revised and updated. Washington, DC: Office of Special Education and Rehabilitative Services.

Schrumpf, F., D. Crawford, H. C. Usadel. 1991. *Peer mediation: Conflict resolution in schools. Program guide.* Champaign, IL: Research Press.

Schuldt v. Mankato Independent School District #77, 937 F. 2d 1357 (8th Cir. 1991).

Schumack, S., and A. Stewart. 1995. *When parents and educators do not agree: Using mediation to resolve conflicts about special education. A guidebook for parents.* Cambridge, MA: Harvard University Center for Law and Education.

Shapiro, J., P. Loeb, and D. Bowermaster. 1993, December 13. Separate and unequal. *U.S. News and World Report,* 46–50, 54–56, 60.

Shriner, J. 1993. *State special education outcomes 1993.* Minneapolis: National Center on Educational Outcomes.

Singer, J. D. (1993). Are special education career paths special? Results from a 13 year longitudinal study. *Exceptional Children,* 59 (3): 262–279.

Skelly v. Brookfield LaGrange Park Sch. Dist 95, 26 LDELR 288 (N.D. Ill. 1997).

Slaikeu, K. A. 1989, October. Designing dispute resolution systems in the health care industry. *Negotiation Journal,* (In Practice Dispute Systems Design: A Special Section, 395–400).

Slavin, R., N. Karweit, and N. Madden. 1989. *Effective programs for students at risk.* Boston: Allyn & Bacon.

Solend, S., and L. Duhaney. 1999. The impact of inclusion on students with and without disabilities and their educators. *Remedial and Special Education,* Mar/April 1999.

Souvin, M. 1980. *The evaluation of college teaching.* Syracuse, NY: National Dissemination Center, Syracuse University School of Education.

"Special Education's Special Costs," *Wall Street Journal,* 20 October 1993, p. A14.

Stainbach, W., and S. Stainbach, and S. Bray. 1996. *Controversial issues confronting special education: Divergent perspectives.* Boston: Allyn & Bacon.

Stakes, R., and G. Hornby. 1997. *Changes in special education: What brings it about: Special needs in ordinary school.* Herdon, VA: Cassel.

Stodes, S. 1982. *School-based staff support teams: A blueprint for action.* Reston, VA: Council for Exceptional Children.

Symington, G. T. 1995. *Mediation as an option in special education. Final report.* Alexandria, VA: National Association of State Directors of Special Education.

Tatro v. State of Texas, 481 F. Supp. 1224 (N.D. Tex. 1979), rev'd., 625 F. 2d 557 (5th Cir. 1980), on remand, 516 F. Supp. 968, rev'd., 703 F. 2d 823 (5th Cir. 1983), aff'd., 468 U.S. 883, 104 S. Ct. 3371, 82 L. Ed. 2d 664 (1984).

Tenth National Conference on School Transportation. 1985. *Standards for school buses and operations: National minimum guidelines for school bus operations* (rev. ed.). Chicago: National Safety Council, School Transportation Section.

Thomas, M. A. 1973. Finance: Without which there is no special education. *Exceptional Children* 39: 475–90.

Thurlow, M. 1994. *Perspective on performance assessment and students with disabilities.* Reston, VA: The Council for Exceptional Children.

Thurlow, M., J. Elliott, and J. Ysseldyke. 1998. *Testing students with disabilities: Practical strategies for complying with district and state requirements.* Thousand Oaks, CA: Crown Press.

Tilly, W. D., K. R. Flugum, and D. J. Reschly. 1996. *Preliminary outcomes of the renewed service delivery system.* Des Moines, IA: Iowa Department of Education.

Tilly, W. D., D. J. Reschly, K. Flugum, P. Atkinson, and M. Sullivan. 1992. *Renewed service delivery system: Perception study.* Des Moines, IA: Iowa Department of Education.

Tucker, J. 1989. Less required energy: A response to Danielson and Bellamy. *Exceptional Children* 55: 456–58.

Twentieth Annual Report to Congress on the Implementation of the IDEA. 1998. U.S. Department of Education.

Vaughn, S., and J. Klingner. 1998. Students' perceptions of inclusion and resource room settings. *The Journal of Special Education* #2, Vol. 32 p. 79.

Verstegen, D. A., and M. J. McLaughlin. 1995. Toward more integrated special education funding and services. *The CSE Resource* Fall: 1–5.

Vitello, S. J. 1990. *The efficiency of mediation in the resolution of parent-school special education disputes. Report from Rutgers: A working paper series.* Washington, DC: Department of Education.

Wang, M. C., M. C. Reynolds, and H. J. Walberg. 1994. Serving students at the margin. *Educational Leadership* 52 (4): 12–20.

"Wanted: More Good Teachers," *St. Louis Post-Dispatch,* 6 January 2000, p. B6.

Weintraub, F. J., and S. Higgins. 1980. *Local special education variables necessary for consideration in developing state special education fiscal policies.* Reston, VA: (ERIC Document Reproduction Service N. ED 201–133).

Weishaar, M. 1997. Legal principles important in the preparation of teachers: Making inclusion work. *The Clearing House* 70 (5): 261–64.

Weiskopf, P. E. 1980. Burnout among teachers of exceptional children. *Exceptional Children* 47 (1): 18–23.

Whelan, R. J. 1996. *Mediation in special education.* Lawrence, KS: R. J. Whelan.

Will, M. 1986. *Educating students with learning problems: A shared responsibility. A report to the secretary.* Washington, DC: U.S. Department of Education, Office of Special Education and Rehabilitative Services.

Witt, J. C. 1986. Review of the Wide Range Achievement Test-Revised. *Journal of Psychoeducational Assessment* 4: 87–90.

Yell, M. 1998. *The law and special education.* Upper Saddle River, NJ: Prentice Hall.

Ysseldyke, J. 1997. *The issues and considerations in alternate assessments. Synthesis report.* Minneapolis, MN: University of Minnesota, National Center on Educational Outcomes.

Ysseldyke, J., B. Algozzine, and M. Thurlow. 2000. *Critical issues in special education.* (3rd ed.) Boston, MA: Houghton Mifflin.

Ysseldyke, J., M. Thurlow, K. Langenfeld, J. Nelson, and E. Teelucksingh. 1998. *Educational results for students with disabilities: What do data tell us?* Minneapolis: University of Minnesota, National Center on Educational Outcomes.

Ysseldyke, J., B. Pianta, S. Christenson, J. Wang, and B. Algozzine. 1983. An analysis of prereferral interventions. *Psychology in the Schools* 20: 184–90.

Ysseldyke, J., M. Vanderwood, and J. Shriner. 1997. Changes over the past decade in special education referral to placement probability. *Diagnostique* 23 (1): 193–201.

Name Index

SUBJECT INDEX